The
Psychic Life
of Muriel,
The Lady Dowding

Cover art by *Jane A. Evans*

Muriel, the Lady Dowding, before a portrait of her late husband, Lord Dowding. She is wearing an amethyst-diamond ring, given her by Lord Dowding to mark their 15th wedding anniversary. He accompanied it with the following lines:

To the love of my life.
Isn't it fun – she's also my wife!

The Psychic Life *of* Muriel, *The* Lady Dowding

An Autobiography

(Formerly published under the title *Beauty Without Cruelty*)

This publication made possible with the assistance of the Kern Foundation

**The Theosophical Publishing House
Wheaton, IL U.S.A.
Madras, India/London, England**

Library of Congress Cataloging in Publication Data
Dowding, Muriel Dowding, Baroness.
    The psychic life of Muriel, the Lady Dowding.

    "A Quest book."
    Originally published: Beauty—not the beast.
St. Helier, Jersey: Spearman, 1980.
    1. Dowding, Muriel Dowding, Baroness.
2. Theosophists—Great Britain—Biography.   I. Title.
BP585.D68A33   1982   299'.934'0924   (B)   81-23260
ISBN 0-8356-0564-7   (pbk.)

Printed in the United States of America

For Pippa and Sarah,
My Granddaughters
& to My Step-Grandsons,
the Hon. Piers & Mark Dowding.

This book is dedicated to those who have helped in its preparation and who have brought happiness into my life – my scribe, Brenda Osborne, my oldest friends, Joan Clark, Brenda Taylor, Betty Midderigh, Princess Helena Moutafian. Also, to Air Marshal Sir Victor Goddard, Patrick Moore, Professor Gough, James Durran, James Distelhurst, Colin Smith, Jon Evans, Prince Galitzine, Desmond Leslie and Neville Armstrong, who asked me to write it. In addition, Jim Tompsett and Margaret Tuches, who have helped me so much in my daily life, and to Ken Johnson who has edited it and became my friend in doing so.

PUBLISHER'S NOTE

In November, 1979, the Rt. Hon. Muriel, the Lady Dowding, was presented with the Richard Martin Award by the Royal Society for the Prevention of Cruelty to Animals. The citation pointed out that this award shares with the Queen Victoria Medal 'the honour of being the Society's highest recognition for an outstanding service to animal welfare.' It is presented to individuals or organisations not necessarily connected with the RSPCA, or for recognition of 'Outstanding meritorious service which may not have been carried out under the direct aegis of the Society.'

Contents

PART TWO

Foreword

by

AIR MARSHAL SIR VICTOR GODDARD

THERE MAY NOT be many of us who have, over many years, known as close friends both Muriel, Lady Dowding and her husband, Hugh – Air Chief Marshal Lord Dowding, Commander-in-Chief of Fighter Command and the famous 'Few.' These latter, it will be recalled, along with many others helping, overcame the mighty Luftwaffe and so won the Battle of Britain in 1940. Because I am the oldest of those friends, I have gladly accepted the honourable but almost needless task of commending this work of love to each one of its many readers.

The almost is my justification. For evidently the authoress, Muriel Dowding, with the utmost good humour has allowed herself to hold two opinions which need correction in this Foreword. Modesty has made her suppose that her role is less important for this Planet than was that of her husband, and that same quality has caused her not to stress the courage which she has evinced as a pioneer – that is to say, as an independent thinker and a courageous exemplar in the many fields of regeneration which will be offered to human beings in the Aquarian age now beginning. Those who choose to follow, themselves being pioneers, will accept the need for this warning.

Let me now give praise to the two brave men who, in turn, were chosen, and chose, to share a vital part of their lives with the authoress and so became her principal helpers. The first, Max Whiting, became an airman in a Lancaster bomber and was overcome, as will be described, by the Fighter defence of Nazi-ism, but not before the birth of their son, David, who has become so important a helper to his mother in their united quest for Beauty Without Cruelty. The second was Hugh

Dowding who, when asked if he felt no bitterness about his treatment by the Government and that even God had not rewarded him, replied: 'But God did; He gave me Muriel.' And I think that it should be more widely known that his very orthodox family – his sister, his brothers and his own son – after his thirty years as a widower, greeted his bride with love and gratitude that that great man had chosen someone who understood and shared his interests so completely.

One other member, this time of the authoress' family, must be mentioned, for she played a very important part in the authoress' life as a healer, notably but not only at the time of her grandchild David's birth. It was by her influence chiefly that Muriel, her daughter, grew up with no doubt in her heart that we lived in a world which, despite its consciousness of material in our space-time existence, is basically spiritual.

I would now commend all my fellow-readers to bear in mind the modesty of the authoress as they read of Man's awakening to the fact that he was given by God the free will to order life on this planet Earth, not merely for the benefit of mankind, but for the protection and evolution of the planet as a whole and, perhaps most notably at this epoch, of the animal kingdom which hitherto mankind has so ignorantly exploited. It will then gradually become more widely recognised that courage and faith which any of us can have for the asking, for both are the gifts of God, are needed for the pioneering in this most vitally important re-generation of the world in which we are privileged to live and to have, each one of us, responsibility.

Victor Goddard.

Part One

We know one day a special journey
    we shall make,
Along a well-worn path ...
    that path that ev'ryone must take,
Friends ...
    family ...
    (and those I've hurt)
    stand by that gate,
But ...
    can I face the animals who also wait?

Edward A. Barton

1 Air Marshal Sir Victor Goddard.

INTRODUCTION

Glimpses of Otherness

PERHAPS IT IS because the Zodiacal sign of Leo was in the Ascendant at the hour of my birth that I normally wake with the lark and feel somehow tuned in to the glorious, majestic symphony that is nature. It may also be because of my natural inclination to a strict vegetarian diet, thanks to which – aside from injuries in a bad riding accident which were put to rights some years ago – I do not know what it is to have an ache or pain in my body.

That is not to say, however, that I have never known illness.

Only quite recently, one of nature's 'warnings' occurred which has ultimately resulted in the writing of this book – something which many friends have been urging me to do for years.

Let me explain how it came about.

Usually, I rise at about 5 a.m. at my home in Calverley Park, and let out my dog, Trudy, and my three cats, Minnie, Jo-Jo and Daisy. I then follow them out into the fresh morning air of the Park to feed the wild birds. Although it is in the heart of Tunbridge Wells and only a few minutes' walk from the railway station and busy shopping centre, the Park always seems so peaceful and verdant that one could almost believe one was living in the countryside.

After dealing with a number of domestic chores, I am normally ready to begin my busy daily working routine at about 9 a.m.

Quite recently, however, I awoke as usual at 5 a.m. and my immediate thought was: Saturday! No secretaries in the house, no letters to dictate, none of the hefty amount of paperwork to get through in running my Beauty Without Cruelty Movement and my other concerns. And yet ... I felt strangely sluggish and lethargic and, when I got up to begin my normal habit of looking after the animals and going out into the Park, I felt even more tired and careworn.

However, as is my custom on Saturdays, I was at my hairdresser's by 8.45 a.m. in time for my regular weekly appointment for a shampoo and set. One moment, I was lying back in the comfortable reclining chair in the salon, relaxing as water was rinsed through my hair. The next, I became slowly and puzzledly aware that I was back at home in bed and the cool fingers of a doctor grasped my wrist to take my pulse.

The explanation turned out to be quite simple: I had been overdoing things for quite a long time and I had collapsed at the hairdressing salon. The doctor ordered me to take a complete rest. As a result, I found myself with at least some spare time to prepare this account of my life.

Which now brings me to one facet of my – to some people, no doubt, unusual – beliefs.

Two major impulses have motivated, guided and shaped my entire life to such a degree that it seems that they are almost 'built in', or that I was 'pre-programmed' right from birth … or perhaps even before.

Although many people will, I feel sure, raise a questioning if not sceptical eyebrow, the fact remains that, without them, my life would most certainly not have taken the course it has.

One of these impulses is an intuitive affinity with the so-called spiritual aspects of life. A deeply-rooted awareness of a quality of 'otherness' which lies behind the physical, ordinary, everyday world in which our gross sensibilities often appear to hold us prisoner. But though our mundane senses frequently get in the way, as it were, I believe that through inborn sensitivity, or through careful training and self-development, glimpses can be gained of the spiritual world or worlds. Fleeting hints and insights from which we can obtain guidance to order our worldly affairs.

Along with such experience there often comes an awareness of order within the living universe itself. A vast pattern which pervades the entire creation, from the greatest super-galaxy, down to the tiniest particle. A pattern which throughout history has been affirmed by philosophers, mystics, saints, psychics, visionaries, mediums, seers, astrologers and other gifted individuals.

A natural extension of these deeply-ingrained feelings is my instinctive and unshakeable love affair with all that lives and breathes – nature and her wonderful works. In particular, the animal kingdom. I have held a lifelong fondness for animals, along with a conviction amounting to certainty that nature's children were not put there to be exploited indiscriminately, as raw materials from which we may obtain non-essential luxuries, such as perfumes and cosmetics, or even necessities, in the form of food, clothing and medication. That is why I am a vegetarian and why I fight so hard to prevent the wholesale cruelty to and slaughter of innocent creatures.

People who are aware of my principles and beliefs often ask me questions about them. They will ask, for instance: given that astrology 'works', do I think it is a good thing to have an awareness of one's personal destiny? To try to answer that, I can draw upon my recent experience.

Because of my interest in the subject, I had known before my collapse at the hairdresser's that I was due to come under what astrologers call 'bad aspects.' And as I lay in bed afterwards, I must admit that I did vaguely wonder if I was dying. Yet, because I had had some astrological indications that things were not going to run smoothly, I had already instructed my secretaries to keep the month of November clear of appointments and engagements. Had I not taken this precaution, based on astrological advice, the doctor's order of complete rest would have resulted in utter chaos so far as my work was concerned.

As my own mother and my astrologer friend Betty Midderigh have observed, the correct approach to astrology is not to rely upon it blindly, like some fortune-telling system, but 'to learn to rule our stars and not allow them to rule us.'

But this is not the sum total of my recent experience. Only about a month before my sudden fainting spell at the hairdressing salon, I had had a sitting with the world-famous medium, Ena Twigg. During it, I received a message via Mrs Twigg from my mother, who died five years ago. My mother had said: 'Poppet, (which happens to be my family's pet name for me) just think what you have come through and do not be apprehensive, for there is much you yet have to do.'

So I realised as I lay in bed that I had received at least some indication that my life should continue, despite the astrological warnings. Although I am not exactly apprehensive of death – for I would love to rejoin my beloved late husband, Hugh – I believe that the actual separation from the physical body is perhaps what might be difficult, possibly even painful, and that is all.

With my mother's message still in mind, I then began to recall what a tremendous help she and many others had been to me throughout my life. I suppose everyone meets those who will guide them on the various important steps forward in their lives – even though they may not realise it at the time. And, looking back on my own life, I began to wonder whether we have complete free will or, if not, to what extent things might be pre-ordained.

While I could reach no precise conclusion on this point, I believe that the various crucial choices I think *I* have made in my life were part of some plan or purpose – although at the actual time I seemed to have had total free will.

Just how important, influential and, occasionally, dramatic such choices have proved, will become quite apparent during the course of my story.

1

Schoolfriends, Fairies
and the Tale of a Rabbit

MY MOTHER CAME from a very strict Protestant family. Her father – my grandfather – Edmund Barnes, hailed originally from Dorset. He had apparently quarrelled with his family and turned up in Ramsgate, a very handsome young man, who became the new organist at the local church.

Each week in the front pew sat the Hydes, who were considered the leading Ramsgate family, and it became quickly obvious that Edmund was very taken with their daughter, Sarah. However, when he called to pay his respects, as young men were expected to do in those days, he was not considered in any way 'suitable' – and he was not allowed to see Sarah.

How they eventually met and where is not known, but meet they certainly must have done. All that is certain is that on Christmas Day, immediately after the service, as everyone was going around and shaking hands, saying 'Happy Christmas' to their friends, Edmund swept Sarah off her feet and carried her out to a waiting coach. They eloped – under everyone's noses – to London.

Because of their treatment of him, Edmund Barnes refused to have anything more to do with Sarah's family. He did well in life, however, thanks to his talents as an organist and pianist and amassed what in those days was considered quite a fortune. He became the first Mayor of St Pancras and continued to hold the office for two more successive terms. In its simplicity, the story of Edmund Barnes and Sarah Hyde, with their clandestine romance, their elopement and his subsequent success, appears to have all the elements of a fairytale. Shades of 'Turn again, Whittington, thrice Lord Mayor of London' on a slightly lesser scale! It did, however, have its more sober aspects.

Edmund and Sarah had three children, of which my mother, Hilda, was the youngest. As a very beautiful girl of eighteen, Hilda had to act as Lady Mayoress to her father because her mother did not feel able to cope with the task. She was very fond of her mother, but I do not think she had much affection for her father, who was very strict, and she hated every moment of her role as Lady Mayoress. She longed to escape from the rather stern and confined upbringing and religious severity of her father.

At a ball one evening, Hilda met Jack Albini, a young man from an equally strict Roman Catholic family. The original family name had been d'Albini, which means 'people of the hills', and the first d'Albini came over to England with William the Conqueror. Eldest sons of the family were therefore always named William. Jack's elder brother was a priest and his elder sister a Catholic missionary in Africa. His other sister was a nun, and two brothers priests.

Jack who, like my mother, felt repressed by the severe religious domination of his family, could see the writing on the wall: if he stayed at home, he would no doubt be expected – or coerced – into following his brother and sisters into the Church. To escape, he went to stay with an uncle in Scotland and, on his supposed return to his parents' home at Bourton-on-the-Water, Gloucestershire, went instead to London, where he got himself a job and never returned to the family fold.

He fell deeply in love with Hilda, and although I think it possible that she was not truly in love with him, she admired him tremendously for having done what she had always longed to do – escape the overbearing atmosphere of a strict and religiously dictatorial family. Neither of them wanted anything to do with religion in any organised sense – they had been over-faced by it. They married against strong family opposition on both sides. Three years later, I was born.

When my mother was told she had a lovely little daughter and saw me for the first time, she turned her face to the wall in despair. In those long ago days, babies were always depicted by adults as adorable little satin-skinned cherubs.

Instead, my mother saw the stark reality: my skin, which

later became fair, was lobster-coloured, due no doubt to the sheer exertion of being born. Nor did she realise that babies were born with rounded, bowed legs – and she thought that I was deformed! In addition, my hair, which could only be described as carrot-coloured, was, along with the lobster skin, an awful combination.

Thankfully, my father thought – or knew – differently.

He immediately took me in his arms and said: 'What a Poppet!' Hence my family pet name.

It was my father again who was responsible for the pet name by which my sister became known. She was born three years later and weighed less than three pounds.

'What a tottie wee thing!' my father said.

From then on, within the family, we were always known as Poppet and Totty, although my sister's name was Hilda Kathleen, while mine is, of course, Muriel.

I can recall asking my parents once why they had chosen to call me Muriel. It seems that my paternal grandparents, who were Catholic, wanted me named after a saint and christened in a Roman Catholic church, while my maternal grandparents did not agree and wanted me christened in a Protestant church.

I do not know how everything was finally decided, but the Protestant camp won out and I was christened in a Protestant church. However, the mixups were not quite over. During the discussions of what I was to be named, apparently, my parents decided on the name Thelma, while Muriel was only one of several alternatives considered.

But due to all the upsets, with the Catholic and Protestant grandparents disputing this way and that, when my father was asked the name of the child at the christening ceremony, his mind suddenly went blank. He forgot all about Thelma and any other names that might have been agreed upon and said: 'Muriel.' It was the only one he could recall of those which had been discussed. So, Muriel I became – without any other fore-names.

I have since learned that names can be highly significant guides to a person's character, under the occult system known as numerology. It involves a number being assigned to each letter of the alphabet. This way, it is possible to calculate the 'value' of a person's name by adding up the numbers which the

2 Lady Dowding's younger sister, Hilda
Kathleen Albini – known as 'Totty.' She
died in 1978.

letters represent. The oldest version of this system is said to be Hebrew, for there have never been numerals in Hebrew script; instead, values were given to each letter.

It is because of this arcane system of evaluating a person's character by their name that, in ancient times, individual names were often regarded as sacred – i.e. secret. This is why so many of the ancient Egyptian pharaohs and their priests had various different names. If an evil person knew the true name of a person, it was believed, he could use it to work magic against that person, in the same way that witches were said to work with portions of hair and fingernails. For that name actually represented a significant element of the person. It is for this reason, I understand, that the deity was assigned so many different names and that the true name of God, or a god, was known only to the highest initiates.

However, like the more superficial, popular systems of astrology, the ancient science of numerology has become debased down the ages. The numerological method of 'reading' a person's character by the numerical 'value' of their name is nowadays somewhat imprecise and rather generalised.

It is also said that the numerical value of a woman's maiden name gives her personality and likely fortune before she was married, while her number derived from a married name is supposed to show how marriage has affected her. Since I have survived two husbands, this becomes rather a complicated process, with highly conflicting 'readings'.

I have also been told that names can have a connection with the remote past. I have often wondered whether my Christian name has any connection with Mu or Lemuria, the legendary lost continent which is held by some to be the Pacific Ocean's counterpart of Atlantis. For I have never been able to discover any actual *meaning* of the name Muriel.

My parents were kind and loving towards me and, in many ways, I believe my mother was very much in advance of her time. Normal nursery tea when my sister and I were children would more often than not consist of a boiled egg with brown bread and butter. We were allowed very few cakes or biscuits and, when I grew up, my mother would sometimes say: 'You have me to thank for your good teeth and skin.' I came to realise that she had brought me up on very similar lines to those of health food diets which are popular today, although I do not think there were any actual 'Health Food' stores at that time. There were, however, plenty of herbalists, who knew the beneficial and curative qualities of many natural plants and herbs, some of which are almost forgotten now.

If ever I talked of fairies – which I saw in many places as a child – my parents would never say: 'Don't tell lies!' They seemed simply to accept that I saw – or imagined I saw – what I said. My paternal grandmother, Mary O'Regan, being Irish, was said to have seen fairies and was also given to premonitions. I think perhaps that it was from Mary O'Regan that I inherited these faculties.

As a child, I had the devious habit of listening to other people's conversations, for in those days, little girls (and boys) were frequently told to be seen and not heard. Taking this rather literally, I suppose, I used to sit under the table, hidden by the tablecloth when Auntie Lily Regan and my mother had tea together. And Auntie Lily would often tell my mother how Mary O'Regan would come rushing round at breakfast time to see her brother Edward – Auntie Lily's husband – and tell him about some dream she had had. These dreams were often of a prophetic or precognitive nature and I used to listen with the most apt attention.

As I, no doubt, inherited some of Mary O'Regan's faculties, I think my own son, David, who is otherwise extremely down-to-earth and practical, also appears to have been heir to them.

Once, when he was almost fourteen, David ran in from the garden where he had been mending his cycle and said: 'Mummy, look – on my left shoulder!' I looked, but saw nothing. Some time later, I asked: 'Did you hurt your shoulder or something?' He replied: 'No. There was a fairy on my shoulder, but it must have jumped off when I came into the house. Evidently, it would not come in, as you didn't see anything, but as I ran out to my bike, it jumped on again.'

I suppose that it is possible that psychological features, as well as physical ones, can be inherited. Perhaps biologists working on the mysteries of the genetic code may discover the secret one day.

Having confessed that I saw fairies as a child, perhaps I had better outline these experiences in a little more detail. The best

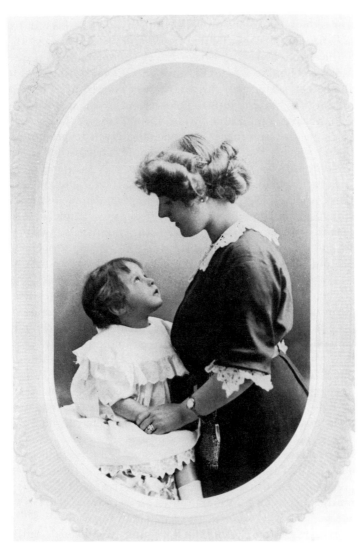

3 'Poppet' as a child: Lady Dowding and her mother, Hilda.

way to describe the fairies is that they seemed to be of a substance similar to that of a soap-bubble; semi-transparent and of beautiful colours. They came in different sizes and during the time my parents lived in London I used to see them in Kensington Gardens, where I was taken daily by my nurse. They were more often than not to be seen outdoors, but I do remember seeing one indoors. I was about eight or nine and at the time staying in Sevenoaks, Kent. I was being sent to get a handkerchief and as I ran up the stairs I saw one, the shiny brass bars of the stair rod reflecting the light through its body.

Seeing fairies was to me as natural as seeing birds and it became hard to realise that not everybody saw them. Many parents, I know, discourage children if they appear to be 'seeing things' or having conversations with imaginary playmates. And yet this is a faculty which a surprising number of children seem to possess and which – even if not discouraged – seems to fade around the age of ten or eleven.

Through my involvement with the Theosophical Society, which I shall describe in more detail later, I came to learn that the ability to see what are commonly called fairies is known as etheric sight – the faculty of being able to see nature spirits, or elementals. These are often described for convenience as sylphs, undines, salamanders, gnomes and dryads, depending upon which element they belong to: Earth, Air, Fire or Water. But they are simply the spiritual forces working within nature which, to someone with etheric vision, are personified. Another form of perception, which I shall also discuss in detail in due course, is the ability to see the spirits of those who have quit this life and are commonly thought of as dead. This is known as astral vision and is quite a different faculty.

I was born into an era and, I suppose, a social level, in which many people had quite large domestic staffs. To a child, of course, such things are at the time taken for granted.

Liza, my nurse, whom I loved dearly, was Danish. There was probably very little to occupy many wives at the time, including my mother, who had a good mathematical brain. At some stage, she met someone who had studied astrology and together they would attend lectures given by a man known as Alan Leo. His real name was W. F. Allen. He was an ardent member of the

Theosophical Society and was one of the most influential and successful astrologers of the early twentieth century. He ran the magazine *Modern Astrology,* wrote many books on the subject and was highly instrumental in the revival and spread of astrology in Britain.

My first cursory introduction to astrology was when my sister and I had just had our day nursery re-papered. Instead of all the little figures of animals which had previously decorated the walls, there were tiny posies of violets everywhere. I decided to add some embellishments of my own and, getting hold of some ink, I drew around all the bunches of violets I could reach.

When my nurse Liza saw what I had done, she said: 'You are very, very naughty and your parents will have to be told!'

She took me downstairs to the drawing room to confront me with my mother.

'That was a very naughty thing to do and you will have to be punished,' my mother said. 'Now, you can choose as your punishment whether you will give up going to tea with Robert on Sunday or to Doreen's party the following week.'

I couldn't believe it. Here was I, having ruined the new wallpaper and yet my punishment was as painless as giving up a visit to one of two friends.

'Mummy,' I asked, 'why aren't you more cross?'

'I am absolutely furious,' my mother replied. 'But I am trying to understand that you find it difficult to be a good little girl at this period.'

I still did not understand. When I asked what she meant, my mother pulled out a paper from among some which she had been studying. She explained that the sea was governed by the moon, while the seasons, which were affected by different planets, governed the growth of vegetation. Humans, meanwhile – and I was a little human, she carefully and patiently explained – were also subject to these influences.

'So I know that at this present time you are finding it very difficult to be good.' she said finally. 'You are only a little girl now, but I want you to remember this as you grow up – you must rule your stars and not let your stars rule you.'

As I mentioned in my Introduction, this latter was a phrase I was to hear echoed years later by my astrologer friend, Betty Midderigh.

*   *   *

I will never be sure precisely why, but the first school to which my parents sent me was Mr Thomas' School for the Sons of Gentlemen, in Porchester Terrace, W.2. I was the only girl.

Looking back, I can only imagine that, either the school was conveniently close to our home at 4 Warwick Avenue, W.2., so that my father could deliver me each day on his walk to his business, or the choice had something to do with my parents' horror of my becoming a 'spoilt' child.

I didn't like it one little bit.

My chief memory of the place was being taken each day into Kensington Gardens where a dreadful game called 'Caesar' would be played. The two head boys, Goodrich and Robert, used to pick the two sides. Then, after all the boys had been chosen, Goodrich or Robert would say, humiliatingly: 'You'll have to have *her*.' Just like that. The implication being, of course, that I would be a disadvantage to whichever team became involuntarily landed with me.

However, they soon changed their attitude. Although I was rather small for my age, I had quite long legs and the boys soon found that I could run very fast – a distinct advantage in their terrible game. They used to push me through gaps in hedges so that I could get into the 'enemy camp' before the other side. A few modest successes at that and I was often picked rather less begrudgingly for the teams – around third or fourth choice.

Robert, who was twelve or thirteen and due to go to public school the following year, befriended me and I became very fond of him. When my nurse used to come along, wheeling Totty in her pram, to take me home, I would beseech her not to put me in the other end of the pram, but to let me walk instead. I simply could not have borne the embarrassment of the other boys – Robert especially – seeing me wheeled off in the pram like a baby.

Instead, I got my way and Robert would often accompany me home. I suppose I have loved few people as much as I came to love Robert. His father had been killed in the First World War and he and his mother lived in an apartment in a large house. Some Sundays, I would go there to tea and he sometimes came to tea at our home. It was one of these visits to Robert that was offered as an alternative forfeit as punishment by my mother over the wallpaper-colouring incident.

Later, when my parents separated, I pleaded with my mother to write to Robert to explain what had happened. But she would not do so because she was afraid that we might be traced through him. So, sadly, I was never to see Robert again. Robert on my seventh or eighth birthday tied a piece of string round my finger and said we would marry when he had got a house for me – he had spent all his money on a birthday present for me and had no money to buy me a ring. My first deep love.

As a little girl, I seldom walked anywhere – instead, I danced. And, on once attending a party at the home of my friend, Doreen – the second of the alternative forfeits – and Huntley Olly, who were children of some close friends of my parents, Doreen danced for us. When she had finished her beautiful display – all executed on the tips of her toes, for Doreen went to ballet classes – her mother asked if anyone else would like to dance. I said that I would like to try. My humiliation in not being able to emulate the graceful steps like Doreen was so great that I ran sobbing to my mother and was practically inconsolable.

Mother said: 'If you want so badly to dance, you shall go to the same Academy as Doreen.'

My grandparents were very shocked and my father was absolutely against the idea, for in the social climate of those days, the idea of dancing, especially publicly on a stage, was regarded as something 'not done.' The world of the theatre – even if it did eventually aspire to the higher, classical spheres – was more generally equated with that of music-hall and was considered vulgar and tasteless.

However, despite the opposition of my grandparents and my father, my mother insisted that I should go to dancing lessons and took me to the Academy of Dancing in Charing Cross Road. I remember that there was a Crosse & Blackwell jam factory next door.

My dancing mistress was a Madame Desmonde. I believe that

she had at one time been a beautiful, professional ballerina, but had had an accident in which she had broken her ankle and could no longer dance herself, but was restricted to teaching. On the floor above the rooms where we practised, the famous, high-kicking Tiller Girls used to rehearse. We never saw them, nor had anything to do with them, but we often heard their feet tapping rhythmically, as we went through our elementary exercises.

My first classes were held on Saturday mornings, but Madame Desmonde also held a morning class during the week which was normally reserved for girls who had actually progressed to the degree where they danced onstage. About five or six of the best pupils from Madame's Saturday class were eventually allowed to attend the weekday sessions and I was among them. But on these occasions, Madame Desmonde rarely paid any attention to us. We stayed in the background and picked up what we could from watching the other girls as she put them through their paces.

Two of the more advanced dancers at this time were Renee Meyer, who some years later played the title-role in *Peter Pan* in the West End, and Gabby Delise, who became quite famous in her day. Much later, I recall seeing Selfridges well-known store and a large portion of Oxford Street draped in black. Gabby Delise, who had been engaged to Gordon Selfridge, had died.

Professional producers would often attend these midweek classes, to pick out girls for work in pantomime for the forthcoming winter season, and my friend Doreen was selected by one to play in *Bluebell In Fairyland*. At the time I was very envious and would have liked to join Doreen, but Madame Desmonde told the producer: 'You cannot have Poppet – she is not to have a stage career.'

For although my mother had had her way in allowing me to take dancing lessons, the idea of me going onstage in pantomime was absolutely unthinkable.

As well as his objections to my dancing lessons, my father did not approve either of my mother's keen interest in astrology, and I believe that this probably represented the beginning of disagreements between them which eventually led to their separation when I was about eight years old and ended in divorce when I was ten.

My parents normally took a house by the sea for about four months each summer, because my mother felt strongly about children being brought up entirely in London. (Our former home in Warwick Avenue has, like so many lovely old properties, since been converted into a number of flats.)

This particular summer, when I was eight, we went to Hove, in Sussex. I remember my mother telling me that we were going to see my grandfather Barnes. My mother, my sister and I, along with our nurse, took a train from Hove to London and went to my grandfather's home, where a lot of mysterious discussions went on. My grandfather then sent a telegram to a farm at Hambledon, near Godalming, in Surrey, to ask if they would take in my mother, my sister, myself and our nurse for a period. (By this time, Liza had returned to Denmark and our new nurse was named Violet.) Apparently, my grandfather had at some time helped the two sisters who ran the farm. It seemed an awfully long time before a reply to his telegram came, saying they would have us to stay.

My grandfather's coachman, who was named Davis, took us to the station and later that night we were put on the train for Surrey. When we got there, I remember, the farm and the village church appeared oddly connected – they shared a sort of party wall at the rear of the farm buildings.

We had a very happy summer at the farm, my sister and I being fascinated by the haymaking that was in progress, and only barely aware that perhaps 'something was going on' between our parents, since our original holiday in Hove had been interrupted and our father left behind.

While at the farm, however, an incident occurred which has branded itself into my memory and, in a way I suppose, was a kind of significant childhood catalyst which helped to cement my lifelong inclination to vegetarianism.

My sister and I had been delighted to see little rabbits hopping about in the fields and, one day, very hungry, we went into the farmhouse for lunch. One of our hostesses brought in a big silver salver as we sat down to eat, lifted the cover – and there was lunch. For one ghastly moment, I thought it was a little cat that had been cooked … and then I realised. It was a rabbit. Just like the ones we had, only a few moments earlier, seen hopping to and fro in the meadow.

I refused to eat and was sent out of the room. Later, my mother came into our bedroom. She said: 'Fancy, a great girl of eight crying! They are being very kind to us and you must not refuse their food. Why are you crying? You haven't been smacked – only sent out of the room.'

I explained through my tears that I was crying for the sake of the poor little rabbit.

My mother nodded understandingly and said: 'I will try and see that you are never given rabbit to eat again.'

Since my early childhood, the eating of animals has always been repugnant to me and I am sure that many children feel the same way. Unfortunately, lots of parents are not so understanding as was my mother and they and school authorities force such food onto them. I realise that there are plenty of people who say that they like – or even need – meat, or believe that it is unnatural or 'unmanly' to dislike it, but I cannot help my true feelings. I think, in any case, that it is simply a case of conditioning; an unwarranted, ingrained habit of our society – and one which considers itself civilised at that – to accede to the slaughter of millions of fellow-creatures, when there are so many equally enjoyable alternative food sources available.

2

More Fairies, More Dancing, Mysterious Journeys and the Case of the Ghostly Nun

TO A CHILD of eight, the events which followed in our lives seemed at the time quite mysterious, somewhat exciting, occasionally frightening and often totally incomprehensible.

While we were still on holiday at the farm, a telegram arrived and my mother whisked herself suddenly off to London, leaving us in the care of Violet. Then, another telegram arrived and Violet told us that we, too, were to return to London.

As we waited for our train, Violet told me that I was to travel as if alone, although she and my sister would be on the same train, and that on arrival in London I was to go on ahead on my own and hand my ticket to the collector. Davis, my grandfather's coachman, would be waiting with the brougham. On no account was I to look back at my sister as I walked along the platform. For some curious reason, Totty was dressed in a boy's sailor suit. She and Violet would take a taxi and join us later at grandfather's house.

As I surmised much later, my father had private detectives out searching for us since our hasty departure from Hove and they would naturally be on the lookout for two little girls travelling with their nurse. Hence our strange strategy at the station and my sister's disguise. At the time, that train journey was quite a terrifying experience. I realise that it might mean very little to any girl of eight today, but in those days it was highly irregular and an unnerving ordeal for me, especially since, at the time, I did not understand what it was all in aid of.

When we all assembled at my grandfather's home, where

mother was waiting, it was decided that the best course would be for us to go away and stay until whatever was going on had blown over. I suppose our cover at the farm had, as they say in modern spy novels, been blown. So my sister and I were to go and stay with Violet's family, while my mother had to remain in London, I imagine for legal reasons, so that the separation could go through.

We had a lovely time with Violet's family. We ate meals in the kitchen and she had two big brothers who were very kind to us. We were not there very long, however, because one day as Totty and I ran in from playing in the garden, we saw that Violet was talking to a strange man in the sitting room. Violet's mother grabbed us and made us stay in the kitchen and keep very quiet. We were not allowed out again that day and, at dusk, Violet's brothers wrapped us in eiderdowns and hustled us across the road to a bakery, like little fugitives in the night. There, we slept in a circular room on a feather bed. Presumably, this was all a precaution in case the strange man, whom I can only assume was one of my father's hired detectives, was still feared to be in the neighbourhood, waiting to snatch us away.

At about four o'clock in the morning, Violet woke us up and we were taken in the bakery van, with its beautiful aromas of freshly baked bread, to a station where we were put on a train bound for London once more.

My father, it seems, had won custody of Totty and I, and we had to return to him. Apparently, his idea was to keep on our home in Warwick Avenue and to get his sister – the one who had been a missionary in Africa – to come and live there and take charge of us. Although we loved our paternal grandmother, Mary O'Regan, and father's family, we had seen very little of the missionary sister. And what we had seen of her we found terrifying.

Naturally, at this prospect, we set up a terrible wailing.

Poor Daddy was almost distraught. Then, what seemed like a miracle happened. He received a letter from some friends named Molly and Albert Epstein with whom, amid all the scurrying to and fro, my parents had lost touch. They had read in the newspaper of the divorce, were very distressed about it and wanted to know what would happen to the children.

Here, I should explain how my parents came to know Molly

and Albert Epstein, since it was through me that they met. During one of the previous summers, as usual, my mother took us to the seaside, taking a house at Beltinge, Herne Bay. I believe the house was called 'Kinfauns.' During our stay, my mother would look after Totty, who was small and delicate, while our Danish nurse Liza took me down by the sea.

Day after day Liza and I would return to the house and I could not eat my lunch. My mother was very worried and when she spoke to our nurse, Liza explained that each day a lady and gentleman had been giving me bars of chocolate from a vending machine.

My mother told Liza that she should have told the couple that I was not allowed to have chocolate like that, ruining my appetite. Liza protested that she had tried to explain, but the couple had not understood her English, which at that time was poor.

Next day my mother left Liza to look after Totty and took me down to the seashore in the morning. The couple were there. When my mother spoke to them they explained that they had been fascinated by this funny, red-haired little girl, who appeared to speak in Danish to her nurse but in English to themselves. My mother explained about the effect of the chocolate on my appetite and, as a result of this rather curious meeting, she and my father became close friends of Molly and Albert Epstein. They were very wealthy and had a beautiful estate in Sevenoaks. As far as I know, they were unrelated to the sculptor, Jacob Epstein, but the playwright Alfred Sutro was an uncle of Albert Epstein.

When the Epsteins contacted my father after the divorce proceedings had been announced in the newspapers, they suggested that, as they had no children, we go to stay with them. My father, naturally, could go down to Sevenoaks at weekends to be with us. And that, roughly, is what happened.

However, my father soon allowed my sister, who was so delicate, eventually to return to my mother. But I stayed on with the Epsteins for about five years – between the ages of ten and fifteen.

It was not the first time that I had stayed with the couple. Shortly after they had met my parents at Herne Bay, I had been invited to be their guest, when I was four, five and six. The

Epsteins used to say to my parents: 'You have two children, we have none: can we borrow Poppet?' And off I would go for several weeks at a time.

When he returned home from business in the evenings, Albert Epstein always liked to walk around his eighteen-acre garden and, as a tiny girl, I would go with him, grasping his hand. He knew that I was prone to seeing fairies and he seemed to understand, because he would often get me to describe them to him.

However, one day, after me telling him about my fairies, he stared at me and, quite seriously it seemed to me, said:

'I am going to put a stamp on your forehead and post you to Sir James Barrie.'

As children will often do, I took him at his literal word and, as a result of pondering the idea, I would save odd biscuits and pieces of cake. Then, when taken out for walks, I would surreptitiously push them through pillar boxes, because I was convinced that these tall, red boxes with their hat-shaped tops were designed so that little girls could be posted to Sir James Barrie, hats and all! I felt terribly sorry for them and, knowing that this would one day be my own fate, I thought it the least I could do to post some biscuits and cake for them to eat while they were waiting for the postman.

I was as concerned for the welfare of the fairies themselves as I became for the little girls I thought were being shipped off, for heaven knew what purpose, to the creator of *Peter Pan*. Whenever the Epsteins' gardener was going to sweep up the leaves, he would coax me into the kitchen first, to give me a hot drink and chocolate biscuits, which I considered a great treat. But the real reason for this bribery was that I used to weep bitterly at the thought that the fairies might be injured or swept away by his broom. Thus, any sweeping operations had to be done in utter secrecy and I had to be kept indoors and occupied in some way, so that I wouldn't know what was going on.

After I had been put to bed in the evenings, the Epsteins would often creep into my room to see if I was all right. And, I suppose in keeping with my earlier eavesdropping escapades under the tablecloth at Warwick Avenue, I would regularly merely pretend to be asleep and listen to what they had to say.

Once, I recall, 'Auntie' Molly said: 'Poppet will not be as beautiful as her mother, but perhaps that is a good thing, as Hilda's beauty did not bring her happiness.'

To which 'Uncle' Albert replied: 'Poppet will be pretty enough. But haven't you noticed she has something which is much more deadly? She could charm a bird off a tree!'

'Oh, I've noticed she twists *you* around her little finger,' Auntie Molly said.

For weeks afterwards, I tried my best to charm little birds off trees. But all they did was stare at me with their little bright eyes and their heads on one side.

It was while staying at the Epsteins, from the age of ten, that I was sent to my second school – Walthamstow Hall, in Sevenoaks. At the same time, I was able to resume my dancing lessons which, with the breakup of my parents and all the moving around we did at the time, were of course suspended. Once settled with the Epsteins, I was able to go to classes held once a week at the Crown Hotel in Sevenoaks. There we were taught to do such dances as the polka and the waltz and various fancy steps, as opposed to the ballet which I had previously studied. However, probably thanks to my earlier experience, I very quickly became the star pupil.

A lady named Mrs. Charlotte Dyson Laurie used to attend to watch the classes and was often my partner in the waltz and polka and she very quickly became one of Molly Epstein's close friends. Mrs. Dyson Laurie was also a close friend of the world-famous prima ballerina Anna Pavlova and took me to see her dance. It was the experience of a lifetime, for I actually saw Pavlova perform the solo dance for which she became most famous – the dying swan. She wore a gorgeous white ballet skirt with a huge ruby set in the middle of her bodice to represent the wound where she had been shot through the heart. She actually danced on glass which gave the appearance of a lake, and it was one of the most beautiful things I have ever seen.

After the performance, Mrs. Dyson Laurie took me backstage at Drury Lane theatre to meet Madame Pavlova and, on another occasion, we went to tea with her. Madame Pavlova set me to the barre and told me to do various exercises and called out particular steps which she wanted me to execute. Then she called me over and, as I knelt at her feet, thrilled and overawed, she asked how old I was. I told her I was eleven.

She said: 'Now if you practise very, very hard and come to me when you are sixteen, I will put you in my ballet.'

I was absolutely thrilled and from then on dreamed of little else but appearing in *Les Sylphides, Swan Lake* and the other beautiful ballets which I loved. On my school reports at Walthamstow Hall, the teachers began to make remarks like: 'We do not know what Muriel dreams about, but she certainly does not pay attention.'

Soon after the Epsteins, no doubt on the instructions of my parents, stopped me from going to dancing classes. From the point of view of a would-be ballerina, this was naturally prohibitive, because these were the very years when my body was developing, my muscles and co-ordination were being shaped and when, strictly speaking, I should have been in constant practice to keep myself supple. Although I did resume some ballet and Greek dancing later when I was fifteen, I was never able to dance so well as I did around the ages of ten or eleven.

I have since been interested to learn, incidentally, that Madame Pavlova was, like myself, a vegetarian and indeed, so are many other well-known dancers.

One of the rules which the Epsteins insisted upon was that I should never stop to talk to anyone on my way to school. I was not allowed to leave the house until 8.50 a.m. and they would be very cross if ever I were late for school, which opened at nine. This meant that I had to run as fast as I could, all the way to school. Whether this was the reason, when I later developed some schoolgirl ailment, that the doctor found my heart was not quite as it should have been, I do not know. But I was taken off all games and was not even allowed to go upstairs. But being taken off games was no great sorrow to me because, apart from riding and dancing, I was not the athletic type.

Now Walthamstow Hall was a strictly Protestant establishment and, I do not know whether it was due to pressure on the part of my aunt (the sister of my father who was a Catholic nun) or not, but I was soon removed from the Hall and sent to a convent school: the Convent of the Holy Child, in Sussex.

I loved this school so much that, had I had a daughter instead of a son, I would probably have sent her to a convent school.

Although I no longer saw fairies by this time, I had always been deeply interested in anything one might loosely term psychic – despite the Epsteins' lack of belief in such things.

On one occasion during the time I was at the convent school, I saw what many people would term a ghost. We slept in cubicles, and the curtain covering the end was always raised back so that any passing Sister might see in and check that all was safe and sound. On this particular night, the light was turned down low and I saw a nun go by and wondered who she was. She passed a second time and I called out: 'Goodnight.' But instead of the usual response, 'All blessed is the Holy Child Jesus', there was no answer.

I crawled to the end of my bed and peered after her to see if I could recognize which of the nuns it might be by her size. She moved silently down to the end of the cubicles and, to my utter amazement – and horror – disappeared through the floor.

The next day I told my form mistress about this unnerving experience and she said: 'Please don't mention it to the other girls.' Yet she did not seem at all surprised.

I think there was something a little strange about the school, because I remember once asking one of the older girls of about sixteen or seventeen why there were very high railings around the banisters. These were on the stairs between the first floor, where we had to line up in white veils and gloves every evening outside the library, before descending to the ground-floor chapel. Eventually, the girl I asked told me that they were not supposed to discuss it, but when she had first arrived at the school a friend of hers had been sent into the library to do a penance. The rest of the school were having supper when they heard a terrible scream. The girl had plunged over the banisters. It was assumed that she had been frightened by something in the library and, in her rush to get downstairs, had fallen.

A second girl, I learned, had also had a terrific fright in that room. On another occasion, a nun had gone into the library to fetch prayer books and, though the school waited and waited for her to come out and hand them round, she had never reappeared. The library was therefore out of bounds.

Despite these rather chilling stories, I was so much at home with the convent atmosphere that the prospect of becoming a nun did pass through my mind. The Epsteins must have got to hear about this, possibly from the Sisters, and I was not allowed to return the following term. No doubt they had reported the knowledge to my father who, still nursing his feelings about the strictness of his own and my mother's religious upbringing, thought it best to have me removed.

I was something over fifteen at this time and I remember Auntie Molly Epstein one day telling me to put on my prettiest frock, as she was expecting a Countess for tea. After the Countess had been and gone, Auntie Molly and Uncle Albert told me that when I was sixteen I would legally be allowed to choose with which parent I lived. I could, if I wanted – although, of course, I would not be so silly, they said – return to my mother. On the other hand, they and my father were arranging that, when I was seventeen in about eighteen months' time, I would be presented at Court by the Countess who had been to tea. In the meantime, however, I would be sent to a finishing school in France.

But all this would fall through should I decide to return to my mother.

They explained that if I made the decision now – at fifteen – I would be allowed to visit my mother, whom I had not seen for some years. The Epsteins told me that although my grandfather was a wealthy man, he so disapproved of divorce that he had allowed my mother only a pittance on which to live and so she no longer had a nice house with maids, but lived poorly in Beltinge, Herne Bay. I could go there and spend a weekend with her and, on my return, make my decision. Naturally, they supposed, I would choose to remain with my father – especially with the promises of finishing school and being presented at Court.

This is one of the occasions to which I referred earlier, when I had complete free will.

I chose to return to my mother and sister.

When my grandfather heard this, I understand, he generously increased my mother's annual allowance by £50.

But because of my decision, I was no longer able to enjoy my large wardrobe of beautiful dresses – I had become known as 'Miss Vogue' in Sevenoaks because of them – and my life became totally different.

By this time, my mother had become very interested in the

Theosophical Movement, founded in New York in 1875 by Madame Helena Petrovna Blavatsky and Col. H.S.Olcott. Although she was not, strictly speaking, interested in spiritualism, which she considered rather dangerous, she did not prevent me from reading about psychic matters. I could have been only about fifteen-and-a-half when I joined the Greater World Association which had its headquarters at Holland Park, London. I didn't attend meetings until many years later, but I used to receive all their literature.

Looking back over my life, the apparent freedom of choice I was given to choose which parent I would live with might still, in a way, have been part of a predestined plan. For the knowledge I received from my mother in this period was to prepare me, not only for my first, but for my *second* marriage!

3

A Past Life,
a Little Girl's Lover
and Mother's Friends the Rats

MY MOTHER WAS undoubtedly the most instrumental among several people who have helped to shape and mould my life and character in so many different ways. And, because we were so close for so long, undoubtedly she wielded the greatest influence. Born under the sign of Virgo, I think her most outstanding virtue was compassion. She was always very non-possessive towards my sister and I, and tended to look upon us not simply as her daughters, but as people, individuals in our own right.

She was also very thoughtful and generous, although she never wasted money, nor anything else for that matter. One incident, which perhaps best demonstrates this selfless side of her nature, occured in about 1929. One day, my sister Totty and I said to her: 'Mother, you simply *must* have a new coat.'

Being one of those people who always believed in paying cash for everything, mother drew out £30 which, at that time, was a considerable amount of money. Off she went to get herself a new coat.

When she returned, Totty and I took one look at the garment she'd bought, then looked at each other. Without saying a word, each knew what the other was thinking. The coat was horrible. It looked very cheap and she could hardly have spent £30 on it. We asked her to explain.

'Well, darlings,' she said cheerfully, 'as I parked the car and got out, I saw little Miss E— going down the road and I thought, I have known you for about ten years and have never seen *you* in a new coat. So I took her into a shop and bought her one, which cost £20. I managed to get one for myself for £10.'

It was so typical of mother.

When I returned to her at the age of fifteen, although she had been living in very reduced circumstances, due to my grandfather's meagre allowance, I was allowed once more to resume my dancing lessons. Along with about fifteen other girls, I became a student at the Herne Bay School of Dancing. The teacher was very strict, which is demonstrated by the fact that she managed to put us through our examinations in ballet, Greek, ballroom and even folk-dancing within only two years.

It was at this time that I met Joan Clark, née Tamkin, a fellow-student who was to remain a lifelong friend. We were almost always paired off to partner each other in the folk-dancing and ballroom classes and, in the School's Annual Display, we were invariably expected to perform at least one *pas-de-deux,* in the form of a minuet, or as a prince and princess in a ballet sequence.

Following our examinations, one day the dancing teacher invited me into her study and said that I could become one of her assistants and take classes for her. But if anyone asked my age, I was to say that I was eighteen. This offer meant that my mother would no longer have to pay for further lessons and I could go on training free of charge.

Although I was not absolutely certain that teaching appealed to me, my limited experience of stage work had taught me that I certainly didn't want to make the stage a career. The idea of grubby dressing rooms, the smell of greasepaint and the hurry and bustle of the theatre, although they may be bliss to some, were quite the reverse of what dancing meant to me.

I think that somewhere in the depths of my consciousness lay a knowledge of having learned to dance previously, in some earlier incarnation perhaps, in a remote era when dancing was an ecstasy, a form of natural religious expression, in which the soul 'spoke' through the body. Although I tried hard to search the hidden regions of my mind, I could not bring out any details of this apparently latent race-memory. I supposed, however, that my dancing classes were simply an outlet for it in this life.

Our tutor told Joan and I that we were to visit schools in the Birchington area, between Herne Bay and Margate, and suggest that we set up dancing classes there. This we duly did, at the Bungalow Hotel, Birchington, and later in Canterbury and Whitstable, as well as teaching a number of classes at the Academy itself. Our reception on these forays, however, was not always entirely favourable. I well remember one unsympathetic headmaster we approached who, when we told him our intentions, simply pointed to the damaged skirting board and wall of one of the classrooms and said: 'That's what happened when we had dancing in this school!'

Our duties as assistant instructors kept us busy most weekdays from 8.30 a.m. until six or seven at night and we seldom got more than £10 or £12 a term.

Among our private pupils at the time were two girls named Gracie Skinner and Cissie Hill. Every night Gracie would go to the concert party on the local Pier to watch a young man tap-dancing and the following day would demonstrate his steps for us. He turned out to be none other than Ben Warris, later of the famous Jewell and Warris comedy duo, and Gracie went on to marry him, although it did not last. Cissie eventually got a job dancing at a well-known London night-club where she met and fell in love with the Sultan of Jahore. Their romance lasted many years and the Sultan took Cissie travelling, built her a modern and beautiful house on the cliffs at Herne Bay, and bought her many expensive jewels. Unfortunately, due to his country's internal politics, they were never able to marry and Cissie was killed in an air-raid on Canterbury during the Second World War. Each day on her birthday for the remainder of his life, the Sultan had Cissie's grave bedecked with flowers.

Around the time of our dancing days, I first began to go out on dates and had a number of fairly regular boyfriends. In fact, just before my seventeenth birthday, I became engaged to one of them. He was older than myself, extremely musical and a very pleasant young man. However, I broke off the engagement about two years later and I think he was very hurt. I became secretly engaged several more times but I always broke it off and I think that this was because, deep down, I *knew* that none of them was the right partner. In order to explain this, however, I must now relate something which had occurred earlier in my life and which I secretly nursed as a kind of half-recognised omen for the future.

From quite an early age I used to have what my father called nightmares and, whenever I did, he was always there to console me.

But later, when my father appeared less and less in my life, there was someone else who came to my bedside to comfort me and reassure me whenever I suffered from these nightmares. He was a figure in khaki, a soldier, and somehow *I knew that his name was Hugh.*

One recurrent dream I constantly experienced seemed to involve a terrifying ritual of execution. I was the intended victim and I believe that my fear of heights and of water stem from these extremely vivid and persistent dreams.

I am always reminded of this dream around Christmastime, when those beautiful flowers called poinsettias are in the shops. For in my dreams, I was some kind of temple girl of about fourteen or so, and similar but larger flowers were featured prominently.

In some way, I had broken my sacred vows and was to be sacrificed, either to the god of the river, or of the crocodiles.

Each time, I stood on a high, narrow platform rather like a diving board. It was decorated with the poinsettia-type flowers. I was petrified, with the noisy clash of cymbals and the chanting voices of a crowd in some festival going on all around me. Then, as if from nowhere, as my terror increased, I would hear the voice of someone whom I sensed was my lover. He would say: 'Don't wait – jump now!' And I did.

I have no recollections whatsoever of my death, nor of how it occurred. All I knew was a feeling of gently drifting downwards. There were no crocodiles nor any other predatory animals and I seemed to be lying on a mossy bank. Then, someone picked me up and, carrying me away, said: 'It is all over now.'

Ever since, the sight of poinsettias has made me shudder. This dream has haunted me for many years and, much later in my life, when I told my second husband, Lord Dowding, about it, he said: 'Do you realise that in all these dreams, death was violent and when very young?' Hugh believed that dreams were sometimes fragmentary memories of former lives which had impressed themselves upon the subconscious because of their dramatic and emotional nature.

I think he was probably correct, because years afterwards I

was to meet someone who appeared to recall an amazingly similar set of circumstances which seemed to belong to a past incarnation. The man in question is a highly respected expert in his own professional sphere, and must necessarily remain nameless here.

He told me that he retains impressions of a previous life which he appears to have lived millennia ago, at Thebes, in ancient Egypt. At that time, it seems, he was a troop commander and recalls an incident in which a girl whose life had been dedicated to serving in the Temple of Isis fell in love with a soldier.

Having broken her temple vows in this way, she and the soldier fled westwards. But they were overtaken by the guards and the soldier was executed on the spot. The temple girl was taken back to Thebes to be ritually slain. The execution had to take place on the west bank of the Nile – the side on which the Sun 'died' as it descended in the heavens each evening before its rebirth in the east the following dawn.

The commander lined up his men in two ranks like a guard of honour, between which the condemned girl was to walk, to a high platform upon which was fixed a plank projecting over the river. Apparently, there was a High Priestess of the Temple who hated the unfortunate girl and who was determined to follow close behind her and, gloatingly, watch her die. The Commander did not approve of this sadistic woman wanting to revel in the girl's death struggles and, as the Priestess moved between the ranks, he stepped forward barring her way. She had a dagger with which she would have liked to attack him, but dared not do so in front of his men. He was surprised to note that she was not supported by her temple maidens and could only assume that their dislike of her exceeded their fear.

As the condemned girl leapt to her death, the commander gave her a royal salute.

The friend who told me this story became convinced – as I did myself – that, because of the curious similarity of our impressions, they may well be inherited memories of past incarnations and that I had been the temple girl in question.

Certainly, there would seem to be no other explanation, barring some strange form of telepathy between myself and this friend, years before we met, as to why both he and I should share such remarkably parallel subconscious experiences. And if it was telepathy, taking into consideration the considerable time and space which separated this friend and I, who was the sender and who was the receiver? And why? Much more important, where did this experience originate in the first place, if not in some actual event, in the Egypt of several thousand years ago?

Which brings me back to my other 'extra-sensory' experience – of the comforting soldier at my bedside, whenever I had such nightmares. I often saw him, he was always in khaki uniform and he always seemed to appear in that twilight state somewhere between waking and sleeping. On one occasion when I saw him, while staying with the Epsteins, I got into trouble.

The Epsteins had some American guests staying for a few days. I had always, as I said earlier, been brought up to 'be seen and not heard' and therefore I always behaved quietly at mealtimes. The American gentleman, who had fascinated me by breaking his boiled egg into a teacup, rather than eating it from the shell in an eggcup, turned to me on one occasion and said:

'You're a honeybunch – can you speak?'

No one had ever called me that before and, as he evidently wanted me to talk to him, I did my best to join in the conversation. The American visitors and the Epsteins had been discussing a play which they had either just seen or were going to see and which was called, I believe, *The Cardboard Lover*. Hoping to say something which had a bearing on their talk, I explained to the American gentleman that I couldn't see *my* lover very often because he was a soldier.

Very sternly, Aunt Molly Epstein said: 'I'm afraid Poppet is too much with the maids.'

Afterwards, she took me on one side and told me: 'Little girls don't have lovers and don't make up such stories.'

I tried to explain that I hadn't made it up, but she would not listen and told me I was never to say such things again.

But I *knew* that in some way my soldier was real and that his name was Hugh. Whenever I was frightened or upset by anything he would be there. And I knew that, when I grew up, I would marry him. I think he must have told me this, because I can remember once asking him if he would come for me on a big white horse, like they did in fairy tales. He said he didn't think so, as it would be disturbing to other people in the everyday world. But he added: 'It would be very grown up, very secret and very thrilling.'

I don't believe I saw him much again after the age of about eleven, until a lot later in my life. But even when I was at the convent school, when the other girls, many of whom were Irish, used to discuss the types of men they would marry, I never joined in these idle speculations, because I *knew* what my man would be like. I don't think I even knew at the time whether his hair was dark or fair or what colour his eyes were – the kind of qualities which the other girls would speculate upon. But I *knew* he was very strong, silent and deeply romantic.

During the early days of my friendship with Joan at dancing classes, we would often have tea together and, one spring day, we took a tray of sandwiches, tea and cakes into the summer-house in the garden. There, I showed her a book belonging to my mother on how to read fortunes in tea-leaves.

My mother, meanwhile, was in the house, actually casting my own horoscope. When we went in after our 'garden-party', my mother told us – and my friend Joan still remembers it to this day – *that I would marry twice and that the second marriage would be to someone with a title, or someone famous.*

My friend Joan was so impressed by this astrological prediction that she actually told another friend about it at the Dancing Studio.

Joan recalls: 'I remember saying to the girl, 'This means Poppet will be a Lady. But, Lady Poppet ... that doesn't sound right. She'll have to be Lady Muriel – I'm going to call her Muriel in future.'

Since then, Joan has always called me Muriel.

Another of my mother's unusual abilities was demonstrated to me during the time we lived at Herne Bay – a faculty which I managed to pick up from her and which, many years later, I was to emulate with rather far-flung repercussions. I will tell of my own experience in its proper place, but here is my first encounter with the phenomenon.

I returned home from ballet class one evening to find my mother sitting in the lounge in total darkness, peering intently out of the window.

'Don't put the light on!' she said in a half-whisper as I came in.

4 Joan Clark, lifelong friend and fellow ballet
student at Herne Bay.

When I asked her what on earth she was doing, she replied:
'I'm watching the rats.'

I should explain. At this time, my mother kept chickens. Not
to be killed and eaten, for she was too fond of them all, but for
their eggs. They were more like pets to us. Currently, there had
been a corn shortage and my mother had discovered that a
family of rats had moved into the garden and were stealing all
the corn.

No doubt the practical thing would have been to put down
poison to get rid of the rats, but my mother felt that it was not
the answer. Instead, she went to see an old friend who was of an
extremely sensitive nature, to ask her advice.

'My dear,' the friend had told her, 'it is all so simple. All you
have to do is to love the rats and when you love them, then you
can explain the situation and ask them to go. This is what is
really meant by those who speak of dominion over the animals,
because it is a dominion of love, not of torture and slaughter.'

'But I don't love rats!' my mother had protested. 'I am very
frightened of them.'

Her friend said: 'People are always frightened of things they
don't understand. May I suggest that when the rats come out at
dusk you watch them and gradually you will be able to
distinguish one from another. When you have got to this stage,
you will no longer fear them and then you must go down the
garden to where they usually are and tell them that you love
them and wish them all well. Then explain about the corn and
ask them if they would leave.'

So, watching the rats for this precise purpose was exactly
what my mother was doing when I got home from ballet class.
Eventually, she became quite fascinated by the creatures and
how they stored the food away in their little larder in the
garden. She was not a particularly tidy person herself, but when
she saw the methodical way they put the corn and other scraps
away, she realised what excellent little housekeepers they were.

Soon afterwards, she was able to go down to their part of the
garden and explain that she really did admire them very much
and had, in fact, grown fond of them. But, as there was a
problem due to the shortage of corn, would they please go
somewhere else.

About three days later an elderly spinster, who owned the

only other house close by, told my mother that she had seen a
whole lot of rats climbing the fence into her own garden. My
mother and I were shocked, first of all to find that her friend's
remedy had worked, and secondly that they had gone to disturb
someone else. We therefore decided that, if we ever had to do
this sort of thing again, we should suggest a suitable alternative
place for them to go and, if necessary, make a pact with them to
put out surplus food for them. This we continued to do and I
have followed this practice all my life ever since, whenever
necessary.

Partly through her study of Theosophical literature, my
mother came to understand that life in all its manifestations
forms an intricate network which ultimately represents one
harmonious whole. And that it is impossible to harm or affect
one tiny part of nature's cycle without it having reverberations
– however small initially – throughout the whole. She also
believed that there must be some omniscient, super-intelligence
directing and guiding the whole of creation and that people's
lives ran in series, as they worked to improve their inner, Higher
Selves, in the process known as *karma*.

To express it simply, my mother equated life with a term at
school: when we died, we were going home for the holidays.

When, eventually, my mother became ill, the doctor suggested that she should move somewhere warmer than the coastal
village of Beltinge, so she took a farmhouse at Crowborough,
near Tunbridge Wells, as a temporary measure while she looked
around for a place to buy.

By this time, my grandfather had died and mother was
comfortably off, though by no means wealthy. When my sister
and I arrived at the farm, there was a fire, flowers and a maid,
and the estate agent himself arrived for supper that evening.
Three weeks later, my mother was engaged to him and they
eventually married. His name was Roy Farrant and, like my
father, he was totally out of harmony with my mother's
philosophical and other ideas and it was not a happy marriage,
although she looked after him well.

Eventually, my mother found and bought a house at Pembury, also in the Tunbridge Wells area. It was a lovely home
with a tennis court, a large paddock and, nicest of all, an
asparagus garden.

Once, when my step-father had been particularly unpleasant, I did suggest to mother that she should leave him. She replied: 'You can't keep on parking husbands – you might get them again if you didn't see it through in this life.'

It was her belief in the cycle of *karma*, once again. As a result of her deep interest in the doctrines of the Theosophical Society, which were in fact a synthesis of various ancient Eastern systems of belief, including Hindu and Tibetan Buddhism, my mother eventually became Lecture Secretary to the local branch of the Society in Tunbridge Wells. Because few of the lecturers in those days had cars, mother would often bring them home to stay for the night.

One of them was a woman who had apparently been cured of cancer of the breast by a group of healers known as the Seekers, whose headquarters were in Queen's Gate, South Kensington. My mother made contact with them and, two or three times a week, went for instruction in healing. The training was very strict and included the detailed study of anatomy, along with all the various methods of treatment for different illnesses. Part of the Seekers' method involved a cleansing process, dipping the hands in water. The healing techniques themselves did not involve the actual laying-on of hands, because their system was to treat not the physical body, but the etheric body, the envelope of subtle, psychic emanations and vibrations which, to some trained occultists, can be seen as the human aura. (Coloured illustrations of this subtle sheath can be seen in a book by the famous Theosophist C. W. Leadbeater, and entitled *Man, Visible and Invisible*. It was originally published by the Theosophical Society in 1901, but has recently been reissued as a paperback.)

My mother learned that the Seekers appeared to be guided by a doctor named Lascelles, who had died some 100 to 150 years previously. He manifested through a natural trance-medium, Mr. Charles Simpson and, through him, taught a form of healing in which he diagnosed the illness. The person then about to perform the healing was instructed as to the form of treatment to be used.

The patient was never actually physically touched. Instead, passes are made about one or two inches away from the physical body. If the etheric body is healed and made whole in this way, it is believed, then so too will the physical body be cured.

Naturally, many people who heard about the Seekers were interested to know exactly who this 'spirit doctor' was and how he came to use Mr. Simpson as a vehicle. So far as I can recall, Charles Simpson worked in the physics laboratory of Canterbury University in Christchurch, New Zealand. One day he received a telegram saying: 'Your wife ill. Come at once.' He hurried home to Dunedin, several hundred miles south of Christchurch, and found his wife in hospital there, in great agony. She was dying of cancer.

Mr. Simpson sat down beside his wife's bed in great distress and prayed to God to take away her pain. Apparently, so far as he knew, he fell asleep. When he regained consciousness, the Sister and the House Surgeon were standing by the door and his wife was smiling at him. All the pain had left her. The House Surgeon called him aside and asked: 'How long have you been doing this?'

'What? Praying?' Mr. Simpson said, puzzled. 'It is the first time I have really prayed.'

'Not that,' said the House Surgeon. 'You have been talking in a different voice and calling yourself Dr. Lascelles. He said your wife would live three months. No power on earth could have instantaneously taken away her pain like that. This has impressed me so greatly that I *believe* she will live three months and I must therefore request you to move her from the hospital, as we need the bed.'

Mr. Simpson took his wife home and she lived completely pain-free for three months and four days – and died with a smile on her lips.

After two years Mr. Simpson re-married and, in 1923, returned to England with his wife and children. He planned to sell an invention and, with the money, to go back to New Zealand and retire to a sheep station. But, as it turned out, the invention had already been patented by someone else, just four-and-a-half minutes ahead of his own application. The shock of this affected his health and he went into a decline. The doctor advised a warm climate but he could not afford to emigrate. In desperation, his wife suggested that he should try to re-contact Dr. Lascelles and, after many prayers, Dr. Lascelles did indeed manifest through Mr. Simpson and simply said to Mrs. Simpson: 'When is he going to start healing the sick?'

Charles Simpson started healing from a house in Kentish Town. His first patient was a case of cancer of the breast and, at first, he felt inadequate. But suddenly his hands started to move involuntarily, making passes over the patient's body, and he found that they were 'controlled', as they continued to be throughout all his time as a healer.

In less than three months, all pain had ceased and the patient's swelling had gone. Several other cures followed and the ensuing publicity in a national newspaper resulted in his being inundated with requests for healing.

'How can we help all these people?' Mrs. Simpson asked 'Dr. Lascelles.' He replied: 'You can pray for them.'

The discarnate Dr. Lascelles dictated the prayers and described the methods to be applied. The Simpsons were to set aside a room, place a table in it, cross upon it and six chairs around it. Mr. and Mrs. Simpson and four other people, or sitters, whom they were told would be 'sent' to them, were to form a Prayer Circle. In a strange way, these four other people who were to sit in on this Circle simply appeared, and their first sittings, for want of space, had to be held in a coal cellar, which the Simpsons whitewashed. Mr. Simpson himself made the altar-table and chairs. At their present headquarters at Addington Park, the Seekers' Trust have a model representation of this first prayer group.

One day, Dr. Lascelles suggested they should buy a house which was worthy of the work they had to do and the Simpsons found an ideal place at 29, Queen's Gate. They prayed hard that they would be able to raise the money needed to buy it. Almost immediately a comparative stranger, whose son Mr. Simpson had treated three times, offered to lend £1,000. A bank manager offered a loan of two-thirds of the house price. But on the day of the auction, Mr. Simpson was still £2,000 short of the sum required when he went off, desperately worried, to visit the sick wife of a retired Army colonel. The colonel noticed the agitated state Mr. Simpson was in and, when the position was explained to him, he turned to his wife and said, quite simply: 'We can do this, dear.' And so the house was bought.

They decided to call themselves The Seekers for they felt that they were seeking the Kingdom of Heaven on earth.

When questioned, Dr. Lascelles said that he had been a doctor when on earth and, indeed, a very accomplished doctor. He could have helped so many people in the state hospitals, but he had chosen instead to be a society doctor. Many of these wealthy private patients were not really ill at all. As he lay dying, his regret at what he could have achieved was so great that he prayed, asking if there was any way he could make amends and he was told that if he could find someone on earth with the same type of psyche as his own, he might be able to heal the sick through this person. He had found Charles Simpson and The Seekers and their work was the result.

What I remember most about Charles Simpson was that he seemed completely uninterested in psychic matters. He was always delighted when I used to turn up with a boyfriend who could talk engineering or motor cars with him. He became particularly fond of one of these young men who was extremely good on cars and mechanical matters and who, ultimately, became my first husband.

Later the Seekers' Trust bought Addington Park, West Malling, Kent, and sold the London premises.

I remember a nurse who worked in a nursing home opposite the original London headquarters and who had often seen my mother's car outside. She asked what went on inside 29, Queen's Gate. She was intrigued, she said, because she had noticed, while in the nurses' sitting room during her time off each week, people going into the premises on crutches and others obviously very ill. Eventually, she had recognised the same people weeks later coming and going without their crutches and obviously so wonderfully improved, if not completely cured, and she was curious to know what kind of treatment they had been getting.

Soon after joining The Seekers, my mother initiated a Prayer Circle, or Absent Healing group, of her own. At our new home in Pembury, we had a loft over a former stable and she converted it into a room where, once a week, six of us gathered. We would concentrate on the names of particular people who were ill or in some form of trouble and try to put the power of prayer to work for them. Although we were only teenagers at the time, my sister and I sat in on these circles. Another of the sitters was the housekeeper of a clergyman and she was extremely clairvoyant. I will always remember her as being so merry and bright and with loving blue eyes. She was quite elderly and completely and utterly selfless. Using her psychic powers, she would often report to us on the progress of different people we were trying to help through our prayers. Much of what she said was later confirmed.

Shortly after the Circle was formed, my mother and I went to the matron of a local hospital, explained about the work we were doing, and asked if the names of patients could be passed on to us so that we could include them in our prayers. The matron was very starchy and told my mother that the hospital had its own chapel. She then showed us an extremely bleak room containing only a few wooden chairs – and then began to usher us out. Just as my mother was about to leave a nurse came in and mentioned a patient by the name of Gregory.

'This is a terminal cancer case and he will be dead in a few days,' the matron said. Then, offhandedly: 'You can have his name if you like.'

Two or three weeks went by, the name having been included in our Circle work, then my mother said: 'I suppose we had better take the name of Gregory off our list – he must be dead by now.' The elderly woman clairvoyant said: 'No, no, he isn't dead – keep him on.'

Some six weeks later my mother received a postcard from the hospital matron to say that the patient Gregory had been discharged as he was no longer in need of medical help. He was cured.

My mother was quite visibly moved and astonished.

'So it really works!' she said.

From then on, she would do anything to try to help those in pain or in trouble, if she thought she could. I can recall one occasion when our local postman, who had a disfigured face, was asked by my mother what was the cause. He told her that it was a form of skin cancer which was quite incurable. On his next call, she invited him in.

'I have a cup of coffee waiting for you,' she said. Then, when he gratefully accepted, she asked: 'Would you mind if I tried to take this affliction away from you?'

The postman agreed and, each morning, my mother would give him a coffee and practise the form of healing she had learned from The Seekers. In time, the disfigurement left the man's face completely.

I do not recall how many people my mother helped throughout her life in this way and through her astrological calculations, but it must have been considerable.

In astrology, when difficult aspects arise in a person's chart, troubles do not necessarily occur singly, but quite often in groups. But if anyone who was particularly anxious came to my mother she would 'progress' their astrological chart. This is a method of calculating the future positions of the planets and their configurations, to get some idea of whether the difficulties a person might be in were of a temporary or a more long-lasting nature.

Often, she would say to really desperate cases: 'Look, hang on. You mustn't even *think* of suicide or anything like that. I promise you that if you persevere for another eighteen months, all will have changed. You will have met someone much nicer than the person you have lost.' Or she might say simply: 'The problems of the moment will soon cease.'

Looking back, there must have been many would-be suicides who took my mother's advice and lived to discover the truth of what the stars indicated.

I think it was during this time that I really took a great deal of meticulous interest in my mother and her philosophies. She had never drunk or smoked and I noticed that she ate no form of animal flesh. When I talked to her about it, she said: 'If I am asking God to make me a channel for his healing, how can I be part of death and destruction by taking the flesh of animals?' Any healers who happen to read my book might like to take note of this point. I have met many Spiritualist healers in my lifetime, but I believe my mother probably achieved more cures than any of them, simply because she made herself a *pure channel* for the power of healing.

Because of my increasing interest in her studies, one evening she invited me along to a lecture at the local Theosophical Society by Fred Ward, who became a famous astrologer in his day.

At the end of the lecture, Mr. Ward asked the audience if any of them would like to give their place, year and date of birth and he would do an on-the-spot horoscope on the blackboard, so they could see how it was done. There were no volunteers and, since I was not then a member, I did not feel I should offer my own natal details. Besides, my mother had already done my horoscope.

Because of the lack of response, Mr. Ward then offered to do the horoscope of any one of a number of famous people whose birth details he had – and read out a list of names. The audience chose the-then Prince of Wales, later the Duke of Windsor.

Mr. Ward began by drawing a large circle on the blackboard, dividing it into the twelve astrological segments of the Zodiac and adding the positions of the planets at the time of the Prince's birth. Suddenly, he faltered, seemed to dry up completely and, making some excuse, quickly finished the lecture – to the mystification of everyone.

As my mother drove him back to our home, Mr. Ward explained.

'I'm afraid I didn't teach anybody much about astrology except myself,' he said. 'I must never again do a public figure's horoscope without having first done it for myself privately. I had to finish the lecture because I didn't know if there were any Press people present, but I'm afraid the Prince of Wales will never be King. There is a tragedy or something in connection with his marriage.'

At the time, Edward Prince of Wales was the darling of international society and it was absolutely unthinkable that he would not make the most marvellous monarch. He was also apparently unattached. It was only some six or seven years later that the newspaper placards began to ask: WHO IS MRS SIMPSON? And, as we watched the sad developments of his abdication and his marriage, we thought back to what the astrologer had indicated.

On another occasion several years later I learned a further important fact about the way in which astrology ought not to be abused – again from Mr. Ward. The astrologer had drawn up a horoscope for my step-brother, predicting that he would be likely to marry in a particular year. At the beginning of the year in question, my step-brother did indeed come to tell me that he was getting engaged and so I wrote to Mr. Ward to tell him how correct his prediction had been. My step-brother was working in London at the time but spent his weekends with me.

On the announcement of his engagement, a number of letters, presumably of congratulation, arrived at my home on a Monday and I kept them on one side, on the mantelpiece for when he arrived the following weekend. As he was opening them, I heard him gasp. He handed me a letter from Fred Ward which said: 'As I thought by your horoscope that you would get engaged and married this year, knowing how expensive this is, if you have a shirt, put it on "My Love" in the Derby.'

And the horse, 'My Love,' had indeed won the Derby – three days earlier, on the Wednesday! I felt really terrible at not having forwarded the letter in time.

When I next saw Fred Ward, I told him what had happened and said: 'You must be able to make an absolute packet for telling the winners in advance.'

'Good gracious, no!' he replied. 'You should never use occult wisdom for personal gain. As people often do crosswords, I sometimes do a horoscope of horses or sportsmen, just to see how astrology works out. The fact that your step-brother didn't get the message in time to act upon it shows me that one should never use such information for personal profit.'

It is true that Fred Ward was a very poor man financially who could, had he wished, have made a great deal of money had he used his powers for gain. But he considered this to be a form of black – or at least, grey – magic.

Over the years, as my mother prepared the horoscopes of many of my friends, I noticed how accurate they turned out.

Once, an uncle brought his charming, second wife-to-be to visit us. Totty and I were in our early teens and we thought it was all very romantic and begged mother to do the lady's horoscope. When she had completed it – after they had left – my mother looked puzzled. She said that she must have been provided with wrong natal information or something, because what she read in the woman's horoscope seemed highly unlikely. The stars indicated that the woman would end her days in an asylum.

Although at this time it was very hard to believe of this particular woman, who was so charming and likeable, in actual fact my mother's forecasts came true. It was only one of many instances in which her astrological predictions proved accurate.

I quite honestly believe that her wisdom, her compassion for all suffering, whether physical, mental or emotional, and particularly that of animals who could not speak for themselves, was the greatest single influence on my life.

4

The Ghost Who Never Was, Marriage to Max ... and the Mystery of 'Clarence'

OUR MOVE TO the Tunbridge Wells area meant a whole new set of friends for Totty and myself – apart from my mother's psychic visitors and the members of the Prayer Circle.

Among them was a young schoolmaster who was extremely creative and who had a particular talent for writing plays and musicals. He loved to put on some of his productions, but could never afford to employ professional actors and actresses. Instead, he persuaded his friends to take part in them, myself included.

He once composed some beautiful music, to which I danced with him, entitled, *The Spirit of Music*. He also put on a revue in Tunbridge Wells called *To Sea In A Sieve*, which was a great success. As a result, he was then asked to produce a cabaret at the Grand Hotel in Eastbourne and it was rumoured that the famous impressario Charles Cochran was to be there. This young man later became famous in his own right – as the playwright, Christopher Fry.

For this occasion, Christopher had written some Eastern-style music and asked me if I would perform an appropriately Eastern-style dance to it. At the time, I was more or less engaged to a boy named Pat. I say 'more or less' because we were very young, in our teens and both his widowed mother and my mother were totally opposed to us becoming officially engaged, let alone even thinking of marriage. But more of that later.

On the evening of the cabaret, Pat took me down to

Eastbourne and we had dinner at the Grand Hotel before the show started. It transpired that there had been a minor setback earlier in the afternoon, because the Hotel had telephoned Christopher to say that they expected him to bring his own electrician to handle the spotlights.

Christopher did not know an electrician who might be available at such short notice, but a friend had suggested that perhaps a young man named Max Whiting might be able to help. After leaving public school, Max had been sent to France and Germany to learn the languages and had worked in a German electrical factory.

When Christopher approached him, Max dropped his week-end plans – and, presumably, the girl who went with them – to rush down to Eastbourne to help out. I had never met him, but had heard of him by reputation. And I had come to loathe everything I had heard. He was reputed to have had an affair with every girl in Tunbridge Wells and stories about the crazy antics he got up to were legion.

He once drove a car down the Pantiles in Tunbridge Wells which, as anyone who has been there will know, is an almost impossible thing to do. The Pantiles comprise a traffic-free, extremely picturesque precinct of historic buildings and shops which are terraced and the area is, to say the least, highly unsuitable for any kind of motor-vehicles.*

As the reputation of Max spread, the young men seemed to admire his 'daredevil' charisma, while the girls adored his striking good looks. But he was the last type of young man to whom I thought myself likely to be attracted. To some people, I am sure, he would have been thought of in contemporary terms as 'a bit of a rake'.

However, it seems that when I appeared in the revue in the Eastern-style dance, dressed in an appropriately diaphanous Arabian Nights-style costume, Max was speechless. After the show, there was general dancing, and Max said to Christopher:

*Historically speaking, the Pantiles evolved as tree-lined Upper and Lower Walks around the site of the original Chalybeate Spring, discovered there by Lord North in the 17th century. Eventually, taverns, market booths and some houses were built and, in 1700, the site was paved with square, baked tiles known as 'pantiles' – hence the name.

'As I have not brought a partner with me, would you please arrange for me to dance with Muriel?'

Christopher pointed out that there were plenty of girls without partners and that I was about to become engaged to the boy I was with, Pat.

'No,' Max said firmly, 'it is Muriel or nobody.'

Already under some obligation to Max for his last-minute assistance, Christopher spoke first to Pat and then to myself, explaining that Max had no dancing partner and, after all, had kindly helped out by attending to the lighting. At length, I agreed to dance with him.

As he whirled me around the floor, I remember thinking: 'So this is that awful wolf. He is good-looking, of course, and he dances beautifully ... but then he would!'

While we were dancing, Max asked me for my telephone number, but I refused to give it to him. I knew he could not get it from the directory, because the number was under my mother's name which, having re-married, was Farrant. I was finally allowed to return to my escort Pat and I thought, with relief, that that was the last I would see of the dashing – but to me, dreadful – Max Whiting.

When the evening was over, as Pat was driving me back to Pembury, he suddenly said: 'There's a car following us – a Humber Snipe.'

It was Max. Undeterred by my refusal to give him my telephone number, he decided that the best way to find out where I lived was by following us home. From that time on he began to call at the house with infuriating persistence to ask me out, but I kept refusing. The next thing I knew he managed to get himself invited most evenings to play bridge with my step-father, my mother and a friend. My mother was very taken with him and, one day, said: 'He is the only one of these boys who come to see you who says anything to your poor parents. I don't know why you never go out with him.'

I explained my reason, but all she did was laugh.

In the meantime, Max continued to insinuate himself into our lives via the bridge evenings, then consolidated his popularity by overhauling our family car. My escorts and I had to step over him and the spare parts as we went out. As he lay beneath the vehicle, repairing it, he would always give us a cheery wave goodbye.

Then, one day he came to me with what I suppose he imagined was an ultimatum. He produced a list of seventeen young men I had been out with fairly regularly and said: 'What have they got that I haven't?'

With all the cruelty of a spoilt young woman, I turned on him and snapped: 'I don't like men who bite their nails, breathe beer all over me and, I suppose, have kissed all the girls in Tunbridge Wells! Now you propose to start on Pembury!'

Furious, Max leapt into his car and roared off up the road at breakneck speed – it seemed like a hundred miles an hour – and I thought smugly: 'That's the last of Max Whiting.'

But no. A month later, he was back again. He turned up with his usual dazzling smile, breathed teetotally over me, showed me some pathetic-looking little fingernails and said:

'There is no cause for complaint about the third matter you disliked about me. Now, when will you come out?'

He asked me to a forthcoming Charity Ball and, while I was trying to dream up some excuse, added: 'It's no good saying that you are already going because my Ma is the Chairman and it was only fixed this afternoon.'

Somewhat reluctantly, I accepted his invitation.

Max and I attended the Ball and while we were there I noticed one of my former boyfriends. He was without a dancing partner, very drunk and behaving very badly. As we swept around the floor, Max asked: 'What's the matter, Muriel? You don't seem very happy.' I explained that I was worried about the other boy, whose name was Gareth.

'I can't have you worried about anything,' Max announced, and promptly took me over to one of his friends. 'Look after Muriel for a moment, please,' he said.

He then collected Gareth, drove him home, put him to bed and returned to the Ball. I was quite moved by this gallant and kind demonstration on Max's part and so, when he next asked me if he could take me out, which was the following week, I accepted.

It was around this time that Pat's mother, who was so concerned about his determination to marry me, decided to take some action. She went to see Mr. Harry Scott Whiting, who was the big white chief of an insurance company office in which Pat worked. (He was also Max's father and was – though no one realised it at the time – to become my father-in-law.) Pat's mother asked Mr. Whiting if her son couldn't be transferred to an overseas branch. This way, she thought, he would be kept away from me and, perhaps, eventually get over what she obviously considered was an immature infatuation.

Being slightly older than Pat, when I heard about this, I wrote to him and told him that we were going to be parted by his being sent abroad. I suggested that it might in any case be better if we mutually agreed not to see each other for one year. If, at the end of that time, we still felt the same about each other, then we would defy our parents.

At this time Pat was living with an aunt in London and received the letter by the late post, which then arrived at 6 p.m.

That same evening, I had been to see a film with Max. In the early hours of the following morning I woke up at home in Pembury and became suddenly aware that there was someone in my bedroom. My mother never bothered to lock the front door. Terrified, I quickly switched on the overhead light. Pat was standing there. He was very tall – six-foot-five – and looked almost as if he were suspended from the ceiling. He had been very much on my mind after I had written to him.

'Pat!' I said. 'How on earth did you get here?'

'I got your letter and caught the next train to Tunbridge Wells,' he explained, 'and I walked to Pembury because the buses had stopped running. Your front door wasn't locked so I walked in. I didn't know which was your bedroom, so I went into one, but the woman in bed there had long hair so I knew it wasn't you and I came out again and tried the next door. I recognised your perfume, so I knew I had the right room.'

We talked over the proposed parting. Pat was against it. Suddenly, we heard a door opening. I said: 'For goodness' sake, get into the wardrobe. It's probably my step-father!'

But Pat was too tall to squeeze into the wardrobe so I told him to get under the bed, which he did, squirming frantically. My step-father went along the passage, presumably to the lavatory, then returned, and the house settled down again. Pat crawled out from under the bed and I told him I thought he ought to leave. He didn't need much persuading – we were both terrified of being caught.

Before he left, however, we did agree that, one year from that same date, we would meet and, if we felt the same about each other, we would marry, despite our parents' objections. Pat was not very happy about the arrangement, but it seemed the only sensible thing to do, because he would in any case have been sent abroad by Mr. Whiting, who had a very influential position with the insurance company for which Pat worked.

I slept late the next morning until, eventually, my mother brought me in a cup of tea. She told me that Aunt Lily Regan, who had been staying with us, was leaving.

'She thinks the house is haunted,' mother said. 'Aunt Lily thought a man came into her room last night and stroked her hair. I told her it must have been the cats, but she won't listen.'

'Mother,' I said, gingerly. 'Will you promise not to be cross if I tell you something?'

It was an awful thing to have to confess – that there had been a young man in my bedroom in the middle of the night. But Aunt Lily, about whom I wrote earlier, was the mother of my cousin and dearest friend, Marjorie Regan, and I was very distressed at the idea of her leaving. Especially since I knew the explanation for her 'ghostly' visitor.

When my mother eventually explained what had happened to Aunt Lily, she said indignantly: 'Well, Hilda, I *do* know the difference between a man and a cat!' And so, Aunt Lily stayed on.

But the incident did not exactly end there. At midday, Max rang and said he had seen Pat on the 8.18 a.m. out of Tunbridge Wells, looking very miserable and, strangely, all covered in fluff and feathers.

'He could only have come down to see you,' Max said, beginning to put two and two together. 'And since I left you at your mother's home at 10.30 p.m. after the film, and saw him at 8.18 a.m., exactly when did you see him?'

There was, as a certain comedian would say, no answer to that. I hung up without saying a word. And mentally chastised our maid for not cleaning under my bed properly!

Max and I went out together for the ensuing eight months. He tried to explain to me how a car works and went into meticulous detail – but I still haven't the faintest notion of the intricacies of the internal combustion engine. But during all this time he made no attempt to make love to me and, still keenly aware of his previous reputation, I eventually began to reflect that perhaps I was the one girl in the world who didn't attract him.

However, during this period, I came to realise that, beneath the veneer of his outward reputation, he was a very nice person. After I had known him for only three weeks, he asked: 'I suppose you wouldn't get engaged to me?' I said: 'Good heavens, no!' He replied quietly that he hadn't thought I would, but that he had felt there was no harm in asking.

Then, about eight or nine months later, Max suddenly kissed me and then burst into tears. I was so surprised at this apparently sophisticated young man of the world weeping that I asked him what on earth was wrong.

'It is just that I love you so much,' he said.

As I mentioned earlier, I had always had a number of boyfriends and had been officially engaged once and unofficially three times. Each time I had avoided allowing matters to progress any further because, in my heart of hearts, I knew that none of them was the man I had seen and known in my childhood waking dreams. Inwardly, I had constantly sought this strong, silent, romantic man who had promised that we would marry, but I could never hope to explain this to any of my would-be lovers. It was so intangible that, as I grew up, I had great difficulty in understanding its full significance myself.

At the time when Max confessed his love, both Pat and an RAF Squadron Leader had matrimonial designs on me and had been to see my father, expressing their intentions. Unfortunately for me, Max also decided that this was the correct and proper thing to do and he called upon my father at his Club.

For the only time I can remember my father was very angry with me and demanded that I should go and see him. He complained that no less than three young men had been to call on him, giving him the impression that they were going to marry his daughter and wanted his consent. He insisted on knowing which of them I intended to marry.

'None of them,' I said.

My father threw up his hands in despair and, for the first time ever, he didn't kiss me goodbye when he put me on the train back to Tunbridge Wells. I suddenly realised that he was deeply shocked and extremely worried.

Looking back, I suppose that, in a way, it was I who brought matters to a head, if only indirectly. Although I had never been one of those schoolgirls prone to 'pashes' on other girls or school-mistresses, the teacher I liked best during my days at Walthamstow Hall had been the gym mistress, who also taught dancing. When earlier, at seventeen, I had become engaged, I discovered that my *fiancé's* sister, Madeleine – Maddie or Mad Cap, as she was known to her family – was none other than my former gym mistress at Walthamstow Hall. Although I eventually broke off the engagement to her brother, she never in any way held this against me. A few years later – at the time when Max was becoming more and more predominant in my life – she wrote to me. She had a growing school of dancing in Worthing and was continually being urged to teach ballet. She knew of my own ballet training and asked if I would consider going into partnership.

I realised that it would be an ideal opportunity to diminish the growing demands which Max was making upon my life, so I agreed to go and live at Worthing and work with Madeleine. We held a number of classes at Warnes Hotel, Worthing.

Max was, of course, furious when he heard of my plans. But Worthing was not so great a distance as to prevent him entirely from seeing me. Quite the contrary. He ordered their family chauffeur, Sydney, to meet him every evening from his train from London and then he would take the car over to Worthing to see me. Every weekend, he would bring me back to Tunbridge Wells and my family.

Eventually, Max's mother came to see me. Could I not consider marrying Max, she asked? She was becoming increasingly worried about him. He would rush off to catch the 8.18 to his job in London every morning and seldom returned home from Worthing before midnight or one or two in the morning. He simply couldn't go on like this. Could I please make up my mind?

Although Max had been proposing to me regularly, I imagine there are few women who have been proposed to by their prospective mothers-in-law.

On New Year's Eve, 1934, I finally made up my mind. I *would* marry Max. We telephoned Mrs Whiting to wish her a happy 1935 and told her the news. No doubt she was greatly relieved.

5   Jack Maxwell Whiting – Lady Dowding's first husband, 'Max', killed in 1944
while serving in RAF Lancasters.

Plans immediately went ahead for the wedding, which took
place at a 13th-century church at Pembury on August 24, 1935.

I was married from my mother's home at Pembury and a big
marquee was set up on the tennis court. The day before the
wedding my step-father noticed that the marquee was smaller
than the one for which he had estimated and insisted on having
it enlarged – a decision which caused an awful commotion on
the morning of my wedding, with workmen scurrying about
everywhere.

My mother and my sister Totty, who was one of my four bridesmaids, went off to have their hair done and our little maid, Clara, was left to bring me breakfast. My mother had insisted that I remain in bed until ten, before getting up to prepare for the wedding. But with all the men hustling and bustling about, making alterations to the marquee, and Clara having to prepare some refreshments for them, I got no breakfast. There were about twenty of mother's guests coming for lunch and I had to be there to receive them, should they happen to arrive before mother and Totty returned from the hairdresser. Thankfully, my own hair and manicure had been attended to the previous night.

Max had made me promise that I wouldn't keep him waiting at the church. 'Whatever you do to me in our future life,' he said, 'for goodness' sake turn up on time!' I had promised that I would.

On my last night at my mother's home I began to think of the man I had thought I would marry – the strong, silent and romantic soldier I somehow knew was named Hugh – and wondered why he had never appeared in my life. I decided that, as he had appeared in khaki uniform, he had probably been killed in some war. In this way, I quite happily rationalised my marriage to Max.

(However, many years later, after my second marriage, I once remarked to Hugh: 'You must have been in the Royal Flying Corps when I "saw" you as a child, yet you wore khaki, I'm sure – not Air Force blue.' Hugh then explained that the Royal Flying Corps had indeed worn khaki, Air Force blue not having been introduced until later.)

Still feeling the pangs of no breakfast, when we eventually sat down to lunch I, being the daughter of the house, was last to be served. Just as my meal was placed in front of me, what did I hear but the extraordinary and distinctive sound of the horn on Max's car. It had once been described as a train calling its young. He was obviously already on his way to church!

Remembering my promise not to be late, I jumped up, leaving my lunch, ran upstairs and started to get into my wedding dress. It was an elaborate affair, designed to resemble an arum lily, and had eighteen yards of white tulle as a veil and train. Dear Elizabeth Edwards, who was the daily help of my step-father's mother, and a competent seamstress, had been assigned to dress me. She decided, instead of tacking the long veil at various points, to fasten it with pins. The result was that I couldn't sit down.

We then discovered that Max, in his eagerness, had gone to the church at 1.30 p.m. – one-and-a-half hours early – for the service which was scheduled for 3 p.m.

So, unable to sit down and certainly not able to eat anything in my beautiful wedding gown, I simply had to wait around until 2.55 p.m., when my uncle, Major Harold Barnes, D.S.O., would escort me to the church.

One of the dramas of the day – and I am sure most brides and grooms have their upsets, major and minor – involved floral decorations. Earlier in the year my mother had told our gardener that there would be a wedding in the summer and asked him to see that the garden was especially beautiful. But although it had been one of the driest, hottest summers, there was little in full flower by August and our garden looked particularly dreary. The gardener said he had plenty of friends who would lend him plants which he could pot in for the occasion. Yet, on the morning of August 24, there was a steady downpour of rain and the gardener was terrified that the borrowed plants might be ruined. With all the problems of reassembling the marquee, the company who provided it were simply not prepared to provide awnings and drugget as well. In all the confusion I cannot remember to this day whether or not the gardener risked potting out the borrowed plants.

All I know is that we arrived at the church in pelting rain. I remember walking up the aisle with my four beautiful bridesmaids, who were dressed in my favourite colours of delphinium, mauves and blues, with matching bouquets and an attendant page-boy in white satin.

The best man was George Weldon, a friend of Max. He looked quite anxious, but Max himself, who had apparently spent the last hour greeting all the guests personally with great enthusiasm, had been mistaken by many of them for the best man. When I joined him at the altar, Max gripped my hand firmly and reassuringly.

I remember very little of the service. Max had wanted the organist to play Gershwin's *Rhapsody In Blue,* but I think it was a little beyond the repertoire of the village church.

There was a slight contretemps as we emerged. The hired Rolls Royce which had brought me there was waiting to take us back to my mother's house for the reception. But the Whitings' chauffeur insisted that, as I was now part of the family, he would drive us back in their car. I suppose that I was quite swept up in the excitement and emotion of the occasion, because I cannot now recall which of the cars took me back to Pembury.

There were between two and three hundred guests and Max and I seemed to spend most of the remainder of the time shaking hands and kissing them. The speeches followed, after which, with Max's help, I cut the wedding cake and sampled a small portion. Apart from that tiny morsel and a few glasses of champagne, to which I was unaccustomed anyway, I had had nothing to eat or drink all day, having missed both breakfast and lunch.

Max had hidden his car to avoid it being festooned with smelly kippers or old boots and horseshoes and eventually, we stole away in another, borrowed vehicle to the place where he had concealed his own. We had just set off towards London, where we were to spend our first night before going abroad, when Max said: 'I thought wives always had lots of luggage.'

I glanced in the back seat.

'Well, there are my hat box and suitcase,' I said. 'Haven't *you* got any luggage?'

Max stopped the car. His luggage wasn't there. He went off to telephone George Weldon. It transpired that Max had put his belongings in a new suitcase which we had been given as a wedding present. He had left it in the hall at Pembury and asked George to put it in the car. Seeing it there, and knowing it was a present, my mother had taken it and placed it in a room along with the other wedding gifts.

George eventually unearthed Max's suitcase and rushed it to us and we finally set off again.

'I suppose the clergyman did give you your passport?' Max asked, a little further along the road.

The procedure was for the wife's passport, bearing her new married name, to be given to the officiating clergyman who would present it to the bride after the wedding service. The clergyman had omitted to do this and, once more, we had to stop to telephone George Weldon. He drove around to the vicar's home, only to find that he was in the bath and George simply had to wait. Eventually, he got the passport and again dashed out to deliver it to us.

At long last we arrived at our hotel in London. And it was there that, I suppose, the effects of not having had anything to eat, a certain amount of champagne to which I was unaccustomed, plus all the other excitement and minor dramas, took their toll. I had never fainted before in my life but, as we went up to our room in the lift, I collapsed. Max had immediately to call the hotel doctor who apparently was very brusque and more than a little suspicious. All that poor Max could say was:

'I haven't even touched her!'

Next day I felt much better and we went to see my father who, with great tact, had not come to the wedding. Then we went off on our honeymoon to La Zoute, in Belgium. While we were there, the lovely Queen of the Belgians, Astrid, was tragically killed in a motor accident. Max and I had seats at the funeral. As a bride, I had nothing suitable to wear – but even the lamp-posts were draped in black crepe.

Max was an adoring, delightful husband and we returned to England excitedly to look for a home. Our original idea was to rent a flat in the Midlands, to be close to the hub of the steel industry, which was Max's business. In 1935, of course, the Midlands were very different from the Tunbridge Wells area where we both came from and we could find nothing we liked. After six weeks of searching, Max's parents suggested that we should look for a nice house which they would buy and Max could pay them back in instalments, as if he were paying rent.

We discovered a delightful little village between Birmingham and Lichfield called Four Oaks and in it, a house which we both liked very much. It stood beside Sutton Park, Warwickshire, which was once owned by Cardinal Wolsey and is, I believe, the largest natural park in England. We informed Max's parents and they came up by train the following weekend to view the house.

As we drove to the station to meet them, Max said: 'Now don't say anything, but I am going down that road at a hundred miles an hour, because if my Ma sees that it is called Clarence Road, it is out.'

When I asked him why, he said: 'I don't know why, but she has a thing about the name Clarence – she thinks it is unlucky.'

Despite Max driving down the road at terrific speed, my mother-in-law was not deceived. In a calm voice, she said: 'Do you think I would let you start your married life in such an unlucky road?'

So, it was goodbye to that particular home.

Eventually, we discovered a house in a delightful little cul-de-sac – the last of twenty houses built by an architect as a hobby. It was a charming place and the kind of home which would be ideal for retirement.

I never did discover the reason for my mother-in-law's dislike of the name Clarence. I suspect that it might have had something to do with the Duke of Clarence, but I cannot be certain. Years later, during my second marriage, Mrs Whiting became very ill and a doctor phoned me to say that he had had her admitted to the Clarence Nursing Home, in Clarence Road, Tunbridge Wells.

Knowing of her aversion to the name, I said: 'You must get her into another nursing home and my husband and I will go and see her at once. She has a thing about the name Clarence.'

'Lady Dowding,' the doctor protested, 'all the nursing homes are full – it is Christmas! This is the only one into which I could get your mother-in-law.'

My husband Hugh and I rushed straight over to see her and I explained to the matron that Mrs Whiting had a hatred of the name Clarence. She was an understanding type and had a notice placed on the door of Mrs Whiting's room saying that under no circumstances was she to discover that she was in the Clarence Nursing Home, or even in Clarence Road. Whether or not my mother-in-law ever found out is impossible to say, but she died there a few weeks later.

Another peculiar aspect of Mrs Whiting's final illness was that, when I looked at the card at the end of her bed, to try to discover her condition, I was surprised to note that it read: 'Vegetarian.' I told the nurse: 'My mother-in-law is not vegetarian.' 'Oh yes, she is,' the nurse replied.

This was most surprising because my in-laws had been quite unsympathetic to my own vegetarianism to the extent that, although they had quite a large household staff, whenever I went to meals there they would serve nothing I could eat. Yet, after all those years and her apparent antagonism towards my dietary inclinations, she had never told me that she too had become a vegetarian, although she was, I knew, fond of animals.

My marriage to Max was a young, gay affair. I suppose we saw every play and musical, went to every ball and had masses of friends.

Three years and one month after our marriage, our son David was born.

5

Married Life, Motherhood and Intimations of Tragedy

OUR DOCTOR, WHO was a personal friend, had become concerned because I had small pelvic bones and he felt that I should not have a baby weighing more than six pounds. He told me: 'Max is already in a complete flap about the whole thing, but I am going to take you to see a specialist.'

During their discussions, which I overheard, my doctor seemed to be in favour of a caesarian operation, but the specialist said: 'She is a very healthy young woman and I am against a caesarian for women under thirty, unless essential. She dances, she rides and I think it is much better to induce the baby.'

They told me that they would come around at 10 a.m. on Friday, September 23, and start off my baby. I remember getting up about 6 a.m. and filling the whole nursery and house with flowers and I had sherry and other drinks awaiting the doctor and specialist, which surprised them.

In my ignorance, I thought that my baby would arrive within the hour but, by Sunday morning, the specialist was again called in. He told Max: 'I don't think we will be able to save both your wife and child.'

Max chose that I should be the one to live. While they were putting me under the anaesthetic, I later discovered, the specialist had wandered out along the passage, looked in the nursery and thought: 'This is a much-wanted baby.' I recall him holding my hand and saying: 'Are you prepared to take a risk?' 'Yes,' I answered.

He did take a risk – and saved us both. But I was very ill and, in fact, failed to respond to treatment. About two days after

David's birth, my mother was sent for, as I was thought to be dying.

I remember my mother coming into my bedroom and touching my nightgown and asking: 'Is this silk?' What a ridiculous question to ask, I thought, when I was feeling so dreadful. But I had forgotten about my mother's training as a member of the Seekers. Apparently, it is difficult to heal through silk.

Being premature, David was fed every three hours and, whenever the pleasant but strictly orthodox nurse was busy doing so, my mother would creep in and apply her healing powers. It seems that I was continually lapsing into unconsciousness, but I remember asking the nurse at one point: 'Am I dying?' And I noticed the tears in her eyes as she replied: 'Do you think I would let a slip of a thing like you spoil my record? I have never lost a mother yet – or a baby.'

The actual details of those hours are vague, but I remember eventually waking up and seeing the nurse, my mother and Max standing there. 'She's not unconscious, she has been asleep!' the nurse said. I turned my eyes towards my mother.

'I feel hungry,' I said. 'I would like some scrambled eggs.'

I had taken no food or liquid for some days.

My mother immediately rushed into the kitchen. The nurse rushed to the telephone. She told the doctor: 'Her mother will kill her – she is going to give her scrambled eggs!'

But, thanks to my mother's powers of healing and the scrambled eggs, I recovered and I went down in medical records that year as a most extraordinary case of recovery. The doctor, of course, knew nothing about my mother's secret healing sessions every three hours while David was being fed.

Six weeks later Max and I went to a ball and danced every dance.

Max was delighted with his little son, but we had not yet decided on a name. He came to me one day and said: 'Look, I have to register the baby. What are we going to call him?'

Our favourite name was David, but Max had already bought me a little Cairn terrier for my first birthday after we were married and we had called him David.

After looking thoughtful for a while, Max said: 'Sad as it is, we may not always have doggy David and, as we both like the name so much, why not call the baby David?'

And so David Maxwell – the latter after his father – our son became.

Max had already engaged a permanent nanny, because he wanted above all things to be able to take me out and about as before, and not have me tied to the baby and nappies. David's godparents, the Epsteins, had sent us a huge white pram. On nanny's first weekend off, I remember trying to push this immense white affair with such a tiny baby in it out for a walk and having great difficulty negotiating the kerbs. A neighbour passing by stopped to peep into the pram at my baby and wryly remarked: 'I understand you have called him after your dog first and your husband second.'

I should, here, say something about the unusual nature of David's godparents. Apart from Molly Epstein, these were George Weldon, the best man at our wedding, and Dr. Lascelles.

In fact, Dr. Lascelles was none other than the spiritual entity who was the guide of the Seekers. At one of our sittings, 'Dr. Lascelles' had already told me that my child would be born with a particular role to fulfil and was being channelled through me because of my work with the healing circles. He said that very often when a soul incarnated it became so immured in worldly matters that it lost sight of its true purpose in life. He said that he would like to become godfather to the coming child to enable him always to realise his correct role.

I asked my father-in-law if he would mind standing in for Dr. Lascelles at the christening ceremony. Mr. Whiting said: 'This is one of your friends that I have not heard about, Muriel. Who is he?' When he heard that it was a doctor who had been dead for about one hundred and fifty years, he almost dropped David.

Thus, David's godparents were, Molly Epstein, George Weldon and, by proxy, Dr. Lascelles. I will explain how Dr. Lascelles' forecast of David's set role in life came true in due course.

Shortly after David's birth, the newspapers were full of the Munich Agreement over Czechoslovakia and, despite Chamberlain's assurances of 'peace in our time,' it was not long before the storm clouds of war were gathering.

Apart from his steel interests, Max had a secondary business in Germany, because he was importing machinery for use in the aircraft manufacturing industry. As conditions became more and more uncertain and ominous in Europe, he became more and more anxious about most of his money being tied up in Germany. He began to drink. At the time, I simply did not understand that he was so tremendously worried and he developed drinking habits which our friends and I found very upsetting.

My father-in-law felt that as our home was in an industrial area, not far from the Black Country, and most likely to be bombed when war broke out, it would be best to sell up. In any case, Max's home business interests meant that he had to transfer his base of operations to Warrington, and so we rented a house in the nearby village of Appleton, in Cheshire.

Max was in a reserved occupation and, because all his friends eventually went off to the war, this contributed to his state of distress and unhappiness and also, I think, a feeling of guilt. His drinking habits grew worse and he began mixing with people with whom he would not previously have associated in the normal course of events. I am afraid that, instead of trying to understand and help him, I behaved like a very spoilt young woman.

At length, I decided that it would perhaps be best if I left him. I told him so. His first reaction was to give all the housekeeping money to our maid, so that I had none. He also put all my shoes in the boot of his car so that I couldn't go out. Finally, he pulled out the telephone cord so that I could not contact anyone. However, the telephone exchange discovered the fault and fixed it. I was then able to phone my father-in-law and explain that I was leaving Max. He immediately came up to see us and persuaded me to stay a little longer.

For some time after David's birth I had had a certain amount of abdominal pain and an operation became necessary. I went into hospital and I think the nurse attending me decided that I was very spoilt, because Max created a frightful fuss and was in and out of the hospital every five minutes with instructions.

About two days after my operation, the first bomb fell in the area. There was a swing-bridge across the river which provided the only road link between Appleton and Warrington and, during ensuing air-raids, this bridge would be swung and left open, closing the road. It meant, of course, that doctors and nurses who travelled in from Warrington were unable to get to and from the hospital.

At one stage during my recovery, a young nurse who was in charge of about thirty patients on her own because of an air-raid, decided that we should all move to the ground floor for safety. On the way down, we became stuck in the lift.

Max, meanwhile, was on the other side of the bridge in Warrington, frantic with worry and unable to cross over to Appleton.

When I was finally ready for discharge from hospital, I still felt that it would be best if I returned to my mother. And so, along with David and doggy-David, I left Appleton and travelled back to Tunbridge Wells. During this time, a peculiar incident occurred which harked back to something which had earlier happened to David.

When he was nearly two, he suddenly developed the habit of calling out in the night. Max and I would rush into the nursery and, with great concern, David would tell us: 'Porker! He's got black feet!'

These frequent disturbances worried us. Max wondered if my strong feelings about vegetarianism had in some way communicated themselves to him. Had he, perhaps, been upset at the sight of a pig – 'porker' – with black feet which he had seen in a butcher's shop? It was highly unlikely, because I did not take David into town. Besides, rationing had made the sight of a whole pig in a butcher's shop a rarity. Fortunately, these upsets over 'Porker', whoever or whatever it was, subsided after about a month and I forgot about them ... until we went to Tunbridge Wells.

One afternoon, David had gone off to tea with a little friend named John and my mother and I were having tea when a young man knocked at the door. He was wearing the khaki uniform of the Royal Army Medical Corps and he had brought a book which he wanted to return to the Theosophical Society and exchange for another. My mother was then Honorary Secretary to the local Society.

The young man, who was Welsh, appeared to have walked the seven or eight miles from where he was stationed to our house and was very tired, so we invited him in to tea. We sat talking for a while, when mother and I noticed that the young man appeared to have fallen asleep. But, when he began to speak in a voice not his own and with his eyes still closed, we realised that he had somehow fallen into a trance state.

A clergyman apparently spoke to us through him. At one point he told us that there was a little black boy who wanted to speak to me through the sleeping soldier. The little boy said:

'David's Mummy? I am Poaca. My name means Peace, but David used to call me Porker. We played together often and were friends until he got frightened. All the children he knew were white children and it frightened him when he realised I was black.'

It was then I remembered David calling out in the night and telling us about 'Porker' and his black feet. A few years later when the war was over, I was again reminded of Porker. For on more than one occasion, his headmaster at Prep School wrote to say that although David was an 'imp of Satan', he made up for this in one way by his friendship with and care of the coloured children in the school, of which there were several from China, India and Africa. He apparently took particular care of the newcomers who were unhappy at being so far from their home countries. He always took vast quantities of fruit back to school with him because he said many there missed fruit so much.

David didn't remember the Porker of his childhood dreams, but I sometimes wondered if his friendship as a baby with a little black boy – possibly on a spiritual level – gave him this understanding of and sympathy for the children of darker-skinned races.

By the time we settled in at Pembury, Max had obtained his release from his classification as being in a reserved occupation and joined the Air Force. He wrote to me and said that he would shortly be having leave and what did I want him to do. I simply replied: 'Enjoy yourself.'

He then informed me that he was coming down to Tunbridge Wells and inquired what kind of reception he was likely to get. David was frantic with delight and wanted to meet him at the station. I couldn't decide whether to take him along to see his father but eventually, because he was so excited, we both went to meet the train.

It was the first time that I had seen Max in uniform and I noticed how strangely older he looked; we hadn't seen each other for eight or nine months. With David clambering all over him, he came up to me and said:

'I love you as much as ever.'

From then on, our life continued very happily, I am thankful to say.

Three years later, he was to be posted as 'missing.'

In the meantime, like many war wives, I went on living at mother's home. In fact, I ran it for my step-brother, my sister and David, because my mother went to Ilfracombe to manage house for my step-father, Roy Farrant, who was now in the Pay Corps. My friend Joan Clark and her son, Skipper, also came to stay with us.

At the time, people were being evacuated from London and billeted on others who had accommodation out in country areas. At one stage my mother was informed that some thirty soldiers would be allocated to her. She explained that I was running the house, was only a young woman and that she did not think that this would be a good thing. The agents then told her that, as she had such a large house, she should let off some of her rooms.

We managed to do this, taking in a woman whose daughter was in a nearby hospital. Curiously enough, the daughter's *fiancé*, who used to come and stay with us, had the same surname as myself – Whiting.

During this time I would frequently consult the playing cards to try to get an indication of future events – a divinatory system which I had picked up from an acquaintance during my dancing days. My sister Totty and I were looking forward to Christmas because Max, my mother and step-father were expected and we had made all kinds of preparations.

When I consulted the cards, however, I could see nothing consistent with our expectations but, instead, the death of a lover, the death of a friend and a funeral from the house. The cards indicated none of the gaiety we expected. I was also very unhappy about the way Max showed in the cards.

In due course, everyone arrived and, on Christmas Eve, the hotel where my step-father's mother lived phoned to say that she had died and would he please collect her, as they did not want a body in the place over Christmas. The only solution was to bring her to our home.

All Christmas festivities were therefore cancelled and – as indicated by the cards – a funeral did take place from home, two days after Christmas.

A few months later, my closest friend and cousin, Marjorie, was killed in a car crash and my former *fiancé,* Pat, had been one of the early RAF casualties of the war, in late 1940 at Rheims.

In addition, Max was not to remain on this earth much longer – being reported missing in 1944.

As a result, I have never consulted the cards since.

*   *   *

It was late in 1943, Max was due home on leave and we were preparing a wonderful Christmas for him. Max got leave every six weeks and, being a member of an aircrew flying Lancaster bombers, he also received extra bonuses which were not available to others: petrol for the car, fruit and chocolates.

I was preparing to go up to Harrods to buy a cocktail dress with some coupons Max had sent me and was going to leave David in the care of my mother and sister. Just as I was about to leave, David asked:

'Has my Daddy been killed yet?'

'Of course not,' we assured him. 'Daddy is coming home on leave next week.'

'I only ask because I had not seen him lately,' David replied. 'But he will be killed, you know.'

Naturally, we tried to assure him that this was not so.

When I arrived at Harrods, I went for a coffee. Someone at the next table was reading a newspaper. The headline said: 70 Lancasters Fail to Return from Hamburg.

I rushed straight out of the store and immediately hailed a taxi and got the train back to Pembury. When I arrived, my mother told me Max had just phoned to say: 'Back O.K.'

I think it was David's foreknowledge of his father's death and his inability to communicate this to those around him which contributed to the asthma he developed a few months later. He became quite ill with bronchial pneumonia and I took him to Kilve, in Somerset, where an aunt had a cottage which she offered us on loan. Here I was to be joined at Easter by my friend Joan and her son, Skipper, along with another friend, Brenda, and her son, John.

As usual, Max came home on leave. We had a very happy time. Before he left, he said: 'Now don't worry, because when the moon is as it is, we don't fly.' Yet I felt there was something oddly, indescribably different about him and, when he kissed me goodbye, he said:

'Nine years isn't nearly long enough to be married to you.'

We continued our daily life at the cottage. As David grew better, each day two of us would take the three boys out, while the third mother stayed behind and prepared high tea for our return.

Another friend, Isobel, whose husband had been killed while serving in the Navy earlier in the War, used to come round frequently in the evenings about that time, when the boys were safely tucked in bed. The four of us would sit round a table and try to discover future events by placing our forefingers on an upturned glass and letting it spell out words from letters of the alphabet placed in a circle. Although none of us exerted any conscious pressure on the glass, it would move and the information which we received in this way later often proved to be correct.

On May 21, 1944, the glass spelled out: PAT, PAT FOR POPPET.

I could only assume that it referred to the Pat to whom I had been engaged and who had been killed in 1940. Then, the glass spelled out again: POPPET BE BRAVE DARLING, PAT.

The following day, Joan and I took out the three boys for a picnic lunch, while Brenda stayed behind to prepare high tea. We had just given the boys their tea and put them to bed when there was a knock at the door. Joan answered it. She looked very strange and pallid when she came back. She handed me a telegram. It was the message which all war wives lived in fear and dread of receiving. It said:

'We regret to inform you that your husband, Jack Maxwell Whiting, is missing.'

It transpired that the telegram should have been delivered at 1 p.m., but that when it came through the local postmistress, who had seen Max on his Easter visit, burst into tears and couldn't bring it to the cottage. Instead, they had sent for a cousin, Dorothy Preedy, at Bridgwater, to bring it to me.

In the dreadful days that followed, one simply lived for the post and the news. But no news came ... only masses of forms to fill in.

In an effort to be encouraging, friends pointed out that Max, who had had such a reputation for mad stunts and crazy behaviour, would be certain to escape. After all, he had the blond good looks which would pass as Aryan, he spoke fluent German and knew the country well.

When I told David that we must pray very hard for Daddy's plane and crew because the aircraft was lost, David looked at me very solemnly and said:

'Daddy is having tea with Auntie Marjorie.'

Marjorie was, of course, the close friend and cousin who had been killed in a car smash some two years previously. I think it was David's acceptance, in his own way, of his father's death which helped to prepare and convince me.

One evening, our friend Isobel, who had introduced us to the improvised 'planchette' with an upturned glass, came round and told us that, one night, while she was experimenting with the technique alone, she got a message from her late husband. He said she was to stop the practice and never do it again because it was highly dangerous. She came especially to tell us and so we also stopped using the glass. Many years later I came to realise that, although this was one means by which one *could* communicate with those no longer on this earth, it was indeed highly dangerous because it could lead to obsession. Also, I understand, messages received in this way cannot all be relied upon, because certain tormented souls and discarnate lower entities can manipulate the glass for their own mindless purposes.

In the event of his not returning from a raid, Max had instructed one of his friends to send on a letter to me. In it, he briefly said:

'If you ever receive this, it means I have not been able to get back to you, but don't worry, bad pennies always turn up and, just as you are about to marry a millionaire, I shall turn up. If I am unable to do this, I will try and contact you through the sources in which you believe.'

Max was always very open-minded about the various subjects in which I took an interest: reincarnation, spiritualism, Theosophy and astrology. And, in a vague way, I think he agreed with most of my beliefs but simply wasn't particularly interested.

There was no possibility of consulting a medium in the little village of Kilve and I knew of no one in Somerset. However, out of the blue I received a letter from a medium friend of my mother, David Bedbrook. He said that, if I thought it might help, he and his wife Betty would come down to Kilve. He had heard from my mother that Max was missing. David and Betty came to the cottage and, during a sitting, confirmed that Max had indeed been killed.

I then had to begin to think of practical matters and decided that I had better ask my mother if I could live in her little seaside house at Beltinge, near Herne Bay. The furniture from the home which Max and I had had at Four Oaks would be far too big and there was far too much of it to fit the little three-bedroomed house. My friend Joan asked if she could buy some of the items, but when he overheard this, David Bedbrook said: 'Don't sell anything. You will go to Herne Bay, but regard it merely as a holiday, because I see you being offered quite a big house and you will need all the furniture you have.'

6

An Interlude: the Case of the Black Elephants

SOME WEEKS AFTER David and Betty Bedbrook had left, I had one of those strange experiences I had had since childhood at different times. I can only describe it as a waking dream for, on properly regaining consciousness after the experience, I noticed that the mantelpiece in my room seemed different in some way – rather like Alice did when she emerged on the other side of the Looking-Glass.

During the experience, there were some black, ornamental elephants on the mantelpiece and, standing by them, was a tall, thin man in grey flannel trousers and a blue-ish shirt and he was tying a knitted black tie. He had greyish hair and very blue eyes. I knew him at once and was so happy to see him, for I realised he was someone I knew and loved dearly. He turned and smiled at me and then started to place the elephants one on top of the other. I laughed with happiness and remember calling out to him.

For his name was Hugh.

My friend Joan shared part of this strange and wonderful experience and, partly to demonstrate that it was by no means pure fantasy on my part, I have asked her to tell her own version of the story. Here, then, is that account, which she has called:

Black Elephants
Mean Happiness

by

Joan Clark

IT WAS DURING our stay at the cottage in Kilve, Somerset, that there occurred what I like to call The Case of the Black Elephants. It was such an unusual experience, both for my friend Muriel and for those of us who shared it, that Muriel has asked me to describe what happened in my own words in this section of her book.

Following the telegram informing Muriel that her husband Max was missing, we could not help sharing her anxiety. We – that is, Muriel, our friend Brenda and our three respective sons – had all been together that Easter and Max had been so full of life, so gay and handsome in his RAF uniform. We found it difficult to believe, even after the telegram, that news would not soon arrive telling us of his whereabouts. Every night we went to bed with a silent prayer for Max and his safe return. But the weeks went by.

One morning I was awakened early by the sound of laughter coming from Muriel's bedroom, which was next to mine. I sat up in bed and listened. Again I heard laughter, and someone talking. Muriel was laughing and she sounded so happy and carefree, I thought: Max has come home! Yet even as the thought entered my head I somehow knew that it was not Max.

I got up and went into the kitchen – it was a single-storey cottage, or bungalow – and Brenda was making tea.

'Did you hear the laughter and talking coming from Muriel's room?' I asked.

'Yes,' she replied emphatically. 'It woke me up.'

As we were talking, Muriel's door opened. We went to her.

'Is everything all right?' we asked.

'Yes,' she said. But she looked at us strangely. 'Why do you ask?'

We told her that we had both heard her laughing and talking to someone.

'Yes,' she admitted. 'I have been talking to a tall, grey-haired man with blue eyes who was standing by the fireplace. He wore a blue shirt, grey flannel trousers and a black tie. There were black elephants on the mantelpiece and, as he stood there, he balanced the elephants one on top of the other. Then he turned and laughed at me. I called to him, "Hugh" and I was laughing with happiness because I knew him so well and was so pleased to see him.'

Naturally, we wondered: had she, perhaps, been dreaming? But Muriel was convinced that it had not been a dream.

'It was too real,' she said, firmly

'But if it wasn't a dream, how could this man have got into your room? And how did you know his name was Hugh? Who *is* Hugh?' we asked.

Muriel could not explain how it had happened, nor indeed exactly what had happened. She repeated that Hugh was someone she knew very well. He was grey-haired, had very blue eyes and was wearing a black tie. Could the tie perhaps be a symbol of death, she wondered?

More weeks went by, with still no news of Max.

One Sunday morning, as usual, Muriel brought the Sunday newspaper into the lounge. As she unfolded it, glancing over the headlines, she exclaimed: 'Joan, look! This is Hugh! This is the man who was in my room!'

She laid the paper on the table and I stared down at a large, head-and-shoulders photograph showing the rather stern features of a man in RAF uniform. Underneath it was the caption: Air Chief Marshal Lord Dowding.

He was the man we knew by repute who had fought and won the Battle of Britain and whose foresight had saved the country from German invasion. As we read about him together, Muriel repeated that she was sure he was the man who had played with the black elephants on the mantelpiece and she was equally sure that, although she had never seen Lord Dowding before, she knew him 'terribly well.'

We talked about her strange, intuitive feelings and one of us, I think it was I, suggested that she should write to ask him if he could help her to get any information about Max. She was hesitant and it was not until some months later, in the autumn, that she was actually prompted to write to him by her father-in-law. By then, Lord Dowding's interest in the fate of missing young airmen enabled him to advise Muriel where to find a medium from whom she might try to seek information. This was the beginning of a sympathetic correspondence between them and, when it was eventually confirmed that Max's plane had been shot down, Muriel, I know, derived much comfort from his letters. Their mutual interest in spiritualism, Theosophy and allied subjects helped her through a very sad and difficult period of her life.

Lord Dowding eventually suggested a meeting and this was the beginning of a firm friendship and a deep, long-lasting love. The morning after they became secretly engaged – which she will no doubt describe in its proper sequence – Muriel went to coffee with a close neighbour.

Several years had gone by since the curious incident at Kilve, but Muriel was suddenly reminded of it. For as she entered her friend's sitting room, there on the mantelpiece, almost as if they were mocking her, stood the black elephants of her 'waking dream.'

As she stared at them in astonishment, her friend said:

'They only came yesterday. Do you know what they are supposed to mean?'

Muriel shook her head.

'Black elephants mean happiness,' the neighbour said.

Some time after the marriage of Muriel and Hugh, I was invited to visit them at their home in Tunbridge Wells. Early one morning during my stay, I was once again awakened by the sound of happy laughter. For an instant, I almost thought I was back at Kilve. I sat up in bed and listened and the laughter came again, just as it had done before, mingling with the sound of a man's voice.

I lay back on the pillows and wondered ...

Muriel's trials and tribulations were at last over. She and her Hugh were truly happy. A dream had come true.

But was that strange experience at Kilve merely a dream?

Or was it, perhaps, a projection of the subconscious into the future, to show her that her despair would not last for ever and that she would attain the happiness that was in store for her?

7

The Crooked Cross and Pentagram, a Message from Max and a Letter to Lord Dowding

IN JUNE, 1944 – only a month after the telegram informing me that Max was missing – the Allied Invasion of Europe took place. Many large army lorries were hidden in the fields of the English countryside, camouflaged from the air.

One day, a friend came around to visit me at Kilve. She seemed to be in a particularly excited state.

'I am sure we will win the War,' she said.

When I asked her how she could be so certain, she asked:

'Haven't you seen all the lorries that are going over in the Invasion?' I said that I had.

'Well,' she said, 'you realise that the sign of Hitler is a crooked swastika – its arms going the wrong way – and that is a sign of destruction. And what have our Allies' lorries got emblazoned upon them, but the five-pointed star!

'If ever you see a picture of a fairy with a wand, you will notice that it has a five-pointed star on the tip. And, by some miracle, the one sign that can overcome the crooked swastika is the five-pointed star which, as you know in fairy tales, always overcomes the power of the bad fairy. There's a great deal of truth behind the tales we learn as children. So ... I just *know* we have got the symbol on our side that will overcome the reversed swastika of Hitler.'

As I was to learn through my Theosophical studies, my friend was quite correct. The swastika is an extremely ancient symbol, not of evil, but of good – its name being derived from the Sanskrit *svastika,* meaning luck, well-being, or good-fortune. It was only after Hitler and the Nazis adopted the swastika as their emblem that the Fuhrer had the symbol of the *Haken-kreuz,* or 'crooked cross' reversed, thus making it a symbol of evil.

The pentagram, or five-pointed star, on the other hand, has for countless ages been regarded by occultists as a powerful magical symbol, employed to invoke beneficial influences and overcome evil ones. With one of its points uppermost, it is said to represent the supremacy of the divine spirit over the four elements. With two points uppermost, however, like the reversed swastika, the pentagram becomes a talisman of evil.

By October, 1944, Joan, Brenda and I were able to leave Kilve and I returned to stay for a while with my in-laws. (Because of the invasion, there had been a temporary ban on travel, to keep the roads clear for military vehicles.) Naturally, like myself, my in-laws were deeply grieved and troubled because Max was missing. To be told positively that a loved one has been killed in an accident of some kind is one thing; but to be informed that someone is 'missing presumed dead' without learning how and where, has a quite different effect. It leaves one constantly wondering and worrying if the person concerned died quickly or in great pain ... or, even more important, if there is any slim possibility that they might somehow have survived. 'Presumed' is a cruelly lingering word in such a context.

The Whitings were fairly orthodox in their beliefs, but they knew of my own interests in spiritual matters and so, when we first discussed the matter of Max, their first question was:

'What are you going to do about it, Muriel?'

The unspoken implication being that perhaps I might consult a medium to try to learn something of Max's fate.

I told them that I would like to go to London, if they would look after David for me, and see if I could get a sitting with a medium. I did not book a sitting because some people – my in-laws included – believed that mediums ran a kind of private intelligence serviie, rather like detective agencies, so that they knew all about their clients in advance. Although I knew from experience that this was not so in the majority of cases and only applied to a small number of charlatans, I wanted to respect the standpoint of the Whitings.

In fact, I had already previously written to try to get a sitting with the world-famous medium of the Forties, Estelle Roberts, only to be informed that she was booked up for almost a year in advance.

I therefore went, without appointment, to the College of Psychic Sciences. Before entering, I took off my wedding ring, my diamond RAF brooch, and was shown into a room on the top floor of 16 Queensberry Place, in South Kensington. A little old woman, whom I later came to know as Miss Topcott, was sitting there. She seemed a kindly person and, barely before I had seated myself opposite her, she said: 'I have your brother here – Max.' Then: 'Oh, he is annoyed at being called your brother – he says he is your husband. You know he is on the other side?'

I was quite speechless.

'He seems to feel you are rather unbelieving,' she went on, 'although you *know* about these things. Why is he holding two rings over your head ... and one of them glitters?'

Although it is true that Max married me with a platinum wedding ring and a diamond eternity ring, I did not consider this evidential, because the information was in my mind and the medium might have discerned it telepathically. On the other hand, it was just faintly possible that Max thought this was one satisfactory way of identifying himself. I tried to keep an open mind.

Miss Topcott then said: 'He wants you to know what happened.'

She then relayed to me what Max apparently told her – that his Lancaster had been flying towards the coast of Norway, when it was pursued and shot down by German fighter-planes. Through the medium, Max said he had one moment of thinking, 'This is it!' and he thought he called my pet-name – Poppet. Then he described what seemed like a fall down a dark tunnel with a light at the bottom. On reaching the base, I was apparently waiting for him and said, 'It is all right, darling, go to sleep.' He put his head on my shoulder and fell asleep. (At the time, of course, I would have been in reality asleep in Kilve – as the incident apparently took place at about 3 a.m.)

Theosophy had taught me that anyone suffering a violent death would not have an easy time. If one dies naturally, the various bodies – the mental, emotional and etheric centres – slowly disengage themselves from the physical and death is quite easy. But in a violent death, this does not always happen smoothly and, as a result, the soul sometimes remains earthbound for some time. The best way to help anyone in this latter situation, it is said, is to persuade them to go to sleep and, during the sleep period, the different bodies can all quietly leave the physical.

So, in a way, the medium's message from Max about the conditions of his supposed death seemed to make some kind of sense to me. But what I could not accept was the assertion that his aircraft was said to have been flying towards Norway, instead of Germany.

'Max,' I said, 'You went to Duisburg.'

Speaking through Miss Topcott, he replied: 'I will try to get you the evidence. But I assure you, the last I saw with my physical eyes was the coast of Norway. I did not go on the Duisburg raid.'

It was not until two years later, when the War had ended, that I received amazing confirmation of Max's message – in an extremely unexpected and indirect way. My step-father was on a train travelling to Tunbridge Wells from the south coast. His only other fellow-passenger in the carriage was a Dane. Since the War had only ended in 1945, it was still a great topic of conversation wherever one went. Quite naturally, my step-father Farrant asked the Dane how he and his family had fared during the War.

'We had one great tragedy,' the Dane said. 'I own a farm that runs down to the sea. I shall never forget the night of May 22, 1944, when we heard one of your great Lancaster bombers fly over towards Norway. The German planes came after it and it was shot down. We were able to salvage part of the plane and most of the bodies and we built a little memorial to them.'

He then showed my step-father a photograph of this memorial, a copy of which I still have. In Danish, it was inscribed: 'To our gallant English Allies.' Around it, carved on the faces of individual stones, were the names of the crew. Among them was J. M. Whiting, Kent. Local schoolchildren kept the little monument decorated with flowers, the Danish farmer said.

My step-father asked if the Danes had officially informed the British Air Ministry of the crashed Lancaster and its crew. The Dane said no. After my step-father persuaded him to do so, it was confirmed that the Lancaster – Max's plane – had indeed been shot down en route to Norway. Because of the great difficulty involved in tracking down the fates of individuals and members of lost aircrews and their particular missions, I have been unable to determine officially what Max's aircraft was doing, flying towards Norway on that night, although I can only assume that perhaps the mission involved dropping someone in Norway.

6 Memorial to a bomber crew: this photograph – the only official record of Max Whiting's fate – was given to Lady Dowding's step-father in 1946, by a Danish farmer.

Naturally, having originally heard on the radio that Lancasters had been sent on a raid on Duisburg that same night, I had found the medium's message about Norway hard to believe. Yet, in the end, Max appears to have produced the evidence I needed to be convinced.

At the actual time of the sitting with Miss Topcott, however, I naturally did not have any particularly convincing and concrete news to give to my in-laws. Before going to London to visit Miss Topcott, I had taken David out in the morning and, on my return, I discovered my father-in-law writing a letter. When he had finished, he showed it to me. It was addressed to Air Chief Marshal Lord Dowding. It explained that his son,

Jack Maxwell Whiting, had been posted missing on May 22, 1944, gave particulars of his squadron, rank and other details and pointed out that there had been no further news of him, six months later. Lord Dowding had written a book about his views on life after death called *Many Mansions,* and my father-in-law thought that, if not by normal channels, perhaps the Air Chief Marshal might help to get news of Max through unorthodox – spiritual – means.

I should at this point make it clear that this was entirely my father-in-law's idea to write to Lord Dowding. For although the man I had seen in my waking vision at Kilve looked very like him, as his picture appeared in the Sunday newspaper, I had dismissed the entire incident as too fantastic for words.

When I had read the letter, my father-in-law said: 'I think I have a better idea. Lord Dowding might be more sympathetic towards a possible young RAF widow than he would be towards an old man.'

So, at my father-in-law's request, later that afternoon I sat down and, with only a few minor alterations, copied his letter in my own hand.

Before describing the events which ultimately resulted from the sending of this letter, I should explain that, by the time I actually met Lord Dowding, I was living at Oakgates. This was a house which my father-in-law had built on top of a woodland, some three or four miles outside Tunbridge Wells. He had first bought some condemned cottages, along with a 500-year-old barn, on the site – and then, to occupy his retirement, he built Oakgates.

War had broken out just as the house was completed and Oakgates had been commandeered by the military as an officers' mess. When I returned from Kilve in 1944, my father-in-law took me out to look at the house and asked what I thought of it. I replied that I thought it was beautiful.

At this time I had been alternately staying either with my friend Joan in Herne Bay or at my mother's house there.

'Is there any reason why you have to live in Herne Bay?' Mr. Whiting asked.

'Merely because I have a house there,' I replied.

'Well,' he said, 'if you like it, it is yours.'

By Deed of Gift, he made over Oakgates to me. Thus, the

words of the medium David Bedbrook on his visit to Kilve had proved correct: 'Don't sell anything. You will go to Herne Bay, but regard it merely as a holiday, because I see you being offered quite a big house and you will need all the furniture you have.'

I was extremely glad I had listened to his advice – and kept all our furniture from Four Oaks.

Because the Army was still using Oakgates, I was unable to move into the house for two years, and so continued staying occasionally with Joan, at my mother's house in Herne Bay, or with my in-laws.

Then, at last, in 1946, I was able to move into the beautiful home my father-in-law had built. Workmen were putting the place back in order now that the military had moved out. All the furniture was stacked in one downstairs room and, what I thought was the silver, was placed in a box beside the bed I was using upstairs. However, I later discovered that the box beside my bed contained nothing but linen. The real box containing the silverware had been left just by the front door all the time!

As the house gradually assumed some semblance of order, being cleaned and repainted and curtains going up at the windows, a little, very thin, greyish cat moved in with me. No doubt taking her cue from the new look the house was getting, she began to clean herself up. At first, she had looked so ordinary that I called her Plain Jane. But once all the dirty grey had disappeared through her meticulous self-grooming, she turned out to be a beautiful, snowy white. Jane was to stay with me for many years, but I gradually collected so many other strays that she eventually took herself off to the nearby home of an elderly lady, where she installed herself graciously as the one-and-only housecat. But she still frequently came around to visit me early in the mornings.

During this period of my life, I read many books on occult subjects and one which particularly interested me was Grace Cooke's *Plumed Serpent,* which was an account of an apparent past incarnation. I wish it were still in print because, along with *The Winged Pharaoh* by Joan Grant – yet another case of apparent retrocognition of a previous life, in ancient Egypt – it is among the best books I have ever read. Some years later, when I tried to obtain the *Plumed Serpent,* I learned that Grace

Cooke had been the founder of the White Eagle Lodge, an organisation devoted to healing and spiritualistic teachings. I immediately joined as a country member, which meant that I received their literature but did not attend meetings. I did not meet Grace Cooke herself for several years.

However, as I had already been a member of the Theosophical Society for some years, now that I was living near Tunbridge Wells again, I began attending the local lodge regularly. There were only about five of us in the study classes and the Lecture Secretary was a dear old lady called Mrs. Lister. She was a friend of my mother and was obviously finding it something of a strain to arrange lecturers, meet them, escort them to the lecture rooms and generally look after them. I took over this job from Mrs. Lister and for fourteen years was Lecture Secretary of the local Theosophical Society.

I felt that it was very disappointing that the lecturers had to face such a small audience as ours. But, I reasoned, if our membership were to increase, we should get really outstanding and much more well-known speakers. I therefore went up to the headquarters of the Theosophical Society in London, and saw Mrs. Holly Salmon, who was in charge of allocating lecturers to various lodges throughout the country. I took with me a list of their five or six top lecturers. When I explained the problem, Mrs. Salmon said: 'How can you expect me to send these lecturers, who are so much in demand, down to such a very small group as the Tunbridge Wells Lodge?'

However, we got chatting and became quite friendly and eventually she agreed to help out. She would, she said, send several top speakers to our lodge, providing that I would also agree to book new ones who were making their debut. I was not to let the other members know that these occasional lecturers were absolute newcomers.

My strategy worked. The result was that we had some really unorthodox lectures – and in due course our audiences grew from a mere five to forty. I enjoyed the work very much.

My mother had, as I have mentioned already, never been keen on spiritualism – certainly not of the kind in which one contacts Aunt Bessie to ask if you should go to Bournemouth or Eastbourne for your holidays, or other such trivia. However, she was interested in all spiritual teachings and, in Pembury, where she was still living, there was a woman who was a natural medium, a Mrs. Wood. They became close friends.

Exactly how it came about I am not certain, but as a result of this friendship, my mother and the medium started what was known as a 'Rescue Circle.' Seven of us – including my sister Totty and myself – eventually sat in on this project.

This circle operated via an intermediary – not a living person, but someone who has passed into an advanced spiritual state after quitting the physical body. But instead of reincarnating on earth in another body, to work out the good or bad karma of past lives, these advanced spirits exist on an intermediate plane. From there they are able to guide and assist those on earth who have the gifts and abilities to seek their aid and to help those who have quit the earthly life, yet find themselves in difficulties.

The guide of our particular circle, who spoke through Mrs. Wood, was named Rahmaman. He explained, through her, that on death, if a person had broken one of the great spiritual laws, such as taking a life, they could not go to their rightful sphere, but would have to spend a period in what he called the 'dark' or 'grey spheres.' He explained that this was not a punishment – as in the Christian concept of Purgatory – but a remedial measure in which the person was able to face up to all the consequences of their deeds in the hope that in future lives they would not be repeated. When the time came for the soul to emerge from the dark or grey spheres, ready to reincarnate, or even to ascend to a higher plane, there was usually no problem. But there were some people who retained a very defeatist attitude, making no effort to progress spiritually. Instead, they might think: Oh, what is the good!

Because the mundane, earthly plane is closer to the dark spheres than the more spiritually elevated planes, it was easier to put these recalcitrant people in touch with those still on earth, than for higher, angelic beings to make contact with them.

Rahmaman's role was to bring these recalcitrants and allow them to manifest through the body of the medium, Mrs. Wood. Our job within the circle was to persuade or encourage them to progress. We carried out this work for some seven years and it only ceased when Mrs. Wood, quite understandably, became physically and mentally depleted through constantly allowing not always very pleasant spirits to use her body as a vehicle. I think she sometimes suffered from a kind of spiritual hangover from these sessions.

As the work went on, I sometimes felt that we were marking time, doing the same things over and over again and, I must admit, doubts did occasionally arise in my mind as to the reality or validity of what we were doing. But there were, at any rate, at least two occasions which I will always regard as sound evidence for the reality of these spiritual operations.

On one occasion we were holding a meeting at my mother's house and so there was no question in my mind, knowing the absolute sincerity and integrity of my mother, of anyone trying to fake evidence there. One of the spirits who manifested through Mrs. Wood was apparently ready to leave the dark spheres but, being very negative, was not making any real effort to do so. Apparently, he had during his earthly existence murdered a groom.

Our usual method was to try to put such people in contact with someone they had loved. I asked this man about his wife. This brought forth a stream of curses. He evidently had no tender feelings for his wife. Then I spoke to him about his mother, but this also drew a blank, as he appeared to have no feelings whatsoever for her. So, in despair, I said: 'Do you mean you have lived on earth and never loved anybody during your whole life?'

His reply seemed very strange: 'No, I have loved nobody except Starlight and I called her that because she had a star in the centre of her forehead. But she was a horse, not a person.'

Just then, all seven of us heard a soft whinnying apparently coming from somewhere in the region the ceiling. The medium's face lit up and the man's voice said: 'Starlight!'

And he was gone. We could only assume that, in some way, he had at last discovered what he wanted. I don't think any of us could feel other than that this was an absolutely genuine case.

Another incident which we found very convincing involved a man who spoke through Mrs. Wood and said he had taken his life that morning. Rahmaman, he said, had explained that this was against the great spiritual law and he would therefore not be able to progress onto a higher plane. Instead, he would have to have a remedial course in a place which was not very pleasant. The time he would have to spend there, however, could be shortened considerably and he would be greatly helped if he could get some people to pray for him.

He told us that he had been a doctor, gave the town in the Midlands in which he had lived, the manner in which he had killed himself that morning and his reasons for doing so. This was at 3 p.m. on a Thursday and it was not until the following day that an account of this man's suicide actually appeared in the newspapers. With the one exception that the newspaper account gave a different reason for his suicide, all the other details were exact, including the name of the town and the method he had used – all precisely as he had informed us via Mrs Wood, the medium.

*   *   *

I received a kindly reply and acknowledgement of my letter to Lord Dowding, seeking information about Max. Then, some months later, I had another letter from the Air Chief Marshal, saying that he rather thought my husband had made contact at a recent spiritualistic sitting. The next time I was coming to London, Lord Dowding said, would I let him know and he would introduce me to his medium. Naturally, still desperate for definite news of Max's fate, I immediately arranged to go to London.

8

Lunch with Lord Dowding,
David Stumped by a Beetle,
the Witchcraft Act and a Proposal

LORD DOWDING'S INVITATION was to lunch at the United Services Club in Pall Mall. When I arrived I was only aware of a very thin, tall man in a grey suit and with grey hair, escorting me into the Club lounge. I scarcely glanced at him. My attention was almost entirely fixed upon the medium to whom he introduced me, a Mrs. Hunt. Over lunch, she did practically all the talking and left hurriedly soon after to go to a matinee, she said, with a friend.

It all seemed to happen so quickly that she did not even bother to give me an appointment for a sitting and, when she left, I felt a little downcast. Until that moment, I don't believe I had any particular interest in Lord Dowding, except for the hope that, indirectly, he might help me get news of Max. In fact, I knew very little about the Air Chief Marshal, except that there had been a lot of public indignation when, following the Battle of Britain, he had been dismissed as Air Officer Commanding-in-Chief of Fighter Comand in 1940.

After Mrs. Hunt had bustled out, Lord Dowding said: 'If you don't have to go at once, would you care to stay and have tea with me?'

As he came around to move back my chair so that we could return to the lounge, I suppose I looked at him properly for the first time.

In that instantaneous glance, I *knew. He was the person I had known as a little girl, the figure in khaki who calmed me after my nightmares and promised that we would marry. He*

7 Formal portrait of Air Chief Marshal Lord
Dowding, G.C.B., K.C.B., G.C.V.O. (Crown Copyright
Reserved).

*was the man I had seen balancing the black elephants at the
cottage in Kilve.*

In my astonishment at this sudden rush of recognition, I
gasped: 'Hugh!'

Then, before I could even begin to feel embarrassed at having
been so over-familiar, he said, quietly and kindly:

'How charming of you to call me that.'

I looked at him. He was older than I, though by how much I
could not have said. He was handsome, distinguished, experienced, a man of obvious fine manners and breeding. I was a
young woman, well-dressed, well brought up, it was true, but I
was young all the same. A young, somewhat bewildered and
distressed war widow, like so many others at that time. And as I
looked at him, I realised suddenly that, although I felt I knew
him, had known him since I was a child, had felt his comforting
presence even later when I received the dreadful telegram about
Max ... he didn't know me at all!

Was it still, then, just some strange trick of time or
psychological make-up, coupled perhaps with a childhood
imagination that had lingered later in my life? Was that all the
explanation there was for making me connect this distinguished
man's appearance with the fantasy-figure of my waking
dreams?

Quietly, we sat in the club lounge the whole afternoon. He
was speaking quietly, of many things. Mostly, he talked of the
lost airmen whose families and dependents he so desperately
wanted to help, by bringing them positive news of their loved
ones, through any available channel, whether by ordinary
intelligence reports, or through the vehicle of a spiritualistic
medium.

I sat listening quietly, almost embarrassed at my innermost
thoughts, turning over in my mind my disappointment at not
having gained any positive news about Max from the medium to
whom I had been introduced. Part of my mind also wondered
about the strange trick of fate, coincidence – or whatever it
was – that had superimposed the image of this man on my
earlier life in such a haunting and unusual way. And yet, he
obviously did not appear to recognise me at all ...

Suddenly, a waiter appeared beside our table.

'Will you be staying to dinner, my Lord?'

Lord Dowding turned to me.

'Do please stay to dinner,' he said.

Suddenly remembering myself, I said rather abruptly: 'Whatever is the time?'

'Seven-thirty.'

'But I have a little boy to put to bed!' I exclaimed. And I got up quickly and, I suppose, rather rudely rushed out of the Club with him running along at my heels. He followed me as I dashed the short distance to Charing Cross Station and as we got there a Tunbridge Wells train was waiting at the platform. He helped me aboard.

Breathlessly, I apologised for my hasty departure, he closed the carriage door behind me, waved ... and the train pulled out. All the way home I thought about him.

'That is the nicest person I have ever met,' I told myself. 'I shall never see him again ... but what a dear person he is.'

Three days later I received a letter from him, saying that he would arrange a sitting for me with a very good medium. He had, he said, taught himself a type of shorthand and, if I didn't feel that it was too personal, he could come along as my scribe if I so wished. He knew, he said, how difficult it was to attend a sitting and to try to take notes. Also, would I care to go to the theatre afterwards and, if so, what would I like to see?

What would I like to see? The man I thought I might never see again was asking me what I would like to see! I wanted to see only him ... that would be enough.

And so, in this rather roundabout and indirect way, the great romance of my life began.

In his book, *Many Mansions,* Hugh had conveyed his belief that, under certain conditions, it was possible to establish communication between this world and the next and, as a result, he had been inundated with letters from widows and mothers with loved ones who had been lost. Some years after we met, I asked him: 'Did you invite them all out to lunch?'

'Only you,' he said. 'Because your husband asked me to.'

When I asked what he meant, Hugh explained that he believed that my first husband, Max, had actually contacted him through a spiritualist medium – to which he had obliquely referred in his letter inviting me to lunch.

'When this airman, Max, came through and had identified

himself to me,' Lord Dowding explained, 'he said, "I wish you would take my wife out to lunch – you will like her." '

So it is true to say that, in an indirect sense, it was my father-in-law, Mr Whiting, and Max, who eventually brought about my meeting with Hugh.

*　　*　　*

My son, David, meanwhile, was by this time boarding at preparatory school, Holmewood House, Langton Green, about two-and-a-half miles from Tunbridge Wells. His form-master at that time was a man who today is known to many millions of people – the TV personality, astronomer and author, Patrick Moore, OBE.

I wrote to Patrick to ask if he recalled any distinct impressions of David as a schoolboy. His answer – a very definite yes – included the following anecdotes. Firstly, on the academic side, he said:

'David was one of eight and I taught him – or tried to teach him – mathematics and history. At mathematics he was good and usually came out top. His history was, to put it mildly, not so good and, so far as he was concerned, Nero, Hitler, Charles II and King Canute might well have been contemporaries … '

On the mechanical side, though, David was apparently quite useful. Patrick recalled how he helped put together an archaic scale on which the boys were weighed at the start of each term, mended an alarm-clock using only a pen-knife and was 'extremely good' at lighting the end-of-term plays. Although he added, perhaps pointedly: 'We never invited him to act!'

But perhaps the most memorable – and amusing – recollection Patrick Moore has of David occurred during a cricket match.

'He was not a scholar and he was not a noted athlete,' Patrick recalls. 'Though I once remember him making about a dozen runs in a house cricket match – and then stopping in mid-innings to rescue a beetle which had wandered into the line of the bowler's run-up.

'The bowler selfishly took the bails off and appealed: Owzat!

'Legal, I admit, but in the score-sheet I recorded: Whiting, stumped saving beetle, 12.'

As a footnote, Patrick added: 'I could not then have foreseen that he would undertake the long and sometimes arduous, even dangerous, journeys that he has since done in the cause of animal welfare. He has saved many animals since that far-off day when he lost his wicket while rescuing a beetle.'

. It was, in fact, Patrick Moore who eventually, at my request, confided to David the date upon which I was going to marry Lord Dowding. I suppose I felt that, since David's father had been killed in the War and he had never really had a close father-figure for any great length of time, his form-master at the school where he boarded was perhaps best-fitted to confide that particular 'secret' piece of information.

I had been seeing Hugh regularly – he had asked me to set aside one day a week for him and, either he came down to Oakgates, or I met him at his London Club. Tuesdays happened to be the days most convenient for me.

As we grew more and more fond of each other, however, there were those people who did not approve of our relationship and who were very determined to put an end to it. I have no intentions of naming them; one is dead and, so far as I know, the other two are still alive. Their combined efforts caused a great deal of confusion and, had there not been such a tremendous link between Hugh and myself, I think they might have succeeded in spoiling our mutual love for each other.

I would like to make it quite clear at this point, however, that none of my husband's blood relatives ever caused any difficulty. On the contrary, they showed me the greatest kindness always and I became extremely fond of them, as I was of my first in-laws, Harry and Mary Scott Whiting. Indeed, I have been fortunate in never having had anything but love and kindness from my in-laws of both marriages.

There is no doubt, nonetheless, that the machinations of the three people previously referred to, delayed my marriage to Hugh, because their combined efforts separated us ... but only temporarily.

Prior to the day he actually proposed to me, Hugh had been speaking in the House of Lords in an attempt to get the Witchcraft Act of 1735 repealed, an effort which, in 1951, succeeded when the Act was replaced by the Fraudulent Mediums Act. As a result of his speech, he was given what looked to me a very imposing document. It was a copy of

Hansard – the official report of Parliamentary Debates – containing the Second Reading of the Act. Hugh came down to Oakgates on the Tuesday as usual, handed me this document and said: 'This is for you.'

I examined it with interest, then said: 'But, Hugh, you cannot give this away – it is yours!'

'I was hoping that all the things that are mine you would now keep,' he said. 'You must know how deeply I love you. And, in spite of the fact that I am old enough to be your father, I was wondering if you would marry me?'

Just then, the door burst open. A little boy who had been staying with us at Oakgates rushed in and said to Hugh:

'I told you not to bring her flowers – she prefers chocolates!'

And smartly exited. The truth was that I had never been particularly fond of chocolates and so, whenever Hugh brought any, I would give them to the little boy. Hence his disdain at seeing the beautiful bouquet of flowers Hugh had brought when he came down.

We laughed over the incident and then, after the boy had gone out of the room, Hugh said:

'Well ... please say yes. Can we discuss dates?'

Hugh thought it might be a good thing if we got married quickly – in about ten days' time. But I pointed out that it was August and David was on holiday, staying with a school friend. It would perhaps be much simpler, I suggested, if we got married when he went back to Holmewood House school on September 23. Hugh agreed and we set the date for the first Tuesday after David's return to school, which was September 25.

'Unless you feel strongly about it, Muriel,' Hugh said, 'would you mind if we were to be married in a register office? There is no reason why we cannot be married in a church because we have both been widowed, but I was hoping that we could get married without any publicity, which would be difficult with a church wedding.'

By then, of course, I knew what a quiet, shy and retiring man Hugh was and so naturally I agreed. He then insisted on going to see my mother at her home a mile away.

We talked of various matters and, two or three times, my mother paused and said to me: 'Are you all right, Poppet – you look very white?'

I was not exactly nervous, but I had suddenly become aware of a big change about to take place in my life. Hugh had overcome all of the difficulties which certain other people had put up to prevent us being together and I knew that we were so deeply in love. I was also full of admiration for his strength in surmounting our problems, for I have always admired such strength in a man. And yet ... to find oneself suddenly faced with an almost immediate marriage and all that it entailed was, I suppose, something of a shock. Hence, no doubt, the pale appearance which had worried my mother.

As we were about to leave, Hugh said:

'I hope, Mrs Farrant, that you have no objection to my marrying your daughter?'

My mother looked at him askance. 'Are you joking?' she said.

Hugh laughed all the way back to Oakgates. As we entered, the telphone was ringing. It was mother, calling simply to say that she hoped we would be very happy.

Hugh explained to her that we wanted to keep our wedding as secret as possible and so only mother, my friends Joan and Brenda, my father, David and, of course, Hugh's family, knew of our forthcoming marriage. My father's reaction was, I thought, even stranger than my mother's had been. When he was informed, he wrote, saying:

'I have seen Lord Dowding on a number of occasions. He is a national hero and a very distinguished-looking man and I can quite understand a young woman falling in love with him. However, I cannot help remembering sitting on the bed of a little girl called Poppet, who was quaking with fear and crying her eyes out because she had to say two words in the forthcoming school play and that I had to go to her head-mistress to get her out of it. So what on earth are you going to do if you marry a famous man?

'May I make a suggestion – that, as you both appear to be deeply in love, you do the other thing for a couple of years and then just quietly make it legal if you wish to?'

When Hugh came down to Oakgates the next day he immediately sensed that something was troubling me. I had suggested that not only should we keep our actual wedding a secret, but our married life also.

Hugh looked thoughtful, then said: 'Yes, but as I am going to come and live in your house, unless there is some very good reason for keeping it secret, don't you think it would be making difficulties?'

I tried to explain to Hugh how I felt; how I had, since being a child, always hated being the focus of attention in large company – aside, that is, from my days at the Dancing Studio.

'Now look,' Hugh said. 'Have I got it right – your only reason for not wishing to marry me is that if you do you might have to make a speech?'

'Yes,' I said desperately, 'that's about it.'

Hugh threw up his hands.

'I can think of a hundred and one reasons why you shouldn't want to marry me, but this is the funniest of all!' he said. Then, more seriously: 'You turn up at Caxton Hall and I'll promise that I will make all your speeches for you.'

He added: 'Of course, as my wife, you will be asked to open this or do this, that and the other, but the majority are not important and you can just politely refuse. But where it is necessary, you will put on your prettiest frock, I will make the speech – and you will receive the bouquet.'

It sounded fine by me.

As Hugh had a house in Wimbledon where he lived with his sister and I had Oakgates and liked living there, we decided that it was best if Hugh moved in with me and left his sister, Hilda, undisturbed.

From the time he began visiting Oakgates, Hugh had become very quickly fond of David. When David was home from school, Hugh would spend lots of time playing with him, helping him to set up his electric train set, organising treasure-hunts, making paper boats and aeroplanes, and telling him all kinds of stories and anecdotes.

Naturally, I thought that David would be delighted when he learned that I was going to marry Dowding. Instead, his response was quite extraordinary.

'Mum,' he said, 'why can't you marry one of your other men? Why do you have to take *my* person?'

I realised that he was not jealous of the idea of me re-marrying at all – just of the fact that I happened to be taking *his person*.

9

Besieged by the Press,
Experiments with Mice and Crackers
and Meetings with Beaverbrook

I BECAME AN 'adopted' Aunt to two young boys – thanks to squatters, a dog named Betty and a pup called Dolly. It happened when I moved into Oakgates after the War. After the military had vacated the premises, a number of huts remained on the site around the house and these had been occupied by squatters. Since there was at this time no man around the house, many of these unfortunate people came around to do odd jobs, to ask to use the telephone, to send for a midwife or for other help.

One couple had a lovely dog named Betty and she would come to see me daily, along with her litter of fourteen pups. On one occasion Betty pushed one of these pups underneath my gas stove and I could not get it out. When David returned home – by now he was a day-pupil at Baden-Powell's Rose Hill School in Tunbridge Wells – he managed to extricate the pup and took it back to the squatters who owned Betty. He was told that all the other pups had been put down. So David brought the 'waif' of the litter back home and we called her Dorothy, gift of God, which became Dolly.

Later, domestic problems erupted between Betty's owners and the wife went back to her mother. In his distress, the husband came to me. I went to see his mother-in-law, explained to his wife how much he loved her and wanted her back – and finally arranged for them to meet at Oakgates. They sorted out their problems, but had nowhere to live, so Hugh got his brother, Ken, to take them on as married domestics – along with their dog, Betty.

In gratitude, the man got me an invitation to the Annual Open Day at Swaylands, a Middlesex County Council home for boys in need of care and protection, where he worked. The headmaster told me how pathetic it was that about nine of the boys never got a letter or a visitor and how marvellous it would be if only they could be unofficially 'adopted' by volunteer aunts.

So it was that I came to take on two of the boys, while my sister and two friends took on others. We took them on outings, wrote to them regularly and – at their request – managed to get them into the Boy Scouts.

In 1951, the Festival of Britain opened in London. The exhibition lights reflected gaily off the Thames and the massive Dome of Discovery and the futuristic Skylon towered above Battersea Park. I decided that I would take David, along with my two adopted nephews – Alfred and another David – to see it. On hearing this, Hugh thought that three boys would be a little too much to manage on my own, so he kindly arranged to accompany us.

The two boys from Swaylands couldn't have behaved better, but my David somehow managed to wander off and get himself lost – at least, so far as the rest of us were concerned. When Hugh and I went to the reception desk and reported missing 'one small boy in grey flannel trousers and a grey flannel shirt,' an official told us that at least one hundred boys dressed like that had already been reported lost! Fortunately, as we were beginning to despair, David simply turned up. He had lagged behind, apparently engrossed by some mechanical exhibit and, when he had seen what he wanted, tried to catch us up. But not before we had spent a pretty anxious three-quarters-of-an-hour.

*   *   *

Our attempts to keep our forthcoming marriage a secret were not entirely successful. Some two weeks before the actual date, Hugh called in at Caxton Hall, Westminster, to enter notice of our wedding. Instead of writing Air Chief Marshal or his titles, Hugh simply registered: 'Hugh Caswall Tremenheere Dowding,' and the address of his Club, along with 'Muriel Whiting, widow.'

At the time, Hugh was also on his way to Westminster Abbey, where he was heading for a showdown with the-then Dean over the Abbey's Battle of Britain Chapel. The reason for Hugh's distress over the forthcoming Battle of Britain service at the Abbey was a matter of precise detail of decor. He had arranged that the beautiful little Battle of Britain Chapel should be in the Royal Air Force colours of blue and silver. Instead, despite the fact that the cleaning of the silver had been carried out and paid for, someone had had it gilted over so that it was in keeping with the rest of the Abbey's gold altar ware. In addition, the altar itself had been draped with a white cloth, covering the carved images of St George and King Arthur which formed its supports, while over the Air Force blue carpet a no-doubt valuable, but old, Persian rug had been placed.

Hugh had not spent more than three-quarters of an hour in the Abbey registering his protest at these deviations from correct procedure and tradition when he emerged to see a newspaper billboard saying: 'Dowding to Marry War Widow.'

It transpired that one of the staff of the William Hickey diary column of the *Daily Express* had been to Caxton Hall, checking on forthcoming marriages and, seeing the entry with Hugh's unusual Christian names of Caswall Tremenheere, had been able to discover who he really was.

At the time, I had gone into Tunbridge Wells to buy a present for my mother's birthday, three days away on September 12. When I got home, between 4.30 and 5 p.m., I was staggered to see about fifty cars outside Oakgates. At first, I wondered if I might have invited some people over and had somehow forgotten or got my dates confused. So I walked past the cars and the house and slipped in through a side entrance.

I had had a lady in, making new curtains for our bedroom, which was being redecorated.

'Whatever have you done?' she said, as I walked in. She told me the Press had not stopped phoning and that all the cars outside were newspapermen, waiting for me to return.

The telephone was still ringing incessantly. I picked it up. It was one of the newspapers, wanting to confirm my engagement to Hugh, to ask the date of the wedding and all the details.

'I don't want to discuss it at all,' I said.

'Do you wish us to issue a denial, then?' the man at the other end said.

'I don't wish you to do anything about it,' I said.

He replied that it would be impossible to do that – wasn't I aware that Lord Dowding had entered notice of our forthcoming wedding that morning? Did I have any children by my previous marriage? Where were we planning to honeymoon? Where would we live? The questions kept coming, thick and fast. I had never been in such a situation before. I felt absolutely overwhelmed. I simply hung up the receiver and thought: So much for our *secret* engagement!

As I don't like to tell lies, I then got the lady who was making the curtains to sit by the telephone and say I was unavailable. Meanwhile, I attempted to pin up the curtains myself. I stayed in my bedroom and it seemed as though I could hear bells ringing all over the house. David then came home from school and, apparently, with the good intentions of trying to protect his mother, had been quite rude to the Pressmen outside.

By about midnight, I peeped out through an upstairs window and it looked as if all the cars had finally departed. I had, of course, tried to contact Hugh in the meantime, only to find that all his lines were busy – no doubt with the Press. He had also probably been trying to get through to me and could not for the same reason.

It really was a nightmare.

Seeing no more cars outside, however, I then remembered that I had left my nylon stockings on the washing line in the garden and that I ought to let out my dog, Dolly, and the many stray cats I had taken in. Followed by this miniature menagerie, I walked around the garden, my nylons over my arm, having retrieved them from the washing line. It was quite dark.

As I turned to re-enter the house, I was suddenly blinded as a camera flash-unit went off in my face. Still blinking, trying to get rid of the after-image of the dazzling light, I realised that there were some newspaper men still hanging around. One had taken my picture by surprise and they proceeded to ask me a lot of questions. I refused to reply.

I don't remember which newspaper they represented, but, despite my refusal to answer their questions, I was quite unnerved to see that they carried on scribbling furiously away in their notebooks. Eventually, I managed to usher them off the premises but, as I was about to close the door, up popped yet another reporter. He jammed his foot in the door and said: 'Look, if none of us have got an interview with you, O.K. But as *some* of them have, I'll lose my job.'

Not wanting to be responsible for his dismissal, I let him in.

Naturally, the next day it was on all the front pages. Yet, curiously, not one of them seemed to have discovered the actual date of our forthcoming wedding.

I later telephoned Patrick Moore, David's form-master, and asked that, since David would be back at school by that time, perhaps he wouldn't mind telling my son the actual date. The other David and Alfred – my adopted nephews – turned up in great excitement a few days later. Seeing the names of someone they knew in the newspapers had been such a novelty to them. When was I going to marry 'Uncle', they wanted to know? (Much to his amusement, Hugh had become 'Uncle' to them ever since the outing at the Festival of Britain.)

When I told them it was a secret and that no one was to know the actual day of our wedding their faces dropped.

'If I tell you,' I said, 'will you promise not to tell anyone?'

They solemnly agreed and so I told them the date: September 25.

Some days after our wedding I met their form-master in Tunbridge Wells and, in conversation, told him that Alfred and David had known the date all along. He simply couldn't believe it. 'Those two boys never breathed a word,' he said.

From September 10 onwards, the Press continued to telephone me daily and eventually I began to recognise their voices. I remember on one occasion a man with a Scottish accent from the London *Evening Standard* saying: 'Oh, you are not in London, then?'

'Obviously not,' I said.

'There is a rumour that you are being married today and all Fleet Street is outside Caxton Hall,' the reporter said. 'Do I go and have a nice quiet lunch, or do I go and tell them that the bride is still in Tunbridge Wells?'

I gave him no clue, one way or the other and I have no idea what he eventually did.

When the day of our wedding arrived, I had a small coffee

party for my mother, my sister and some local friends. One friend, Reta Harrison, along with my sister, came with me to the wedding, but by way of precaution, we did not leave from Tunbridge Wells station. Hugh was waiting for us at the barrier at Charing Cross.

It was a beautiful day and we walked across Green Park to Caxton Hall. As we entered the building, Reta heard a man say: 'That's Dowding!'

Although the register office ceremony is quite short, by the time we emerged there were men with cameras running everywhere in the street and some reporters had already managed to station themselves outside.

Assessing the situation, Hugh noticed a man about to get leisurely into a taxi by the kerb. He stepped quickly over and said to him: 'Sir, my need is greater than yours.'

Before the poor fellow could react, Hugh bundled me into the cab and we went off to the United Services Club, where we were joined for luncheon by Hugh's family, Sir Arthur Dowding and his wife, Kara (the other Lady Dowding), Hilda his sister, my friend Reta and my sister Totty.

Naturally, Hugh had already inquired previously where I would like to go for our honeymoon, but I had asked him if he would mind very much if we didn't go away immediately. He said he didn't mind at all, but thought all brides wanted honeymoons. I explained that I could not go away and leave my animals. They were all strays and most of the cats were terrified of men, not being used to having them around the house all the time. They had always made themselves scarce on Hugh's visits. The only pet Hugh had actually seen at Oakgates was Dolly, my dog, who followed me around like a proverbial shadow.

Since Hugh's car was at the time in for repair, after the luncheon we returned to Tunbridge Wells by train. I had been married in a shade which is probably most becoming to my colouring – red hair and a fair complexion. My frock was a pale, subtle colour that was somewhere between blue and green. It was a simple style with matching shoes and I suppose the only item of my ensemble that might have been easily identified with a wedding was my hat. It was decorated with orchids and a veil.

I thought it was extremely pretty, but when we got into the train, Hugh whispered: 'Take your hat off, take your hat off!' I was rather hurt, thinking that he didn't seem to like it, but I obediently took off the beautiful hat and Hugh immediately placed it under the seat!

I then became aware that the man sitting opposite us in the carriage was reading an evening newspaper. On the front page was a prominently-displayed photograph of Hugh and myself – and my distinctive hat. Thanks to Hugh's somewhat abrupt strategy, I don't think any of the other people who got into our carriage recognised us, although we noticed that, like the man opposite, they were studying the same newspaper photograph.

We arrived home to a cascade of congratulatory telegrams and masses of beautiful flowers that bedecked the entire house.

Being married to Hugh was the most marvellous experience. He was a wonderful lover, the most gentle and protective of men, and a delightful companion. We had many mutual interests, which grew and developed as we became more involved in our beliefs and causes and the days and weeks seemed simply to slip by. We were completely and totally happy.

When we had been married for about three days, Hugh came to me and, in his quiet way, said knowingly: 'I can quite see why honeymoons abroad were out – I have counted fifteen animals so far.'

'Well,' I said, 'now you have seen the lot.'

We then set about hiring a cook and more domestic help so that by January we were able to leave the animals in good hands and go for an official honeymoon in the picturesque mountain village of Grindelwald, in Switzerland. As a bachelor and a widower, Hugh had spent a great deal of his spare time there. Sadly, while we were there, we learned of the death of King George VI.

Hugh was a marvellous skier and he would take me out to try to teach me ... not, I might add, very successfully. Although he would always choose an area in which there was perhaps only one obstacle, such as a tree, as if by some magnetic force, I seemed constantly to head straight for that particular hazard. He also tried to teach me to ice-skate, but with similar, none-too-impressive results. Besides, I had during my days at Four Oaks with Max, suffered a back injury as the result of a riding accident and, perhaps, such sports as ski-ing and skating, with their requisite attention to balance, were not the best of pursuits in my own case.

In the afternoons, Hugh would often go off on his own. He would point to the top of some nearby mountain and say: 'That is where I am going.' And, anxiously, I would await his return. As soon as he got back, we would have marvellous Swiss cream-cakes and hot chocolate.

It was on returning to our hotel one day that we found a crew of radio technicians had moved in, set up their equipment and wanted Hugh to make a broadcast. As a public figure and an acknowledged expert skier, he was often in demand.

The amount of money one was allowed to take out of Britain at the time was very small. But the hotel management were so pleased with the publicity they got through having Hugh as a guest that, although we occupied the bridal suite – the best in the hotel – they begged us to stay on and we were able to extend our honeymoon rather longer than our money would normally have lasted.

At one stage during our honeymoon, Hugh said: 'I don't think I shall ever write my autobiography, but *you* may be questioned at a later date about certain matters.' He then told me of his distress at the way he had been dismissed as Commander-in-Chief of Fighter Command – after the vital role I knew he had played in the Battle of Britain. Apart from this one occasion, since the War had been over some years when we met and married, he seldom referred to those days.

*   *   *

As I have already mentioned, Hugh was always very sweet with children. An incident which demonstrated his understanding, particularly of my son David, occurred one Christmas, shortly after Hugh and I were married. David, still quite small, followed me into a chemist's shop and, while I was making my purchases, I overheard him asking for something mysterious at another counter. What, I heard the assistant inquire, did he want an explosive for? His reply was that it was to make the 'bang' in a home-made cracker!

I was terribly worried and, despite my attempts on the way

home to discover exactly what he was up to, David stubbornly refused to tell me. I immediately ran to Hugh.

'He's up to some terrible mischief,' I said. 'For goodness' sake, stop him!'

Instead of rounding immediately on the boy and putting him through a stern third-degree, Hugh bided his time. Eventually, he wandered casually into David's playroom.

'I understand you've got some sort of explosive, David,' he said, quietly. Pause. No reply.

'If you want to lose an eye or a limb, of course, that is your concern,' Hugh went on, still keeping his voice calm and steady. 'But if you are going to do anything of that nature, you must take it right out into the field so that you don't damage Mummy or the house. I'm sure you realise that this is only a fair request to make.'

Hugh turned and left. About ten minutes later, I heard David scurrying along the passage to his step-father's study.

'By the way, Dad,' I heard him pipe out, 'I've decided not to make a cracker.'

I breathed a sigh of relief and at the same time my admiration for Hugh's subtle understanding of the minds of children was reinforced. Then, to my horror, 'Dad' said: 'I suppose you've never tried putting treacle in a pillar-box, have you?'

Of course I realised, having made such a suggestion, Hugh was enough of a psychologist to know that David would not then go ahead and do such a thing. And even if he had, it would no doubt have had far less drastic results than fooling around with explosives!

*   *   *

One day, our cook came to Hugh and I and asked if we could get some poison, because she thought there were mice in the kitchen. I told her firmly that she was to do nothing and that I would attend to the matter. Remembering my mother's experience with the rats at Herne Bay, I waited until cook was in bed, then went into the kitchen. I announced to the mice that this was not their rightful place and that as soon as the snow had gone, would they please leave and make their home in the toolshed? I promised that I would make sure food was left for them.

The mice disappeared from the kitchen. Then suddenly, a lot of those insects known as silver-fish appeared in the lounge. So, once again, when all the house was quiet, I made similar suggestions to those I had made to the · mice. Again, it worked – the silver-fish vanished.

No sooner had this problem been dealt with, a rat or some other small rodent was apparently nibbling a hole in the ceiling. Once more, I used the same technique.

Hugh, who watched this operation, was at first completely mystified and then quite intrigued. After a great deal of thought, he finally voiced his own opinion.

'You know, darling, I don't think that when you talk to these creatures they actually prick up their ears and say, "We have to go, although Muriel loves us," ' he said. 'I think rather it is because you mean no harm to these animals and are giving out, for want of a better description, a love-ray to them. In fact, you are making the most difficult of contacts between the angelic kingdom and the human and, therefore, the guardian of that group of rats, mice, whatever-it-is, listens to your reasonable request, because it is given with love for their charges, and removes them.'

Not long afterwards, Hugh was in the House of Lords, speaking on the Cruel Poisons Bill. I began to wonder why he was so late in returning. Then my mother telephoned and said that the Press had been on to her about something Lord Dowding had said in the Lords. Before long, the newspapers were also on to me and it emerged that my husband, in speaking against the use of cruel poisons, had said: 'In actual fact, there is no need to use anything of this sort at all. My mother-in-law and my wife merely speak to the animals and they remove themselves.'

The Press were upon us like a swarm of locusts. There were even interested scientists calling to ask questions.

I tried to explain to them that there was nothing peculiar about what I did, about my voice or anything else – it was something anyone could do, provided it was done with genuine love for the creatures one was trying to remove.

The result was that most of the English newspapers carried

stories and, some of them, cartoons. I still have an original by Giles of the *Daily Express,* which he sent to us on this occasion.

The story also made the international Press and we began to receive many letters. One was from a missionary who had been sent out to the East and had been horrified to discover that there were no mosquito nets. On complaining, all he had been able to make out was that they were not regarded as necessary, at least, not by the locals. That night, a monk had emerged from a nearby Buddhist monastery, sat in prayer and drawn a kind of circle on the wall. As dusk fell, all the mosquitos and other nocturnal insects became attracted into this circle and the village had a completely insect-free night. When dawn broke, the insects dispersed and everyone took their chances. But at night, no one needed a sleeping-net.

Another letter came from some monks, presumably Buddhist. They said they had read with interest of Lord Dowding's speech and that what he had been practising was well known in the East under the name of some tremendously long word we could not decipher but which, the writer indicated, meant 'loving kindness.' They were, he said, so interested to hear of someone in the West doing the same.

Yet another letter came from a man who had been hunting with two companions in a forest. I do not now recall the country, but it must have been close to the equator, because the night fell very quickly. As they were making their way through the forest, they saw a light shining in the window of a little hut and they headed for it. A very charming, cultured man was apparently living there. He gave them food and turned out to be a perfect host. They asked if he were not afraid, living in the midst of the forest, with all kinds of dangerous animals around. 'Of course not,' the man replied, 'they are my friends.'

The stranger had obviously made a tremendous impression on the three huntsmen and, as they left him and made their way to a nearby village, they experienced a strange feeling of regard and humility for the animals they had originally sought to hunt. Back at the village they asked about the man and were told that he had once been a famous doctor, but had given up money, fame and everything to live quietly in the forest, communing with nature. He treated the people of the village

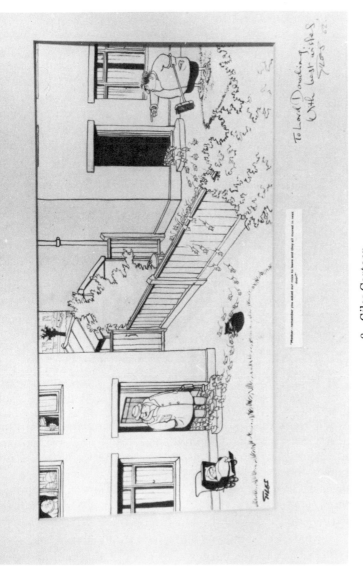

8 Giles Cartoon

and their animals, and any other wild creatures which had in any way been hurt apparently sought him out automatically.

*   *   *

One of the first of Hugh's personal friends I was to meet was Lord Beaverbrook. He told me that I had married the most splendid man in the world and that I was to regard him as always at my service in any way. Then he turned to Hugh and said: 'She is lovely and, as always, your judgement is correct.'

For years, Max Beaverbrook had apparently been inviting Hugh to his villa at Cap d'Ail, in the South of France, or to his other one in the Bahamas. Hugh, who was normally reserved and retiring, disliked these social affairs and had always declined to accept the invitations.

But once he had met me, Beaverbrook saw the opportunity of coercing Hugh into accepting.

'I have no lovely lady to be my hostess at Cap d'Ail,' he said. 'Will you ask your husband if I may borrow you?'

Somewhat stiffly, I replied: 'I never go *anywhere* without my husband.'

'Oh, bring him along then,' Beaverbrook said casually, 'if you must.'

This was his sly way of compromising Hugh into going to his villa. At meals, Beaverbrook could not very well have another man sitting beside him, so I was always placed next to him, with Hugh on the other side.

It would seem that Beaverbrook did his own housekeeping at Cap d'Ail. Every kind of animal food was served – except to myself, being vegetarian. For some reason he would order no vegetables – not even potatoes – for his other guests.

I was asked by one guest if I was a vegetarian on account of my figure. (Before a number of spinal operations, as a result of my earlier riding accident, which upset my thyroid, I had always been 33-23-32 and had a good, clear, fair skin, as do most vegetarians.)

'No,' I replied. 'I don't like animals being killed on my account.'

It was almost as if I had told the most dirty joke. There was an utter, shocked silence.

'It's a matter of religion with her,' Beaverbrook put in, 'and I admire her for it.'

One of the Rothschilds who was present then asked if I didn't enjoy the drama of the bullfight. Nothing, I said, would ever make me attend the torture and slaughter of an animal.

That evening, Hugh told Beaverbrook: 'I think my wife was wonderful. Would you arrange that *I* have vegetarian food also for the rest of our visit? I wish to support her.'

It was the kind of quiet reassurance which Hugh constantly extended towards me throughout the whole of our married lives. Later, he too became a vegetarian, but not through some slavish deference to my own beliefs; he decided to do so as a matter of experience, gained personally.

It was Beaverbrook's habit to fly his incoming guests into Cap d'Ail in a private aircraft and those leaving would fly out on it. But first, all ingoing and outgoing guests would lunch together, in a kind of potpourri social melting pot. Beaverbrook had a somewhat wicked sense of humour and once organised his private air-transport scheme so that a famous divorced man, about to leave, was suddenly confronted by the arrival of his ex-wife and their son. Beaverbrook also liked to try to compromise people in conversation – then to stand back and see what developed.

He told us once that he had the Editor of the *Financial Times* coming to visit, a man who had recently been converted to Catholicism. 'How amazing,' Hugh commented quietly. 'I can understand anyone brought up in that religion being a Catholic, but not a man of intelligence becoming one.'

On the day of the new guests' arrival, Hugh had gone down to bathe on Beaverbrook's private beach. Back at the house I was introduced to the newly-arrived editor.

'I want to introduce Lady Dowding,' Beaverbrook said, 'who will convert you to spiritualism. Her husband thinks no man of intelligence could become a Catholic.'

And with that wicked barb, Beaverbrook disappeared – but only into the next room, where he could eavesdrop on how his poor guests squirmed on. Fortunately, however, I managed to catch Hugh returning to change and told him what Beaverbrook had said. As it turned out, both Hugh and I got on well with the Editor.

Whenever he was at one of his retreats, Beaverbrook liked to pretend that he was no longer a part of the *Daily Express* and *Sunday Express,* although I occasionally used to overhear him in his private office, dictating his editorials.

One other incident I remember at Cap d'Ail, where Hugh and I were usually so happy, was when my husband found me one day in the bathroom, sobbing. I could not explain my tears; I simply felt so lost and lonely, for no apparent reason. Hugh wrapped me in a towel and helped me dress for dinner. As we were leaving our suite, he asked the chambermaid who had last occupied the room.

The maid answered that it had been the recently-widowed Lady Norwich. I can only think that I somehow 'picked up' or sensed psychically her grief for there was a deep love between herself and her husband, just as there was between Hugh and myself.

The last public occasion on which I saw Max Beaverbrook was at a party at Lord Northcliffe's at which Winston Churchill was the guest of honour. My husband had never had any contact with Churchill since, having successfully masterminded the Battle of Britain, he was then removed as C-I-C of Fighter Command.* We went as guests of Lord Northcliffe, but Hugh did not take me into the room where Churchill and Beaverbrook were. However, Beaverbrook eventually came over to Hugh and asked: 'May I borrow Muriel? I want Churchill to see her.'

He took me in and presented me to Churchill, who dropped to one knee and kissed my hand.

As Beaverbrook escorted me back to Hugh, I asked: 'What was that all about?'

'Winston always has an eye for a lovely woman,' Beaverbrook said.

I asked if it had been some kind of message to Hugh and Max said that maybe it was 'a bit of both.'

I can recall Hugh telling me how, during the Battle of Britain when he was desperate for aircraft, Beaverbrook got the parts that were needed for the assembly lines. He had a number of the leading manufacturers down to London and called Hugh in on the meeting. Hugh sat behind Beaverbrook who, when a

* See Robert Wright: *Dowding and the Battle of Britain*

manufacturer said he did not have the parts required, would say: 'How many *have* you got, then?'

The manufacturer would give a figure. Beaverbrook then opened a drawer in his desk and took out a card which only Hugh, being behind him, could see was blank.

'Oh no,' Beaverbrook would say, 'you have so-and-so' – and name some vast figure. He would then add that this enormous amount would have to be delivered by a particular date. In this way, Beaverbrook bamboozled the industrialists and the parts rolled in, enabling The Few to have the planes they needed.

The very last time I saw Max Beaverbrook was some three weeks before his death in 1964. We had been invited to lunch at Cherkley by Christopher, his second wife, who had turned Max's private cinema into filing rooms. (The cinema had originally been a ploy so that, after dinner, Beaverbrook could send his guests in to watch a film while he held private conversations with those he particularly wanted to see.)

The only noticeable difference in his appearance since the previous time I had seen him was that he was in a wheelchair. I was wearing a rather striking hat and he said: 'Muriel, I never thought I'd see you in feathers, or any animal product.' So I took off the hat and showed him that it was made, not of feathers, but of nylon fronds.

Despite his various idiosyncracies and wicked sense of humour, I think Max was a wonderful person. Had he lived, I believe that Britain might have been saved from the Common Market, which both he and my husband were totally against. After all, Britain had the Commonwealth, which she badly let down, and did not need to join. And since we joined the European Community, everything that once cost a penny is now twice that amount – and even more.

Certainly, his role in Wartime Britain cannot be minimised. In 1971, only a year after my husband's death, the distinguished historian A. J. P. Taylor made this clear. In a lecture to University College, London, Mr Taylor said that in May 1940 only two men in high positions in Britain believed fighter aircraft could put up a good defence.

'One was Lord Dowding and the other was Lord Beaverbrook,' he said.

'Instead of the supine direction of the Air Ministry, it was

Beaverbrook's drive that supplied the planes. He did it the unorthodox way.' The Air Ministry had said that it was impossible to 'cannibalise' aircraft – to make one efficient plane from damaged ones.

'Beaverbrook disregarded this advice and at the end of the Battle of Britain there were more cannibalised aircraft in the air than there were new ones,' Mr Taylor said.*

Beaverbrook was a very Christian person, in the truest sense of the concept, and he helped many people. I am sure that, had he survived, he would have ensured that all widows of former Services personnel got suitable pensions. That some of them do not is a wrong which the late Airey Neave was so keen to put right; in fact, he once asked me if he might use me as an example.

My first husband, Max, to whom I was married nine years, had given his life in Bomber Command in Lancasters in 1944; and my second husband, to whom I was married nineteen years, was Air Chief Marshal, the man whom many people feel helped to save Britain from the Nazi invasion. Yet I get no pension from either husband from a grateful nation.

I only hope that I do not live beyond the time when the money which Hugh left me runs out. Like Hugh, I believe that whatever comes to one in life is a lesson one has to learn. Economy is one lesson and I hope I have learned it in this lifetime.

*Daily Express (London), January 20, 1971.

10

Under Psychic Attack, Physical Threats and the Spiritual Uplift of Dorothy Kerin

To DESCRIBE MY first encounter with what occultists call the Powers of Darkness, I must temporarily go back in time now, to 1949, before I married Hugh, while I was living at Oakgates and David was still at prep school. An extraordinary series of events led me eventually to believe that there was at that time and later some malignant force bent on my destruction.

First of all – an incident which, at the time, I barely considered significant – a bus on which I was travelling was involved in a collision and I was rather badly bruised. Shortly afterwards, I was walking my dog on Southborough Common when a huge branch from a tree fell with a resounding crack – missing me only by inches. Then, my father-in-law telephoned and asked if I remembered a former housekeeper of his, whom he and his wife had engaged for a short period, a Mrs. S—. She had apparently written to him and was obviously very unhappy and wanted to return.

'I would like to give this woman a holiday,' Mr. Whiting said, 'but, if there is anything I have learned, it is not to have an ex-housekeeper to stay, with a present housekeeper also on the premises.'

He asked if I would mind having Mrs. S— to stay with me and offered to pay any expenses. Naturally, I agreed.

Mrs. S— arrived, a nice-looking, seemingly charming woman. Apparently, her husband had died twelve years previously and she had worked as housekeeper to several other people, in addition to my in-laws. But it emerged that she had never been able to get over her husband's death, long ago as it had been, and her mind seemed constantly to be preoccupied with thoughts of suicide.

I tried to put across to her my own beliefs and teachings on the subject, which I had learned from my Theosophical studies and by direct spiritual experience in the Rescue Circle and Absent Healing groups which my mother had run. I explained to her that if she broke the great spiritual law by taking her own life, she would not, as she seemed to think, automatically be reunited with her late husband. Instead, she would probably be lonely and unhappy in a state of spiritual limbo, until the proper time for her 'death', or elevation to higher spheres, came. I tried desperately to impress this idea upon her, much in the same way that my mother had done in the past with others.

After about three or four days, Mrs. S— took to her bed and would not get up. I telephoned my father-in-law, who sent his own doctor to see her.

'I cannot find anything physically the matter with her,' the doctor said. 'But I would like her to see Mr. McDowell, who specialises in mental conditions, because I think her illness is in the mind.'

He explained that this specialist came regularly to the Kent and Sussex Hospital in Tunbridge Wells on Thursdays, but first always called on himself at 2 p.m. If I could take Mrs. S— along to his surgery, he said, he would persuade Mr. McDowell to see her before he went on to the hospital.

On the Thursday morning, Mrs. S— seemed to be in a very strange mood. I managed to persuade her to come downstairs, but she then shut herself into a little sitting room and began to scream and carry on in a terrible way. Then, I heard the sound of knives being sharpened – a number of carvers were kept in a canteen of cutlery in that same room.

I went in. She was standing there with one of the large, finely-honed carvers in her hand. As calmly as I could, and trying to exude love and friendship, I said: 'Please, please remember what I told you. You will be so lonely if you take your own life.'

With a chilling smile and in a very matter-of-fact voice, she replied: 'You have been so kind to me, dear – I am taking you with me!'

Somehow, still keeping my eyes upon her, I managed to back out and close the door behind me. It was now my turn to shut myself away somewhere – and quickly. I was alone in the house … except for a woman whose mind had obviously become unhinged. I chose a small closet in which there was a telephone. I rang my friend, the healer Dorothy Kerin, who lived at Burrswood, Groombridge, about three-and-a-half miles from Tunbridge Wells. Normally, it would have taken some time for her to answer the telephone but, as it happened – call it fate, or what you will – she happened to be walking through the hall of her home and picked up the receiver immediately. Quickly, I explained my desperate situation.

'This is an attack by dark forces,' Dorothy said. 'I knew you would experience this. Now don't be frightened, I am going straight into Chapel to hold you and this poor woman in the Light. Go back to her without fear and try to calm her down.'

I had great faith in Dorothy Kerin's spiritual awareness, her tremendous faith and her powers as a healer, which will be elaborated upon presently. Her home at Burrswood had its own beautiful chapel and it was there she would be going immediately to try to put beneficial, balancing spiritual forces into play. I did as she suggested.

When I quietly re-opened the door of the sitting room, Mrs. S— had stopped sharpening the knives and was simply standing there.

'It is very cold in here,' I said softly. 'Come into the lounge.'

Almost somnambulantly, she did as she was told, leaving the knives on the table and following me out. I tucked her up on the lounge sofa in a blanket and brought her a hot drink.

I then telephoned a taxi driver I had hired on previous occasions and explained that I had an appointment with the doctor at 2 p.m. and would he help me get a patient into the cab if I had difficulty. He agreed. But when he arrived at 1.45 p.m., I had no trouble persuading Mrs. S— to go out and get into it.

At the doctor's surgery, Mr. McDowell came in. When he saw Mrs. S— he immediately stepped over to her, shook hands and asked: 'What are you doing here?'

'I am staying with Mrs. Maxwell Whiting,' she said, pointing to me. The doctor turned and eyed me quizzically.

'What does she mean, she's staying with you?'

'That is perfectly true,' I said. 'She has been staying with me for ten days.'

Mr. McDowell then took me outside and said: 'Do you know that I certified that woman for trying to murder her sister and attempting to commit suicide?' I shook my head. 'Who is in the house with you?' the specialist asked.

'My son, who is only a little boy. But he is away at boarding school,' I said.

'I cannot leave you alone with her. She cannot wander about, staying with people.'

He then telephoned my father-in-law and we all had to meet at Oakgates and be present while Mrs. S— was re-certified by two magistrates and two doctors. When the Black Maria-type van arrived to collect her, I walked her out to it and put one of Dorothy Kerin's books, *The Living Touch,* in her hands.

'Tomorrow,' I said, 'I will go and see this great healer. Do not despair.'

Meekly, Mrs. S— climbed into the waiting vehicle.

Next day, I went to see Dorothy and told her the whole story. And, thanks to her, within two years, Mrs. S— was released as cured. At least, so far as I am concerned, it was thanks to Dorothy – her powers of prayer were tremendous, as she demonstrated throughout her life.

I asked her what she had meant by my being 'under attack by the Powers of Darkness.'

'Poppet,' she said, looking steadily at me, 'when I first met you, I immediately knew certain things. One was that you have a Work to do.'

Thinking of my interests in Theosophy and spiritualism, I asked: 'Do you mean occult work?'

'No,' she replied. *'Your Work is with the living.* I can only tell you that before anyone does a Work, they are tested to the hilt and I have experienced the Powers of Darkness before any major project I have put into operation. I know at the moment that you are under attack by these powers, but you will be protected by the Powers of Light, so do not fear.'

I had first met Dorothy Kerin three years earlier at her Home of Healing, at Ealing, and was fortunate enough to know her for some twenty-five years. She helped me tremendously and I learned and absorbed much from her. Along with my mother,

Hugh, and the psychic Grace Cooke, I consider her to be one of the greatest souls I have met in this lifetime and an important influence on my life. Such was our affinity that I sometimes think that I may have known all four of them in some previous incarnation and that I am only one of many people to whom they each, in their own ways, have been an inspiration.

The person best fitted to give an impression of the elevated level of spirit of Dorothy Kerin is my friend, Kathleen Davis, *née* Burke-Collis, who was closely associated with Dorothy for about twenty-six years. In fact, Hugh and I did a good deal of our secret 'courting' under Dorothy's wings. Here is what Kathleen has to say:

'I lived with Dorothy Kerin for eighteen years. Outwardly she was surrounded with beauty; God's beauty and the beauty she had created for God; beauty that had been poured out to her and that she in turn emanated; beauty that had been thrust upon her ...

'And yet she longed for one thing only, to remain poor in spirit to serve her Lord.

'Sixty-five years ago on February 18, when a young girl, she lay dying, after five years of complicated diseases, her emaciated limbs on a bed of cotton wool, being watched by her mother and fifteen other people, waiting for her to draw her last breath. Instead, she did nothing of the sort and, to the amazement of the onlookers, this girl suddenly sat up in bed, surrounded by a golden light. She spoke:

' "I am well ... I must get up and walk." '

'She had been told, apparently by some divine spiritual agency, that she was being sent back to "heal the sick, comfort the sorrowing and give faith to the faithless."

'During the War, Dorothy was again instructed by an inner voice to adopt nine orphans and it was then, in 1946, that I went to help her look after them. The first few months were a testing time and I was sustained by a force that was not my own.

'It was later that this extraordinary lady taught me that to wallow in self-pity gets you nowhere and that there is other strength than our own to draw upon at all times. There were many other lessons to follow, but Dorothy constantly taught that obedience is the key that unlocks the door to spiritual experience, and should be the corner-stone of our lives. Obedience, she often said, is better than sacrifice.

'For sixty-five years Dorothy tirelessly used all her strength and energy to comfort and re-direct and, because she was a channel for the Living Touch of her Lord, to heal. Worn out physically, she would give her undivided attention and counsel to all who sought for help.

'Sometimes, she longed to run away from it all. Often, she expressed her longing to be able in her old age to retire to a little cottage and there to live a life of intercessory prayer and communion with God, and with the beauties of nature which she so dearly loved. The life of selfless service she led was, to my mind, the expression of true poverty: no time to call her own, no privacy ... nothing but endless problems and suffering borne vicariously on behalf of those for whom she spent hours in intercessory prayer.

'She plodded on, unbending to personal sorrows, patiently bearing the hurtful and ignorant criticism from the outer world. One thought always remained uppermost: to serve the Lord she loved so much.

'Several newspapers have referred to Dorothy's "country mansion" and "mink cape", thus spreading a false impression of the reality. Burrswood, in fact, was purchased for the sum of £8,000, realised from the sale of the Ealing Home of Healing. The "mink cape" was beaver, which so many remember, for she virtually lived in it in the winter. It had been the lining of Bishop Loyd's* overcoat and she loved it. It was worn and mended and re-mended until it literally hung together by a thread.

'Dorothy never lost an opportunity to earn an honest penny and there was never any waste.

'When we first moved to Burrswood, the parkland was full of prize daffodils. We were taught how to bunch these professionally and during the short time they lasted we sent them twice a week to market. This meant long hours of stooping, picking and still more intensive hours of bunching, into the night. Dorothy always worked the hardest and got through twice as many blooms as anybody else and, as the spring advanced, she would

* Bishop of Masik, in India and later of St Albans, Herts.

make her famous posies, which she did in the bathroom in the early morning, long before anyone else was astir. In this way, money was made for the furtherance of her healing work.

'As for the gifts which were showered upon her, I will give one or two of the more unusual examples.

'Over the Drawing Room of the Chapel House stands a very beautiful bust of Our Lord, made of white alabaster. It is very heavy. One day a brother and sister, refugees from one of the Iron Curtain countries, called to see Miss Kerin. After a long interview, the sister opened their suitcase which, she said, contained all their worldly possessions. Out of it, she took the head of Christ.

' "It is for you," she said. "It has been all over Europe with us and my brother has often begged me to sell it, but I could not … and now I know why. It is meant for you."

'Dorothy's post was always most exciting, for there was rarely a letter without an enclosure of some sort – stamps, pound notes, cheques, in large and small amounts, given by all kinds of people.

'One morning a shoe-box arrived, unregistered and post-marked Birmingham. There was no name. It contained £500 in pound notes.

'Our Lord told Dorothy in latter years to "draw deeply from my boundless store." And, again and again, there was tangible proof of the fulfilling of his promise of the earlier years: "I will provide."

'During the fifteen years from 1948 to 1963 that Dorothy lived at Burrswood, she built and built. She prayed and the money came, just when it was needed, and always just enough for what was necessary.

'The last achievement was the building of the Church of Christ the Healer, which she saw in a vision and had construct-ed in obedience to her Lord's command: "Build this Church for me."

'Our Lord also told Dorothy to "go and tell my children what I have wrought in thee" and to "be awake when I come." In the latter years Dorothy was asked to tell her story in churches and pulpits all over Europe, America and Sweden and, during the Healing Service that always followed, many cures were wit-nessed by packed congregations. Literally, the blind saw, cysts disappeared and the lame walked. Old and young people and animals all responded to the healing power channelled through Dorothy from the One Source. Her complete and utter faith in the power and love of Christ brought Him right down beside one.

'One day at the Service at Christ the Healer, a young man carried up a King Charles spaniel to the altar. It was paralysed in its hind quarters. After being ministered to, the young man put down the dog, turned and walked back to his seat. The dog followed, moving perfectly. I still have a photograph of the dog, which the owner sent to Dorothy. It was signed on the back: "In gratitude for making me well, The Marquis of Boodles."

'Horses, birds and especially dogs, all responded to Dorothy's healing hands. A Father Browning of Tysoe, in Warwickshire, invited Dorothy to take a Healing Service in his church especially for animals. On this occasion, his own dog, a rare Chinese breed, was ill in its basket. It was made well and lived for many more years. It was difficult to get away after this Service, as many people rushed home to bring their animals and even thrust them through the window of the car as we were leaving.

'Dorothy Kerin was born in the Victorian era, but her Spirit had moved into the New Age. She once told a close friend that she knew she had been one of the women at the foot of the Cross.'

*   *   *

I can wholeheartedly endorse Kathleen Davis' impression – for which I am grateful – of the spiritual purity and greatness of Dorothy Kerin. I can also add a little anecdote of my own – again concerning an animal.

This time, it involved Dorothy's own pet spaniel, Bruno.

He was a beautiful brown colour and followed her everywhere – even into Chapel. On one occasion Bruno hurt his paw rather badly and Dorothy carried him into the Chapel for healing. A day later, while she sat writing, Dorothy became aware of Bruno going in and out of the Chapel with something in his mouth. When she looked, she saw that he had brought in his broken 'doggy toys' and laid them on the altar steps. In some way, Bruno must have discerned how Dorothy had 'mended' his paw – and wanted her to do the same with his 'toys.' Dorothy felt such faith could not go unrewarded. She sat up most of the night, fixing the toys for her dog.

I had first been taken to meet Dorothy at Ealing by my mother, because the injuries to my back, sustained in a riding accident during my first marriage at Four Oaks, were giving me pain.

Dorothy was a very devout Anglo-Catholic. By then, I had been influenced by the Protestant, Roman Catholic and Jewish faiths, along with my other interests in astrology, Theosophy and spiritualism. Practically every osteopath and naturopath seemed to have a different theory about the pain I was suffering and one doctor put me on a very strict diet. After a few months, I found that I could neither eat nor drink.

Dorothy immediately made me swallow the yolks of two raw eggs along with a rusk biscuit.

'Forget your diet,' she said. 'It has made your inside completely raw. The egg will cover that and the rusk will prove the roughage.'

Thanks to her, my pain was temporarily eased.

When we first met, she greeted me as if she recognised me.

I asked her if she believed in reincarnation.

'How can I not, when I *remember?*' she said.

We became great friends – a relationship which continued throughout my marriage to Hugh and until Dorothy's death in 1961.

Whenever Hugh and I invited her over to see us, we would say: 'Do you want to come alone? There are so many who would like to meet you.'

'I want to come alone,' she would say.

Dorothy's attitude towards vegetarianism was quite simple.

'What was good enough for our Lord is good enough for me,' she said.

Perhaps at the time it seemed a curious thing to say. But then, the Dead Sea Scrolls had not been translated. They indicate that the Essenes, who compiled them, were vegetarians. And many people believe that the Teacher of Righteousness, mentioned in the Scrolls, was Jesus himself. There is a theory gaining more and more support that the 'missing' years of Jesus – between the time when he was found talking with the Temple Elders as a youth and the beginning of his ministry some eighteen years later – were spent being trained and prepared as a member of the Essenes.

The Dead Sea Scrolls were first discovered in 1947 by a 15-year-old Bedouin boy in a cave near Qumran, at the north-western corner of the Dead Sea. In the ensuing ten years, more caves containing fragments of the Scrolls were discovered, along with the ruins of the Khirbet Qumran monastery, where the mystical Jewish sect of the Essenes had its headquarters.

When they were eventually deciphered – most are in Hebrew, others in Aramaic and a few in Greek – it was found that the Scrolls represent more than 500 books, about 100 of which are alternative versions of the books of the Old Testament. There are also commentaries on the Old Testament and descriptions of the life and disciplines of the Essene community.

Both Hugh and I became very interested in the Scrolls and my husband at various times entered into a detailed correspondence with different translators of the fragments, a process that went on over a period of twenty years. This included the scholar John Marco Allegro, who became a personal pen-friend.

Some seventy years before the discovery of the Scrolls, a Jew named Moses Shapira had turned up at the British Museum with what he claimed was an early version of the Book of *Deuteronomy*. It was declared a forgery by contemporary archaeologists. But, following detailed examination of the Dead Sea Scrolls, John Allegro wrote, in his book *The Shapira Affair*: (1965)*

'The Essenes believed themselves to be God's Elect, on whom He would found His coming Kingdom at the end of days ... Their writings are therefore of supreme interest to students of the New Testament and Christian origins, for they come from the crucial period before the birth of Jesus when breakaway movements within Judaism were paving the way for Christianity.'

At the end of his book, John Allegro concluded that the

* See also John Allegro: *The Dead Sea Scrolls* (Penguin, 1956); Geza Vermes: *The Dead Sea Scrolls in English* (Penguin, 1962).

Shapira scrolls were probably themselves part of the Dead Sea collection, which were not discovered until 1946.

Years later, the Vatican, which had meanwhile secured control of the publication and findings of its archaeologists on the Scrolls, had made no formal announcement. It seemed almost as if there might have been a plot to cover up the idea that orthodox Christian scriptures of the New Testament might be inaccurate or, at least, incomplete.

Hugh made up his mind to ask a Question in the House of Lords on the Vatican delay. But he was taken ill and the Question never got asked.

*   *   *

However, to return to Dorothy Kerin. It seems from the foregoing that she somehow anticipated the suggestion that Christ had been an Essene – and therefore, a vegetarian. She certainly had tremendous spiritual awareness on a level which few people attain. I believe that Dorothy's mission was to try to re-introduce healing to the Church. I have myself witnessed her laying her hands on the head of a patient who was suffering from cancer and who was cured in the twinkling of an eye. She had immense love and wisdom and, along with my mother and Grace Cooke (about whom, more later), I owe a great debt for their guidance and friendship, which helped me on many occasions.

A second psychic attack upon me occurred when I decided to let part of Oakgates while David was at boarding school and I was alone in the place. I had a charming military couple for a few months, but they were posted to another part of the country. Then, a couple turned up on my doorstep to inquire about renting a wing of the house. They appeared to be simply a middle-aged couple, but I later learned that they were not actually married.

It quickly became apparent that this couple were having the most terrible quarrels and, although there was little contact between us and I practically never spoke to the man, the woman seemed in some way to be jealous of me. On two occasions, I tried to sort this out with her and for a short time all was peaceful. Then, a friend of my mother, who was a medium and lived a few miles away, came over to see me.

She told me that my husband Max had been in touch with her psychically and asked her to warn me always to lock my bedroom door, as the woman in the house meant to harm me. Max had added that although it was always his labour of love to protect me, it would prove very difficult if I didn't lock my door.

Returning from London one evening, I found the man in my hall. He seemed to be in an agitated state and told me that the woman had been looking for her 'little yellow pills.' It seemed that she had worked for the Milk Board during the War and these pills were put into milk in a particular ratio. I presume they were some kind of preservative. The man seemed to think, however, that if taken neat, the pills were highly dangerous. Immediately calling to mind the terrible rows they had had, I said: 'People who threaten suicide seldom do it.'

'She does not intend to kill herself,' he said.

I therefore assumed she intended to kill him.

But he added: 'It's you she wants to kill, so I thought I had better warn you.'

Not very long afterwards, the woman came to me and told me Oakgates was haunted. I said I was quite sure that it was not, but she insisted that somebody had tried to strangle her during the night.

That afternoon, the medium friend from Pembury arrived. She said Max had been through to her again while she was having lunch and had asked her to impress upon me once again that I must not forget to lock my bedroom door. Max had said that he thought the woman guest in my house was perhaps a little psychic, because he had seen her moving towards my bedroom with an object in her hand and, when he told her that if she harmed a hair of my head he would strangle her, she shot off back to bed, pulled the sheets over her head and there was not a peep out of her for the rest of the night.

No wonder, I thought, the woman thinks Oakgates is haunted!

A few weeks later, the man went to see his mother and the woman and I were left alone in the house. She knocked at my door.

"Don't be nervous,' she said. 'Because if anyone comes

prowling around, I will protect us. My mother and I always kept this under our bed.' She produced a huge policeman's truncheon. Undoubtedly, this was the 'object' Max had seen her holding as she made for my bedroom.

Normally, I would have dismissed the couple from the premises immediately. But I had been told through spiritualist channels that, in a sleep state, I had offered to take in this couple to try to prevent a tragedy. After one more terrific row, when the woman's common-law husband returned, she took herself off. I then immediately gave the man notice.

A year or so after our marriage, Major Wellesley Tudor Pole came to stay with us at Oakgates. It had been Major Tudor Pole – T.P. as he was known to friends – who had instituted the Silent Minute during wartime. This involved setting aside one minute at nine each evening – wherever one happened to be – for a silent prayer for peace. At T.P.'s request, and with the support of King George VI, Mr. Winston Churchill and his Cabinet, the BBC restored the voice of Big Ben to the air on Remembrance Sunday, November 10, 1940. This was the signal for the minute of prayer each evening – and it thus became known as the Big Ben Silent Minute. Many millions of people, at home and overseas, on land, sea and air, observed the practice for many years to follow.

T.P., who died in 1968, was an ex-soldier of the First World War, a businessman and traveller – and a man with a highly developed spiritual awareness. Rosamond Lehmann, who was his friend and collaborator until the time of his death, described him as 'a Master: an incomparable Seer, infinitely adept in out-of-the-body travelling.'*

According to his own book, *A Man Seen Afar*,† T.P. could in some mystical way transcend time and space and appears to have been a witness on the periphery of the Crucifixion.

Recalling my own experiences which Dorothy Kerin had interpreted as a kind of testing in the form of psychical attack, I asked T.P.:

'Do you believe in the Powers of Darkness?'

---

* See *My Dear Alexias*, Extracts from the Letters of W. Tudor Pole to Rosamond Lehmann, (Neville Spearman, 1979).
† Published by Neville Spearman

'Indeed, I do,' he said.

I explained what had happened to me and asked: 'If God and goodness are supreme, how can the Powers of Darkness be allowed to do these things to people who do not appear to have done any harm?'

Spiritual power, said T.P., was very precious and could not be misused. If spiritual power were to be put behind a project or a person, they first had to be tested, to ensure that they were capable of wielding it properly for good and, indeed, that they could actually endure such power, physically, mentally and spiritually. To try to elaborate upon this concept, T.P. later sent me a poem, *The Secret of Time and Satan* by Edward Carpenter, from which I quote the following extract:

> And so at last I saw Satan appear before me – magnificent, fully formed.
>
> He stood there erect, dark-skinned, with nostrils dilated with passion;
>
> (In the burning intolerable sunlight he stood, and I in the shade of the bushes);
>
> 'Come out,' he said with a taunt, 'Art thou afraid to meet me?'
>
> And I answered not, but sprang upon him and smote him;
>
> And he smote me a thousand times, and branded and scorched and slew me as with hands of flame;
>
> And I was glad for my body lay there dead; and I sprang upon him again with another body;
>
> And he turned upon me, and smote me a thousand times and slew that body;
>
> And I was glad and sprang upon him again with another body –
>
> And with another and another and again another;
>
> And the bodies which I took on yielded before him, and were like cinctures of flame upon me, but I flung them aside;
>
> *And the pains which I endured in one body were powers which I yielded in the next; and I grew in strength, till at last I stood before him complete, with a body like his own and equal in might* – exultant in pride and joy.

Then he ceased and said, 'I love thee.'
And lo! His form changed, and he leaned backwards and
  drew me upon him,
And bore me up into the air, and floated me over the
  topmost trees and the ocean, and round the curve of the
  earth under the moon –
Till we stood again in Paradise.

The italics are mine. T.P.'s view was that you would be tested up to the hilt – as Dorothy Kerin had said – and, if you came through the test, what was planned for you to do in this life would proceed and spiritual power would be put behind you. If you failed the test, there would be another time, another place. I think this was what Dorothy and I had experienced.

And yet, at the time, it seemed fantastic that I, who had loved dancing and had had so many boyfriends, was destined for any kind of spiritual work.

But evidently, my testing had taken place during these years. And it prepared me for my Work, which I began in earnest ten years later – for animals – which, as Dorothy had so rightly foreseen, are 'the living.'

*   *   *

I ought here to give a word of warning to anyone who becomes interested in psychical or spiritual matters. Many people tend to plunge into such areas without proper under-standing of what they are doing. Those who have read the book or seen the film of *The Exorcist* may have noticed how the central character, the child, was playing with a ouija board in the early stages of the story. This is very probably how she – and others in real life – became the victim of demonic possession. And it applies whether one takes an objective or even a psychological view of the phenomenon of possession.

Soon after we were married, Lord Dowding and I attended a group in London who were working to free those who had become obsessed or possessed and it was extraordinary to note how many of them had been dabbling with a ouija board, a planchette, or a table and an upturned glass.

Some years later the same thing happened to another person involved in a spiritual work. In this case, those who wished to help and knew how to break this astral domination were rejected – as Dorothy originally was in the first case. Now, the man in the first case helped to break the domination in the second instance, because it could have been prolonged throughout a number of incarnations.

Astral domination is not, however, quite the same phenomenon as possession. It can arise through group work when either an astral entity, or even a person within the group, consciously or unconsciously gains domination over someone. Even in such a seemingly innocent situation as a healing group or meditation group, it is always essential to 'seal' oneself both before and after. The reason for this is that, in embarking on such work, the participants 'open' themselves psychically – and malignant entities can often take possession, even in the guise of benign ones.

There are various ways of sealing oneself for protection, some of which are more complex than others. The methods of those who practise ritual or ceremonial magic, for instance, which are too complicated to enter into here, involve the use of a protective circle with symbols, candles, oils, incenses, gestures and phrases, along with ritual implements such as daggers, swords, wands and pentacles.

Another, Eastern technique is rather simpler. It involves sealing the seven major chakras, or subtle bodily centres, by mentally drawing a circle enclosing a cross around each chakra in turn. This should be done both before and after meditation, healing or whatever psychical group work is being embarked upon. The seven chakras, with their Sanskrit names and locations are as follows: 1. Muladhara (base of spine, below the genitals); 2. Svadhisthana (spinal centre, above the genitals); 3. Manipura (navel); 4. Anahata (heart); 5. Visuddha (throat); 6. Ajna (between the eyebrows – the 'third eye' region); 7. Sahasrara (immediately above the cranial suture – the 'thousand-petalled lotus' of advanced Yoga techniques).

There are various books available giving a more detailed description of the chakras and their supposed functions, such as *The Serpent Power* by Arthur Avalon and *Kundalini* by Gopi Krishna. But these are essentially concerned with highly advanced and complicated systems of Tantra or Shakti Yoga and are not really suitable for the layman.

If the concept of the chakras is too difficult to remember, the simplest method of protective sealing before spiritual or meditational work is to surround one's entire body mentally with a circle of light and to seal it with a cross over the heart. That way there is little danger of being dominated by any astral entity or of becoming obsessed.

11

An 'Impious' Inquiry, Hugh the Vegetarian, the Coat that Cried and the White Eagle Lodge

HUGH, WHOSE FIRST wife had died in 1920, first became interested in spiritualism following the Battle of Britain. At that time he had been inundated with inquiries from wives, mothers and relatives, all of whom had had loved ones posted as lost or missing in the RAF. He simply wanted to do his best to help them.

He consulted his local priest, asking what happened to people after they died.

'You must tell them it is God's will,' the priest said. Hugh, dissatisfied, then put the question to his bishop. He was told quite simply that it was 'impious to inquire.'

This did not satisfy him in the least either, and so he spent eighteen months or more, reading the various literature on psychical research, mediumship, materialisation, messages from 'beyond' and theories of survival. It was as a result of this research that he wrote his book, *Many Mansions*.

I would like, however, to make one point absolutely clear. Contrary to the misapprehension of many people, *Lord Dowding did not win the Battle of Britain through spiritualism*. He did not, in fact, begin to study the subject until about three or four years after the Battle, when he had retired.

After the publication of *Many Mansions,* a friend took him to a private circle, at which he met his first medium, a nonprofessional who appeared to receive messages from lost airmen. In some cases, Hugh was eventually able to put the bereaved in touch with these spiritual entities – and it gave many of them great comfort. As his interest grew, he wrote a second book, *Lychgate,* reaffirming and expanding his earlier opinions about the possibilities of survival after death.

When we met and discovered our mutual interest in spiritual affairs – he from his desire to help the bereaved, myself as a natural extension of my own studies in Theosophy and healing – we became frequent visitors to the Spiritualist Association of Great Britain. It was Hugh, in fact, who laid the organisation's foundation stone at its London headquarters in Belgrave Square, in 1955. On one occasion when we went there, my husband saw an old lady going up the stairs. 'Muriel,' he said, 'I want you to meet her.' And he took me upstairs and introduced me to Miss Eva Lees.

Normally, Hugh was not particularly good at recognising women and remembering their names. So I said: 'Well, that was particularly clever of you to have recognised her.'

'That is someone I shall never forget,' he said. 'She is the daughter of the famous medium of the Victorian Age, James Lees.'

Hugh went on to tell me that some years previously, Miss Lees had asked to see him and told him the real identity of Jack the Ripper. I had always been interested in the mystery of the man who had so horribly murdered and mutilated so many women in Victorian times. I asked him to tell me the story.

Apparently, during the time of the murders in 1888, a young man had had a vision of where the next murder would take place. He had advised the police, but at the time they were receiving so many thousands of letters that they ignored his claim. I understand that James Lees' aunt was at Court and mentioned the 'vision' of her nephew to the Queen. 'If he has another vision, he is to send it to the head of police,' Her Majesty said – and they were to act upon it. The Queen made her wishes known to Scotland Yard.

At length, James Lees wrote and said that he knew where The Ripper lived. By pre-arrangement, he led the police to a particular house in London and said: 'He is in the upstairs room.' The police knew the house, which was owned by a well-known person, and they did not believe that The Ripper could be there.

'If you like to ring at that bell,' Lees told them, 'you will find there is a black dog sitting at the bottom of the stairs.'

The police rang the bell. A dog barked and, when the door was opened by a servant, a black dog ran out to them. An inspector then asked to see the mistress of the house. He questioned her about her husband and, so Hugh was informed, the replies gave the man away.

The whole thing is supposed to have been hushed up and the man, a doctor, was locked away in Broadmoor. Meanwhile, it is said, a mock-funeral was held from his home, with a coffin containing only bricks.

The Queen later sent for Lees and asked him to be her personal medium in trying to contact her beloved Prince Albert. Lees apparently explained politely that he had much more pressing work to do and that Her Majesty would find a perfect medium at Balmoral. This turned out to be John Brown. He hated London so much that the Queen spent much of her time at Balmoral so that, through Brown, she could be in touch with her late Consort.

A book written many years later, *The Final Solution* by Stephen Knight, gives an account of the whole business.

Life with Hugh was never dull, always fascinating, and he was always ready to listen to another person's point-of-view before making any judgement. As we grew to know each other more and more, our already-established mutual interests began to overlap increasingly.

One day, Hugh got a somewhat disconcerting insight into the physical realities that lay behind the art of healing. It happened after a local clergyman, who occasionally called on us, became very interested in the spiritual healing with which my mother and her circle had been occupied. I took the minister to tea at mother's home.

She offered to teach him The Seekers' method of treating the etheric body without the laying on of hands. To demonstrate, she asked me to stand up and, first dipping her hands in water, she began to make various passes around my body, just as The Seekers do.

I then left because I wanted to be back in time for Hugh returning from London. As I walked home I began to feel weaker and weaker and, by the time I arrived at Oakgates, I practically collapsed into Hugh's arms. He took me upstairs, asking what the matter was. I told him about tea with mother and the clergyman. Hugh rang her.

'I was demonstrating on her,' my mother told him. 'I drew from her but didn't give back strength to her.'

So Hugh quickly drove over, collected my mother in his car, and brought her to me to give me back the energy she had sapped. As well as surprising Hugh, the experience also gave me an inkling of just how powerful The Seekers' method of treatment could be.

Whatever area of spirituality I happened to delve into, Hugh always tried to take an active interest with an open mind. In the summer of 1957, my husband and I were introduced by a mutual friend to Princess Helena Moutafian and her husband Artin, at supper at the Cavalry Club. The Princess was then expecting her first child, which she unfortunately lost at birth.

When the following year Helena and Artin were expecting a second baby, Hugh and I, who had become close friends with the couple, discussed the possibility of astrologically fixing a time and date for the birth – by caesarian section – so that it would be successful. My mother and I examined the aspects for early November, 1958, and we finally decided, after many calculations, upon November 6 at 9 a.m. This was because Jupiter – The Great Protector – would be in good aspect.

The surgeon who was to perform the operation was, quite naturally, mystified when the Princess told him of her decision over the time and date she had selected for the birth of her second baby. But she kept him in the dark until after the baby was born.

It was a beautiful baby boy born, as planned, on November 6, and Helena was splendid. Soon afterwards, the surgeon was enlightened as to how Lady Dowding and her mother had planned the birth, aided by astrology. He was very pleased, he said, that the stars had had a favourable aspect at the time of birth.

In the same way, we also chose the date of birth for Helena's second son, Mark. Once more everything went splendidly and she now has two handsome, grown-up sons to whom I am unofficial godmother.

As I have already mentioned, my husband eventually became

a vegetarian like myself – although not through any attempt on my part to persuade or convert him. I had, of course, been a vegetarian for many years before we married and he would sometimes say that he knew I was perfectly right. He wondered, however, if perhaps I wasn't fifty or a hundred years ahead of my time. Eventually, he believed, everyone would become vegetarian.

When we had been married a year or so, I asked him if, seeing that he had a seat in the House of Lords, and was himself a flesh eater, he couldn't do something to get animals more humanely killed. He looked at me in astonishment.

'Aren't they?' he asked.

That, I said, was what I was really asking him to find out.

When you are a member of the House of Lords and plan to speak on a subject, you jolly-well have to know your facts thoroughly.

During the next few weeks, Hugh would go off early in the mornings without telling me where he was going. This was most unusual because we were extremely close and he would often ask me to accompany him, wherever he might be going. Nor did he normally keep secrets from me.

Instead, however, he began returning late at night and shutting himself in his study. He was obviously disturbed about something but, although we had such a close affinity, I did not want to pry.

However, Sunday arrived and it was time for Hugh to carve the joint of salt beef. He stood up slowly, looked across the table at me and said quietly: 'Would you mind sharing your vegetarian dish with me? Don't ever get any animal flesh in the house on my account again.'

From that time onwards, both Hugh and David became strict vegetarians. Hugh had, he later explained, been out early in the mornings to visit three slaughterhouses. What he had seen there had disturbed and disgusted him so deeply that he could no longer bring himself to eat meat.

As a result of these experiences, he campaigned successfully to get the humane killer enforced for use on smaller animals, such as pigs and sheep. Until then, it had only been used on bullocks and larger cattle.

Later, he also tried hard to get ritual slaughter abolished. But the only thing that he was able to achieve in this direction was the enforced used of the casting pen. This meant that when an animal was driven in for ritual slaughter, instead of being set upon by eight men and thrown upon its back, it was driven into a rotating cage – and then its throat was cut. Not a very pleasant procedure and not, as some people think, a necessarily quick death, but certainly not so terrifying for the poor animal as being attacked en masse and roughly manhandled.

During his inquiries into this question, Hugh and I visited the Imam of the Woking Mosque in Surrey. He told us that in the Islamic faith, God was regarded as an understanding God and that if ritual slaughter were against the law of the country in which Moslems lived, then the Lord would understand.

Probably more than half of the people who are vegetarians are what I call 'health vegetarians.' And it is undoubtedly a very healthy diet. Others are simply unable to bear to sit down and enjoy the flesh of some animal; it is, to many of them, akin to cannibalism. Yet others become vegetarian from a desire to make spiritual progress and it certainly does refine and purify the body. Many of the great clairvoyants, seers and occultists have been and are strict vegetarians.

My personal belief is that, perhaps twenty years or so from now, England will be mainly vegetarian. So many children being born today will by then be grown up and, maybe as I did, will have a natural aversion to eating the flesh of animals. Another thousand years or more and perhaps the majority of people on earth will be vegetarian. The next step after vegetariansm is, of course veganism – in which not even dairy products are consumed. Eventually, I think, mankind will reach the stage when only the gifts of the earth – the fruits and nuts of grove and orchard – will be consumed, so that vegetation itself is not destroyed.

Following this – and it may be a million years hence – we will probably live on *prana* alone. I was once asked at a lecture what *prana* was and a Hindu gentleman in the audience stood up and said that if one looked at the sky near the sun, little specks of light could be seen – and that was *prana*.

It is, in fact, a Sanskrit word meaning 'life-force' – the mysterious essence which pervades all living creation. Advanced Yogis, with their complex and difficult breathing exercises, are said to draw *prana* from the atmosphere into their spiritual and biological systems, which is why they can fast for many weeks, or even months, on end, or put themselves into cataleptic states in which even their respiratory and circulatory systems appear to have ceased functioning. *Prana* is probably what the mystics, saints and spiritual alchemists, who were never reputed to eat, survived upon.

From a health point of view, humans have the long intestinal systems of the nut, grain and fruit-eating mammals; in other words, vegetarian. We have nails rather than claws, and the forcing of decaying flesh through these long intestines puts a great strain on the bodily system. It has been noted among the animals that the strongest are vegetarian – the elephant, ox, gorilla, horse and cow. They also have much sweeter-smelling breath than carnivorous species. The carnivores – cats, dogs, lions, etc., – do not have such long intestinal tracts and their lives are, by comparison, shorter.

In youth, human beings get rid of a lot of the acidities and impurities of a flesh diet through sport and exercise, but as a person grows older these acidities are more than the blood stream and filtration systems of the body can cope with, and they form deposits within the various ducts and glands. These become the breeding grounds for many of the aches and pains of middle and old age: rheumatism, arthritis, even cancer.

I am often told: 'But all life preys one upon the other.' That is true. But I believe that when human beings change, when they evolve into a higher stage both physically and spiritually, so gradually will the animals.

There has already been the case of one lion which refused to eat flesh. Her name was Little Tyke and although the people who brought her up with other flesh-eating lions were not vegetarians and tried to force her to eat meat, Little Tyke lived on eggs, cereals, milk and fruit. She was so beautiful that she was used in films and could be put among any other creatures – including adults and children – with absolute safety.

I saw a film of this beautiful creature some years ago. Unfortunately, after spending a day under the hot arc-lamps of a film studio, her human companions put on their coats to go home, while Little Tyke contracted pneumonia and died. I firmly believe that she was a kind of prototype in animal evolution – a pointer to gradual future trends.

People also sometimes argue: what will happen to all the cows, sheep and other cattle if everyone became vegetarian? But it is hardly likely that everyone would become vegetarian at the same time. Like all change and evolution, it would be a gradual process.

In any case, when an animal is needed for food or any other by-product, its breeding is more often than not forced and intensified. Through the rapid strides that have taken place over the last fifty years in industry, commerce, agriculture, energy and science, people's minds will be accelerated towards the things that really matter. Negative thoughts and difficulties which we are experiencing now could equally be re-directed to more positive areas of thinking – and conservation would really come into its own.

We vegetarians always find it rather strange when, in a car, bus or train, we hear non-vegetarians enthusing over the beauty of little lambs gambolling in the fields. One finds it difficult to restrain oneself from asking: 'Oh ... and do you like them with mint sauce?' It is odd to us how people can sit down to a meal and do not identify it in their minds with the corpse of an animal they have elsewhere found so loveable – in its natural habitat.

For the benefit of those children who, in the future, will represent the forerunners of the new, non-flesh-eating evolutionary step of mankind, I should like to quote the following poem, by my friend, the late Elspeth Douglas Reid:

LULLABY

*(For a baby who will not be fed
on flesh of beast, bird or fish)*

> Sleep my little one,
> Sleep my pretty one,
> Sleep and rest
> On mother's breast.

No beast shall die to give you food
No bird's soft wings be stained with blood
So you may rest
On mother's breast.
Sleep my little one, sleep.

Unharmed by you shall fishes swim
Weaving through every weedy nook,
Like silver fire, in waters dim,
Nor ever struggle on barbed hook,
Sleep my darling, sleep.

Sweet your foods be, sun-warmed fruit,
And the garden's happy loot;
Glowing colours, red and gold.
No calf shall cry, no lamb be sold.
Sleep my little one, sleep.

When you are grown I wish for you
No power or wealth, but heart of true
Compassion towards each bird and beast,
From sky-borne eagle, to the least
Small whiskered mouse that fearful flies,
That you may look into their eyes
Compassionate, and unashamed,
Nor be for their sad murder blamed.
So sleep and sweetly rest, sleep and rest,
Sleep and sweetly rest.

Naturally, as a vegetarian and spiritualist, I believe that in matters of health, spiritual healing and the less orthodox methods are often the best. I became disturbed, however, when, despite visits to various osteopaths, naturopaths and healers, the pain in my injured back kept returning. Eventually, it became so acute that Hugh had me admitted to a nursing hospital and an operation was performed. The surgeon in charge then very wisely sent me on to the Woolwich Hospital to see another prominent specialist and surgeon, Geoffrey Knight.

He found that my fall in the riding accident – which he

correctly diagnosed as having happened twelve years previously – had caused a tumour at the base of my spine in which all the nerves had become entangled.

'You must have been in agony!' Mr. Knight said. A second operation would, he informed me, be necessary.

'Yes,' I said, 'please operate as soon as possible.'

However, Hugh was reluctant. He thought I was too weak to undergo a second operation so soon. However, the surgeon assured me that I had made the right decision.

I went straight into the theatre on the same trolley on which I had been wheeled up from the X-ray Department and the operation was performed immediately.

For several weeks, I remembered nothing, but I believe that the nurses turned me over every four hours because I was paralysed. My surgeon, whom I came to believe I had somehow met in a previous incarnation, used to visit me daily and stick pins in me, which I did not feel.

'For twelve years I have had X-rays for this, that and the other,' I told him.

'It is unfortunate,' the surgeon said, 'but it seems that many doctors do not know how to read X-rays properly. I have looked at them all and they showed no injury to the spine, but I could see perfectly well the result of your fall. If only I could have had you here even six weeks earlier, it would have been so much easier.'

It was rather a bitter pill to swallow – realising suddenly that it was orthodox medicine that had saved my life and taken away the pain of twelve years. Why, I wondered, had not spiritual healing been wholly successful?

Then I reasoned that if an experience were part of the lesson of life, one would perhaps not be so grateful to any spiritual healer who quickly and conveniently took away that essential experience. The lesson would then have to be learned in another life and the suffering would have to be borne again. That, I believe, is why some people are not successfully healed or do not respond to healing – it is part of the plan, of the cycle of *karma,* of their own particular lives.

One incident which occurred during my recovery period in hospital will always remain in my memory. In retrospect, it now seems almost a prophetic indication – an omen, if you like – of the way in which I was eventually to become so deeply involved in animal welfare.

A woman who was visiting another patient in the hospital asked me one day: 'I see you are a vegetarian. May I ask if you wear furs?'

I said no, I didn't. When asked why not, I explained that I did not approve of the cruelty involved in killing animals for such luxuries.

The woman then told me that her four-year-old son had a godmother of whom he was extremely fond. One day she came to visit and the child refused to go anywhere near her. This was most upsetting to his parents, because he had previously always been so delighted to see her. When they questioned him afterwards, the boy explained: 'I couldn't go near her. *She had on a coat that cried.*'

The child had evidently picked up vibrations of cruelty from his godmother's mink coat.

During this period, I had a letter from Grace Cooke, to whom I have briefly already alluded. Before explaining what she had to say, I shall now give a brief account of this remarkable woman – yet another important influence on my life. I am indebted to one of Mrs. Cooke's daughters, Mrs. J.G. Hodgson, for providing much of the background details.

For several years I had been a country member of Grace Cooke's White Eagle Lodge – receiving the literature, but not attending meetings. Eventually, however, I met Mrs Cooke and became a full member. What attracted me to the Lodge was that, although its teachings are by no means as comprehensive as those of the Theosophical Society, it was along very much the same lines and I feel that nothing but good can result from belonging to either of these organisations.

Grace Cooke was born in 1892, the youngest of nine children. Before she died in 1900, Grace's mother promised the family that if there were any truth in survival after death, she would find a way to bring clear proof to them. So far as the family was concerned, this promise was fulfilled abundantly by detailed messages from their late mother and, as a result, Grace was brought up in an atmosphere of full spiritual awareness.

As a young girl, Grace showed signs of unusual seership and often unconsciously gave convincing proof to various friends that their loved ones continued to exist after death. In her early teens, she first became aware of her lifelong spiritual guide and teacher, an entity who eventually identified himself as White Eagle and said he had been an American Indian chief of the Iroquois tribe. He told her that, together, they had much work to do in the future.

People often ask why so many mediumistic spirit guides seem to manifest themselves as Red Indians, Tibetans or Hindu sages. The answer seems to be that it was among these peoples – and other so-called primitives, such as Asian shamans, Eskimos and African medicine men – that spirituality was allowed to develop freely and naturally, without the complex dogmas and largely man-made rules and regulations of ortho-dox Western religious systems. When the time was ripe for spiritual awareness to emerge in the West, these entities – often advanced beings who had forsaken the *karmic* cycle of constant reincarnation to teach from higher planes – manifested them-selves to those who were naturally sensitive to their presence.

Grace Cooke's first call to service in the spiritualist movement occurred in 1913 when she was asked to stand in at a meeting, because the intended guest clairvoyant had cancelled at the last moment. Leaving her infant daughter with a friend, she took the platform and gave such a successful demonstration of her clairvoyance that she was asked again and again to that particular spiritualist church. Soon the news spread and she was travelling every Sunday and often on week-nights to churches all over London. In this way, for more than twenty years, she brought comfort and hope to thousands of bereaved, giving them absolute conviction that their loved ones, many of whom had been casualties in the First World War, lived on.

During the early years, White Eagle was known to Mrs. Cooke only as a strong and radiant presence who provided support and protection in her work. But in the late Twenties, he began to take control, speaking through her for short periods at first, at groups she conducted at her home and at various spiritualist centres.

As the White Eagle Lodge itself affirms, through its spokes-man, Mrs. Hodgson: 'Gradually, the quality of his wisdom and deep understanding became ever more apparent and he became a much loved friend and counsellor to many who sought his advice.'

By the early Thirties, while still attending meetings and giving demonstrations of clairvoyance all over the country, Mrs. Cooke was working regularly with the Stead Library and the Marylebone Spiritualist Association (now known as the Spiritualist Association of Great Britain), giving counselling lessons. White Eagle himself also began to give trance addresses through her and soon became acknowledged as a wise and illumined teacher, uplifting and inspiring to all who heard him. It was at this time that Sir Arthur Conan Doyle died (1930) and, through the various happenings described in *The Return of Arthur Conan Doyle,* a book written with the help of Mrs. Cooke by her husband, Ivan, indicated his desire and need not only to give his friends on earth proof of his survival, but with White Eagle's help to put right some of his own misconceptions about life in the beyond.

In order to give these teachings adequate expression, under the guidance of White Eagle, Grace and Ivan Cooke took premises at Pembroke Hall, Kensington. In February, 1936, they founded the White Eagle Lodge, which was to be a non-denominational Christian church, a centre of light and healing, run entirely under the guidance of the spirit. At the start of this work, White Eagle gave instructions for the formation of healing prayer groups which were to be held weekly for the treatment of patients unable to attend the Lodge. The entire work was dedicated to healing the sick, comforting the bereaved and teaching people how, through mind control, they could radiate a light which would heal not only individuals but nations.

The original premises were bombed in September 1940, but almost immediately, guided by White Eagle, Mrs. Cooke and her family found new premises at 9, St Mary Abbots Place, Kensington. These were dedicated – through Mrs. Cooke – by White Eagle on March 22, 1941, and the work continued throughout the war years. It is still the London Centre of the White Eagle work.

From this time onwards, the teachings began to be issued in books and in a monthly magazine, *Angelus.* Grace Cooke also wrote two books of her experiences in past lives – now in one volume and entitled *The Illumined Ones* – and her all-time classic, *Meditation.*

As the Second World War drew to its close, White Eagle was again urging Mrs. Cooke to search for further premises, this time in the country, where a centre of peace and healing could be established, eventually to attract people from all over the world for spiritual training and guidance. Despite gloomy predictions of bank managers and financial advisers, in a remarkable way, Mrs. Cooke was led to premises near Petersfield, Hampshire, which, through seemingly miraculous donations, she was able to buy.

White Eagle's new centre was called New Lands. By 1966, the guide was again urging expansion of this centre – in the building of a White Temple on a hill at New Lands, which was to be a meeting place for heaven and earth and a prototype for New Age temples all over the world. Thanks to friends, disciples and subscribers, the money was raised to go ahead and the Temple was completed and dedicated by White Eagle, through Mrs. Cooke, on June 9, 1974, her 82nd birthday.

Two years after its completion, Grace and Ivan Cooke retired from public service, but their work of healing and illumination goes on through the religious trust which they set up. Mrs. Cooke died on September 3, 1979, aged eighty-seven.

During the time that I was in hospital, following my operations, I received a letter from Grace Cooke. She said that White Eagle had told her that all I had been through was indeed partly *karmic* and partly a 'cleansing' operation in preparation for a Work I had to do. I would, she assured me, become ninety-five percent whole again.

At the time I received the letter, the idea sounded extremely unlikely. Yet, within a year, I was able to walk and the paralysis had left me, except for my left foot and a patch on my thigh.

All pain had gone and I felt extremely healthy. I think also that many of my vanities had dispersed as a result of this period of illness, this critical experience. And, because of my own suffering, my feelings for the animals who suffer in vivisection and in many other ways in which man exploits them, had intensified.

As a result of these feelings, I began to write some rather ghastly magazine articles on cruelty to animals, none of which were accepted. Originally, my intention had been to use this period of convalescence to study astrology in more depth and detail. But because I do not have the necessary mathematical expertise, it would not have been a successful project anyway.

Astrology is not, strictly speaking, a psychic science, although a highly-developed intuition and intelligent deduction can play an important part. It is rather a mathematical discipline, involving degrees, minutes, latitudes and longitudes. Although my nurse was extremely clever and tried to help me, while Hugh worked out the more complex calculations, we never got beyond preparing one or two horoscopes. They did, however, turn out to be surprisingly accurate.

However, my mind kept returning to the animals and I realised at length that this was the field in which my work lay and that my own sufferings had really been a preparation for it. I remembered how ill my mother had been at Herne Bay, shortly before she took up her healing. And I realised that – as explained independently by Dorothy Kerin, Tudor Pole and Grace Cooke – many people who are about to embark upon a Work must first experience an illness or setback such as my own.

12

A Fear of Flying ...
and the Flying Saucer Mystery

DESPITE HAVING BEEN married to two Air Force men, I had always had an aversion to flying. I think it was mainly because I have a horror of heights – possibly due to the recurrent nightmare, or retrocognitive dream, which I have described in Chapter Three. Even when we went on our delayed honeymoon to Grindelwald, Hugh and I travelled by boat and train and, until much later, always got about in this rather laborious and time-consuming manner.

What helped to alleviate my phobia of flying, however, was an invitation from Queen Juliana of the Netherlands to a conference at her summer palace at Het Oude Loo. The letter of invitation also included air tickets.

Immediately, Hugh said: 'Don't worry, darling, I can soon convert them into boat and train tickets.'

But I felt that I really could not go on being so silly about the matter. 'Don't do that, Hugh,' I said. 'I will fly.'

He put his arm around me and said: 'You really will be all right, darling.'

We duly arrived at the airport and when we boarded the plane, Hugh held my hand very tightly. He told me to blow my nose as we began to climb, to relieve the pressure on my eardrums. It seemed as though we were barely off the ground before we were coming in to land again. I wondered what I had previously made such a fuss about.

On our arrival, the Queen's Lady-in-Waiting told me not to curtsey on meeting Queen Juliana, as she did not like it. By that evening, when we all met, the story of my fear of flying must somehow have filtered through to Queen Juliana's immediate retinue. But, in the process, it must have become thoroughly garbled, because the Lady-in-Waiting came up to my husband and said: 'I understand that this is your first flight?'

Hugh was the kind of person who never used four words where two would do. With only the slightest hint of inner amusement playing about his eyes, he answered drily: 'Not quite.'

We found Queen Juliana absolutely charming, so much prettier than her photographs showed her, with her marigold hair, her lovely skin and blue eyes. The meetings were completely informal and, in fact, the Queen herself served the lager to her guests.

At the time, I was still suffering considerable pain in my back and at one stage I slipped away quietly upstairs to get a couple of aspirins. The Queen, noticing my absence, made inquiries and Hugh explained about my riding accident. When I returned, Queen Juliana asked if I would like to meet Gret Hofman, the healer who had helped her daughter, Margriet. (Queen Juliana's daughter developed eye-trouble as the result of her mother contracting German measles shortly before the child's birth.)

I gratefully accepted and the following day we had an interview with her. As we did not speak Dutch and the healer did not speak English, there was little actual conversation. Yet I felt somehow more at ease during the remainder of our visit – thanks, I believe, to meeting her.

On our return, we were appalled to see that there was some kind of a crisis in progress at the Netherlands Court, brought about, it would seem, by Prince Bernhard, over Queen Juliana resorting to spiritual healing for her daughter. There was even talk of abdication. My husband felt that all this was some kind of cover-up for other, less apparent reasons for the estrangement of Queen Juliana and her husband; that little Gret Hofman, an ordinary village woman, might possibly be considered another potential Rasputin; or that the Queen was influenced by her for other reasons than the desire to bring healing to an ailing daughter, as would any mother. The whole episode made us very sad for the Queen and the kindly, unobtrusive-seeming, little Gret.

One impression I particularly retain about Queen Juliana was that she seemed Queen not only of her people but, in a true sense, of her land. When one of the first oil-tanker disasters occurred off the Dutch coast and seabirds were covered in oil, she personally broadcast to the nation and to schools the treatment that should be extended to these unfortunate creatures. I believe that, as a result, the schools actually set up centres to which children could take the birds to be cleansed and treated.

Hugh and I enjoyed our visit very much. So much so that we had just about grown used to the march-march-march-click of a sentry outside our bedroom when it was time to fly home.

*   *   *

My work as Lecture Secretary to the Tunbridge Wells Lodge of the Theosophical Society continued during my marriage to Hugh. In 1953, a sensational book appeared, entitled *Flying Saucers Have Landed,* by Desmond Leslie and George Adamski.*

We managed to get the co-author Desmond Leslie down to Tunbridge Wells to speak and we were absolutely packed to the doors for this lecture. Although the book and its sequels have since been attacked and have had many various critics and detractors, Hugh was always inclined to keep an open mind on such subjects, and never condemned outright anything which he had not personally investigated thoroughly. The abbreviation UFO, meaning Unidentified Flying Object, was already in use among RAF personnel and, since people did report seeing what were called 'flying saucers', Hugh believed that they existed. Exactly what they were, of course, was quite another matter, which has not been satisfactorily resolved to this day.

However, we both became extremely interested in the subject and in Desmond Leslie, an electronics expert and son of the Irish novelist Sir Shane Leslie. He eventually told us how he came to write his manuscript to which Adamski later added his own experiences. Desmond had been browsing in a friend's library when his eye was caught by a slim volume called *Atlantis and Lemuria* by W.J.Scott-Elliott, published by the

* Neville Spearman Ltd., 1953; revised edition, 1970.

Theosophical Society in 1893. He opened it at random and discovered a chapter entitled *The Vimanas*. It contained allegedly ancient accounts of flying objects, described as 'round, glowing in the dark, and propelled by some unknown, etheric force.' This was in 1950, shortly after the modern revival in sightings had occurred and, thanks to a casual description by the American airman Kenneth Arnold, they had become tagged by the popular Press under the rather glib and unworthy classification of 'flying saucers.' (In fact, all that Mr Arnold said was that the objects, which he saw over Mount Rainier, Washington State, seemed to skim along 'like saucers' over water.)

Desmond read on, anxious to discover the sources of such way-out information, and found references which claimed that some of the material had been obtained clairvoyantly, by reading the so-called Akashic Record. This is believed by many occultists – both inside and outside Theosophical circles – to be an invisible, etheric sheath enveloping the earth and which picks up every thought-form, every action, however microscopic, and keeps it permanently recorded for eternity like some giant, psychic computer, or hologram. According to occult doctrine, some are able to hook into this vast sensorium as if it were a telephone exchange – and 'read' what is recorded there. Madame H. P. Blavatsky, co-founder of the Theosophical Society, claimed that she gleaned much of the vast information contained in her books, *Isis Unveiled* and *The Secret Doctrine,* in this way.

Desmond decided that if, indeed, the chapter on the Vimanas were a true account and not merely the wildest fiction or embellishment of folk-myth, there should be *some* surviving records, even from ante-Diluvian times.

He searched through the Oriental section of the British Library and his hunch was well rewarded. Ancient Sanskrit sagas, forming sections of the *Mahabharata,* the Hindu *Vedas* and the *Samarangana Sutradhara* and other little-known classics of eastern literature made his eyes pop. For not only were UFOs described, but what appeared to be atomic bombs, laser beams (not discovered, or at least, put to use, by then) and other even more futuristic and weird weapons, were portrayed in graphic, poetic and literal detail. He became convinced that

UFOs must have existed throughout all history and, indeed, subsequent research by many other authors seems to indicate that he may have been correct. Although, let it be added, such research is by no means exhausted and the debate over whether our ancestors were visited by extra-terrestrials whom they took to be gods, continues.

At first, publisher after publisher rejected Desmond's manuscript. One of them, he told us, even turned it down on the grounds that it might have upset the Astronomer Royal! But all this procrastination was working in Desmond's favour. For it gave time for a Polish-born American, and amateur astronomer, George Adamski, to enter the picture. Adamski claimed to have contacted, or been contacted by, a being in a 'flying saucer' and accompanied his claims with some controversial photographs.

The company of T. Werner Laurie, headed by that brave pioneer in such *outré* areas of speculation, Waveney Girvan, jumped at the opportunity, persuading Leslie and Adamski to marry their writings into a single volume. It duly appeared as the world best-seller, *Flying Saucers Have Landed,* before either author had actually met the other.

When dying of cancer years later, Girvan was said to have been visited on his deathbed by two magnificent-looking strangers who identified themselves as space-people. They thanked him for all his work and he died happy.

Later, Hugh and I were to meet Adamski. Despite all that may have been written subsequently, my husband's impression was that Adamski was a totally sincere person and that he believed he had had this amazing experience of seeing a UFO land and speaking to its occupant. Personally, I am inclined to think that this encounter – whatever it was – may have been of a telepathic or spiritual nature, outside the normal compass of everyday, ordinary human experience.

Adamski was so obviously filled with awe and reverence towards the being that he met, he felt he was almost a god.

Still on the topic of UFOs, I remember a man once asking for an interview with my husband. He said he had been driving along in his car and had seen what looked like a little parachute descending in a field. He had stopped and gone to see what it was. He said it was a kind of book, made of some material that was neither copper, tin, nor aluminium. In fact, the implication was that it was of some substance not of this earth. There was a lot of writing inside the book-like object, along with what appeared to be a key.

Hugh studied the book very carefully during the man's visit and, apart from the fact that he said it was somewhat like the ancient, wedge-shaped writing known as cuneiform, he could not in any way understand it. The man, who apparently was a doctor, took the book-object away with him and we never heard from him again.

Although many instances involving alleged UFO sightings are as inconclusive and mysterious as the foregoing, I feel that it is too soon to dismiss the subject entirely. More and more people working in parapsychology are currently edging towards the idea that there is some as yet undetermined connection between UFO experiences and psychic phenomena. The psychologist Jung was perhaps the first to note this link in the latter part of the Fifties. Maybe it will take another Jung of the future to unravel the mystery once and for all …

Part Two

'I firmly believe that painful experiments on animals are morally wrong, and that it is basically immoral to do evil in order that good may come – even if it were proved that mankind benefits from the suffering inflicted on animals. I further believe that, in the vast majority of cases, mankind does not so benefit, and that the results of vivisection are, in fact, misleading and harmful.'

– Air Chief Marshal Lord Dowding, G.C.B., G.C.V.O., C. M. G., speaking in the House of Lords, Thursday, July 18, 1957.

13

Anti-Vivisection
and Beauty Without Cruelty

THE SPIRITUAL IMPULSE to devote my life to working for the welfare of animals had already been indicated to me. What I really needed was a crystallisation of that impulse – a positive direction in which to aim my energies and activities.

It was in 1957 that this was realised. That was the year in which I joined the Council of the National Anti-Vivisection Society.

Of all the terrible cruelties perpetrated on animals by man, perhaps the most calculated and obscene is that known as vivisection – experiments on still-living animals. By its very nature it is cruel. Pain, suffering and distress are inseparable from this method of research.

From time to time I had drawn my husband's attention to various anomalies in the law, allowing the infliction of pain and cruelty upon animals in different ways. Always, he supported my views and, whenever he could, tried to draw public attention to these iniquities. Thus, on July 18, 1957, he made a speech to the Lords in which – upon my prompting – he drew attention to the abuse of the law on cruelty to animals. Here are some extracts from that speech:

'The first Royal Commission on Vivisection was followed in 1876 by a Bill called the Cruelty to Animals Bill. This Bill was humane in intention and in drafting. Its most important provision was that no potentially painful experiment should be carried out on animals without an anaesthetic, and that if an animal was likely to awake into a state of severe pain it should be destroyed while still unconscious. The Bill prohibited absolutely the performance of painful experiments on dogs, cats and the horse family.

'I have spoken of the "Bill", because during its passage through Parliament it was considerably modified. Various provisions were introduced which enabled almost every item in the Bill to be evaded.

'Seven different certificates were introduced, under which experiments could be performed without anaesthetics. For example, the animal need not be killed before recovering consciousness; and experiments without anaesthetics might be performed on dogs, cats and horses. All these certificates could be given if it was claimed that the object of the experiment would otherwise be frustrated. At a later date, after another Inquiry, terminating in 1910, the so-called "pain" clauses were introduced. These stipulated that if, during any of these experiments, the animal appeared to be suffering pain which was severe and/or likely to endure, and if the main result of the experiment had been achieved, then the animal should at once be painlessly killed. This, of course, was a futile provision, because, apart from the vivisector himself, there was no judge as to the intensity of the pain or its probable duration.

'It was also laid down in the Amendments which were made to the law at that time that if it appeared to an inspector that an animal was suffering severe pain he might order it to be killed forthwith. That, too, was a dead letter, for there is no recorded case of any inspector ever having given such a direction. Nor, indeed, has any prosecution ever been carried out against any vivisector since the passing of the Act in 1876. It is true that offenders are occasionally admonished and warned, but that is generally owing to some irregularity in the certificates which they hold; and no penalty is attached to such warning or admonition.'

These, then, were the basic underlying faults of the Cruelty to Animals Bill, as my husband and I saw them. But expressed in these straightforward terms they may mean little to the average layman.

What is really calculated to tug at the heartstrings most painfully, of any person who professes to be an animal-lover, is the section of his speech in which he went into details of what was actually done to animals in laboratories in the name of research:

'There is another aspect of the present law which urgently

demands attention. I refer to the absence of any adequate definition of what constitutes an anaesthetic. A true anaesthetic causes loss of all consciousness, sensation or feeling; and this was undoubtedly the sense in which the word was intended to be interpreted by the original Act. But in the *Lancet,* in the *British Medical Journal* and other professional publications, operations are described which have been performed under drugs that are not true anaesthetics at all.

'For instance, dial anaesthesia was used at Cambridge University during the tearing out of the eyes of cats. Dial is defined as a "sedative and hypnotic for nervous insomnia and to induce narcosis in conditions of severe agitation." Amytal was used when dogs had their abdomens cut open and horse serum injected to produce shock. Amytal is defined as a sedative and hypnotic and as a preliminary to surgical anaesthesia. Nembutal was used during the smashing of cats' legs with eight to a hundred blows of a hammer. Nembutal is described as a basal narcotic in conjunction with inhalation anaesthesia. It is chosen for its brief duration of action. In this case it was administered one hour before the operation and so those cats had no palliative at all to their pain. Those experiments were carried out in Edinburgh.

'Urethane is a mild hypnotic which produces normal sleep without after-effects. This was used instead of an anaesthetic during an experiment involving the repeated dropping of a metal rod on to the thighs of small rodents extended on a heavy anvil. That experiment was done at Oxford.

'Then there is the drug known as curare. That was at one time fairly extensively used in this country and is extensively used abroad today. It is not an anaesthetic at all; it is a paralysant which paralyses the animal so that it cannot struggle or cry out but it is left with all its sensations unimpaired. I am glad to say that the use of curare as an anaesthetic is forbidden in this country. At the same time, it is permitted in conjunction with another anaesthetic and, when it is used in conjunction with these so-called anaesthetics of which I have been talking, then you get paralysis of the animal and no dulling of the pain. These cases are all quoted from accounts written in the medical and physiological Press by vivisectors themselves.

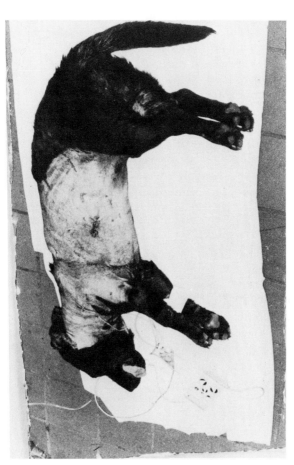

9 This stray, black, short-haired mongrel was used in New York for a heart transplant operation – simply so that a young doctor might practise. The hospital, built and equipped by millions of taxpayers' dollars, did not even provide a recovery room; the floor had to suffice. *Photograph © Jon Evans* F.R.G.S.

10 Its exposed stomach tissues treated with acetic acid, this unconscious dog was then placed in a cage at the Tokio State University (Todai) Experimental Animals Centre. Later, an ulcer would form which would be treated by drugs. *Photograph © Jon Evans F.R.G.S*

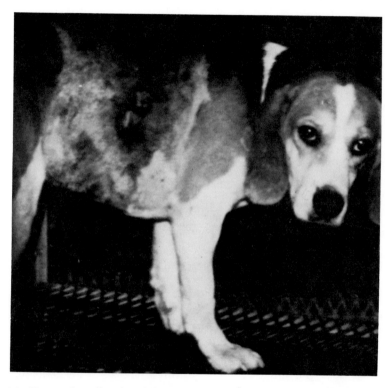

11   Doomed to die: the ultimate fate of this beagle, upon whose body tumorous excrescences were experimentally induced at a New York university training hospital. The dog cowered and showed signs of great stress when approached and was not even provided with anything for comfort – such as a blanket – in its steel mesh cage. *Photograph © Jon Evans* F.R.G.S.

'When one asks oneself what goes on behind the closed doors of laboratories to which the public has no access, it is only reasonable to suppose that the most shocking experiments never appear at all in print to which the public has access ... '

As I have already pointed out, one cannot make a speech in the Lords without having the facts. Here are a few more:

Latest statistics issued by the Home Office show that during 1978 no fewer than 5,195,409 animals were used in British laboratories for a wide range of purposes: the development and testing of drugs, pharmaceutical products, vaccines and sera; the development of weapons and riot-control agents; behavioural studies, including stress-inducement by electrical and other means; the study of the results of surgical intervention, or the biological action of some compound on an animal which may or may not be useful in saving or prolonging life.

The type of procedure to which animals are subjected is virtually endless and there is now general recognition that animals used under the archaic Cruelty to Animals Act of 1876 are liable to suffer severely. Sweeping and drastic reform of the law is necessary to give some measure of protection to laboratory animals.

When I joined the NAVS I became – along with others – an advocate of the proposition that the anti-vivisection movement should not merely condemn the use of animals for research. In addition, I believed that researchers should be encouraged to develop existing alternative techniques and methods of investigation to their full potential. The ultimate object, of course, being that the use of animals would eventually be rendered altogether unnecessary.

This particular line of thought had arisen from a meeting my husband had, following his speech in the Lords, with the-then Home Secretary, Rab (now Lord) Butler. Lord Butler had expressed the view that no government, whatever its political persuasion, would dare to move on the vivisection problem, unless the medical profession agreed.

The Home Secretary's remarks gave emphasis and encouragement to the more progressive leaders of the anti-vivisection movement, and enabled Wilfred Risdon, who was General Secretary of the NAVS from 1957 to 1967, to raise the question of encouraging the development of alternatives at a Council meeting in January, 1960.

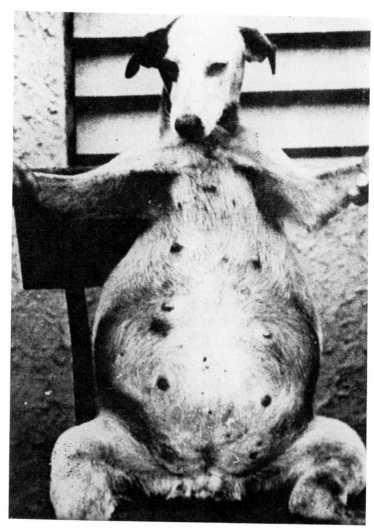

12   This dog has been force fed. It will be killed and
the state of its liver examined. Animals are force fed
with alcohol, cosmetics and other products so that a
firm can say the product has been laboratory tested.
Photograph © Hans Ruesch.

In the meantime, however, my determination to do something positive to help animals in my own way, took an unusual turn of its own. I believe that the seed for this particular outlet of my work had been planted back in 1946, when I was a war widow. I had been unpacking cases which had gone into storage while I was waiting to occupy Oakgates, when I found several brands of face creams bought as presents for friends years before when they were becoming scarce. They were in varying degrees of decay ... except for one jar, which was in perfect condition.

A friend in the beauty business told me the reason: the firm who had made that particular cream had not used any animal ingredients. The incident made a great impression on me. It made me realise that so seemingly innocent an item as a jar of face cream could be as responsible as a plate of meat for some poor creature's suffering, or death.

It has long been a sore point among anti-vivisectionists that no animal welfare inspector – not even a senior RSPCA official – is permitted, under the Cruelty to Animals Act, to enter premises for live animal experiments for inspection purposes. The Home Office has fifteen such inspectors, many of whom have themselves held licences to vivisect.

During his inquiries into such matters, Lord Dowding discovered that many inspectors were purely cursory in their approach to laboratory work and dealt mainly with documentation rather than animal welfare.

After my second marriage in 1951 'and, no doubt, largely inspired by my vegetarianism, I began to receive a number of letters asking for information – including details about animal-free cosmetics. In trying to track down this information for my correspondents, I became interested more and more in the subject, but with no definite plan in mind.

Then, in November, 1958, my husband was speaking at the annual Spiritualist Association's meeting at the Royal Albert Hall. As I sat in the audience of some six thousand people, I was appalled to note the number of people who were obviously concerned with spiritual values – and yet who were wearing fur coats and other items of clothing made from animal products. Spiritualists tend to talk a lot about 'vibrations' and I began to wonder what must have been the vibrations of terror and suffering, emanating from the skins of those animals.

The following day, my friend, the writer Sylvia Barbanell and her husband Maurice, the Editor of *Psychic News,* came to lunch. Sylvia had read some of the beautiful and sensitive poetry of the *diseuse,* Elspeth Douglas Reid, another friend, and was very anxious to meet her. So I had invited Elspeth, along with her husband, Stanley Sharland, to join us.

After lunch, Sylvia, Elspeth and I went upstairs to powder our noses, and I mentioned how appalled I had been to see so many furs at the supposedly 'spiritual' meeting the previous day. I said I really felt that I ought to try to do something about it.

'But what *can* you do?' Sylvia and Elspeth asked.

'I don't know yet, but I will do *something,*' I said.

'Count me in!' they chorused.

The three of us arranged to meet at a vegetarian restaurant the following week to discuss the best course of action.

As we were sitting there after our meal, two more friends, Dr. Monica Latto and her sister-in-law, Dr. Barbara Latto, happened to walk in. They were attending a wedding reception upstairs, but they came over to say hello and, when they heard what we were discussing, they said: 'Count us in, too.'

Eventually, the five of us decided that the best thing to do would be to put on a fashion show in a London hotel, showing people what they could wear as an alternative to animal fur. At this point, Ian Johnson, who was doing the public relations for the NAVS, offered his help and literally became godfather to the movement we were to found, since we had no money to pay for public relations advisers. He did it simply out of the goodness of his heart and a lot of publicity was eventually given to the forthcoming non-fur fashion show.

But it was not as simple as all that.

What the trade then called simulation furs was material which was warmer than wool or tweed, because it had a graduated, fur-like substance in it. This was being made up into coats, under the trade name of 'Simulated Furs.' They were not terribly good in those days, but they were a very warm alternative to the use of animal furs. They were sold chiefly by furriers as a cheap imitation of fur and some of them – although we never used this type – would have an animal-fur collar.

I went to every furrier who stocked these simulated furs in

Regent and Oxford Streets, but their lack of response was most discouraging. I was asked by some of them what I was being paid to do this and, when I said that nobody was paying me anything, I do not think they believed me. I was also asked: 'Is your husband aware of what you're doing?' When I told them that not only was he aware, but that he supported it, I doubt if they even believed that.

We managed to obtain the use of the ground-floor of a newly-opened London hotel for our fashion show – although we still had no one prepared to lend us the garments to put on display. A furriers' named Manards, whose premises were near the BBC, were the last on our calling list. When I went there, one of the brothers who ran the business, Cyril Kirsh, saw me. I told him our intentions and he slowly went back over what I told him:

'You want us to lend you the simulated fur garments and help you to put on a fashion show of simulated furs? You also want a label put in these coats to show that they are not animal fur?'

Then he said: 'Well, it will take about three weeks to get the labels printed. And anyway, what do you want put on them?'

After getting over the shock of actually finding someone who was prepared to co-operate, I began to wonder just what slogan should be put on the labels.

By this time, the group of women working with me had grown from the original four – Elspeth, Sylvìa, Monica and Barbara – to about twelve. We had not called committee meetings as such, since it was such an informal business and we were not even an official organisation. Yet we were already beginning to be asked what our name was.

'People are calling us Lady Dowding's Young Ladies,' my collaborators told me at the same time reflecting that the name recalled the impressario Charles Cochran's up-and-coming stars of the Twenties and Thirties.

'If that is what you want,' I said, 'of course. But what *do* you really want to be known as? Remember, we are not even an organisation. Write and send me your suggestions and we will discuss them when we meet again next month and we shall choose the best.'

One or two had sent suggestions, but I cannot remember any

of them. However, on the day that I went to London to visit Mr. Kirsh, I received a letter from Sylvia Barbanell. Although she had been unable to think of a suitable name, she said, her husband Maurice thought we were 'Beauty Without Cruelty.'

And that was that. I realised that if I delayed for a month telling Mr Kirsh what label to put in the coats, he might have second thoughts about the whole venture. So I told him: 'Beauty Without Cruelty.'

'I think that is very good,' Mr. Kirsh said. 'It is not offensive and perfectly true.'

I bought a coat and, when I attended the next meeting of our group, I showed them the label: Beauty Without Cruelty.

'I am very sorry,' I explained, 'but I had to jump the gun.'

And that was how we came to get our name.

I later asked Maurice Barbanell whether his phrase had been his own idea or whether he thought it was in some way inspired.

'Well, let us see how it works out,' he said. 'If it is successful – then I think it was inspired.'

There are, I understand, something like six hundred animal welfare societies in Britain. The last thing I wanted was to form simply another one. For three years we fought against this tendency and regarded ourselves merely as the backroom girls to the entire animal welfare movement, trying to find alternatives to cruelty.

The resultant paperwork involved meant that Hugh had to employ a secretary for me. The postage bills were trebled and this small group of women, working with only their dress allowances, pin money – call it what you like – kept the rapidly growing movement going.

The original London fashion show was a great success. Hugh attended and spoke of the cruelties behind the fur trade and beautiful models paraded up and down, showing off the alternatives.

We were then invited to take the show to fourteen other cities, including Glasgow, Edinburgh and Carlisle. As I was so terrified of public speaking, my husband always came along and made the speeches and introductory remarks. We had some awful journeys, lugging all the garments from trains and trying to find taxi-drivers who would take the huge trunks to our destinations was not always easy.

About this time I saw a documentary film on the cruelty and slaughter of the great whales, the largest living mammals, the greatest warm-blooded creatures in existence. Many scientists are now convinced that the whale is more intelligent than man.

To see harpoons shot into these majestic creatures – devices which would explode in their insides, so that they had a ghastly and lingering death – made me ask: 'Why are the whales killed? For what are their bodies used?'

To my horror, I was told: 'Soaps, margarines, cosmetics, perfumes and many other things.' My mind quickly flashed back to the uncontaminated jar of face-cream I had found in the packing case back in 1946.

Since everyone uses soap, we of Beauty Without Cruelty felt it our duty to try to obtain a soap which did not contain whale-products and to draw up lists of other products that were not the result of tortured animals' bodies.

Although we were not able to include them on our animal-free products-list, we received great help from the manager of the Coty company, who put me in touch with the source of supply of ingredients used in cosmetics. I may say, however, that when I first turned up wanting to know which products did not contain animal ingredients, he was not at all pleased to see me.

'Don't you think we have a big enough headache without you coming along with this idea of not having animal ingredients in your beauty preparations and soaps?' he said. At length, however, he was helpful.

One of the things I learned was that animal ingredients, either from whales or by-products of the slaughter house, were the bases of most cosmetics and soaps. Civet from the civet cat, ambergris from the whale, musk from the gentle little musk deer and castoria from the beaver – all were used as fixatives in perfumes. So I immediately went to a well-known herbal shop, thinking that they must be the answer. But no ... although they used various herbs in their creams, lotions, soaps, and so on, they also used these animal bases. I left some money with this company and asked them if they would have a non-animal foundation cream made up for me. Eight months later they wrote to say that this was not possible.

I then spent something like two hours with one of the biggest cosmetics firms in Britain and asked them to produce a range of cosmetics which had no animal ingredients. I had since discovered one of the most closely-guarded secrets of the trade – that cosmetics were tested on animals, sometimes in the eyes of rabbits, sometimes by force-feeding until their guts burst and they died. Lipsticks, cosmetics and dyes were often tested in this way. This company didn't.say it was impossible to produce non-animal-product cosmetics, but they said that to produce a new range would be very costly and that the demand would not be sufficient, they felt, to warrant the outlay.

When I brought this disheartening news to the group of women working with me, a new member, whom Dr Monica Latto had introduced, Kathleen Long, said: 'During the War when cosmetics were so hard to get and also because I didn't like what they put into them, I made up my own. Before my marriage, I trained as a chemist.'

We asked Kathleen if she could make a range of cosmetics, but she said: 'I couldn't make a range in my back kitchen, but I could do the formulae and I could get a firm to make them up.'

We sent one of Kathleen's formulae to several manufacturers. The two best of these were Boots and John Bell & Croyden, chemists in Wigmore Street. Since Boots had their own animal laboratories, we decided we would use John Bell & Croyden and that they would make up our first cream. We were greatly assisted by their chief chemist, Mr. Benjamin.

The first cream actually cost us £125 to produce, of which £50 was donated. It was eventually put on sale at John Bell & Croyden. With the minimal profit we made from this cream, we then produced the next – and all the profits from Beauty Without Cruelty cosmetics were ploughed back into the funds to produce the next non-cruelty item.

It has taken almost twenty years since those early, tentative beginnings in 1959, but we now have a complete range of beauty care products, cosmetics, soaps and perfumes.

We chose purple and gold as the house colours for Beauty Without Cruelty products, because Kathleen Long and I not only loved the colour purple, but because we knew it was the colour of Jupiter, the great benefic, while gold is the colour of the sun. Purple is also, incidentally, the colour of the New Age and, I suppose, Beauty Without Cruelty is a New Aquarian Age movement. It is noteworthy how, over the past few years, purple, which used only to be worn by royalty or in mourning, has suddenly become very fashionable. All of which makes it an ideal choice for Beauty Without Cruelty.

As our work continued, I began to get countless letters from people all over the country and from many other parts of the world, asking where they could buy non-animal-fur products, perfumes, soaps, and cosmetics, if they came to London. At the time, there was no simple answer. One had to spend a great deal of time shopping around, which only the dedicated could do if they happened to live within convenient travelling distance of the capital. All of us realised the need for somewhere where people who wanted to follow our example and our way of life could go.

In short, we needed a shop window on our range of goods.

The rents of London shops were far beyond our means and so I went to a world-famous London store and asked if they would have a Beauty Without Cruelty section. The director to whom I spoke was rather taken with the idea and said he would raise the matter at the next board meeting. He thought it possible that we might be allowed a small department for one year. If that paid off – we would be in. If it didn't, of course, we would be out.

About two weeks later I received a letter to say that the remaining directors felt we were too controversial to be included in their store and that, out of loyalty to the companies with whom they already did big business, they could not include Beauty Without Cruelty.

At the time we were meeting in the house of Constance and Ralph White. Constance was a member of our working group. When I gave them this disappointing news at their Bayswater home, Constance said: 'Well, you know, we have a very nice garage. It is brick and attached to the house and I am sure Ralph would not mind keeping his car in the road. Would you like it as a boutique?'

In those early days, our membership numbered only women. So, when someone asked: 'Wouldn't we have to get permission from the council?' I think most of the women, as with one voice, said: 'Don't let's inquire.'

The next thing, dear Ralph's car was parked in the road and the garage was painted and decked out: apple blossom pink walls, with a lovely purple carpet which had been donated to us and purple velvet curtains to hide the garage doors.

We went to the scruffiest-looking second-hand shop we could find and bought about nine mahogany cabinets which had long ago been used to display China ornaments. They were glass-fronted. The shopkeeper asked why we wanted so many and, sitting on a wooden crate, we told him the story of the genesis of Beauty Without Cruelty. At the end of our tale, the tears were running down his face. He got out his barrow and delivered the cabinets, helped us clean them up and, when I asked him how much we owed him and got out my cheque book, he said: 'It's £32. But, my dears, I can't charge you more than £16. God Bless you!'

We put all our non-animal cosmetics, along with the simulated fur samples, non-leather handbags, gloves and shoes, etc., on display. Of course, we couldn't possibly afford to pay an assistant to run the boutique and so this group of dedicated women took it in turns to serve in the shop. When it was my turn, I used to go home and spend rather a lot of time adding up the sales. As I have already mentioned, I was not very good with figures. I remember on one occasion taking a particularly long time: I simply could not get the figures to work out right.

'You know,' I heard Hugh say to David, 'I think Mum uses her toes as well as her fingers!'

Then, after letting me struggle for a little while longer, my husband came over and said: 'What's the difficulty – you seem to be taking a long time, darling?'

I explained that the figures just wouldn't come out right.

'Well,' he said, good-naturedly, 'if the housekeeping can't supply the difference, perhaps a loving husband could. What *is* the matter?'

'The matter is,' I said, 'that I have too much money, not too little!'

'Oh, my goodness,' Hugh said. 'That means that you have done somebody down.' Yet I could not imagine who.

From then on, whenever it was my turn to serve in the boutique, for the sake of the family honour, Hugh would accompany me. He would sit behind the curtains, reading a Hammond Innes novel. I would make out the bills, shove them through to him – and back through the curtains would come the correct change.

. We used Constance's garage for eleven months and had a non-stop stream of customers. This proved to us that there was a definite demand for our expanding line of non-cruelty products. We also realised that the garage wasn't anything like big enough. With three customers in at the same time, we were packed out.

My healer friend Grace Cooke, who had become one of the Trustees of our movement, offered us the drawing room of the White Eagle Lodge in St Mary Abbots Place, Kensington, and we moved there for a time. Betty Bedbrook, the wife – now, widow – of the medium David Bedbrook, ran this operation.

Then our solicitor pointed out that we could not keep switching from pillar to post in this rather underground manner and that we really ought to get a proper shop.

'What with?' I asked him – all of our profits were poured back into producing and providing further non-cruelty products. He said that now we had a lot of members I should write to them and ask if they would invest in Beauty Without Cruelty so that we could buy a shop. If people were going to invest, he pointed out, one could not rent premises, but must buy them.

I was very dubious as to whether anybody would give sixpence towards this venture. But, within six weeks, £22,000 had come in, and we were able to buy a freehold property in Upper Montagu Street, W.1. It was a very charming premises and we were all so thrilled with it. Unfortunately, however, it was not in a shopping area and although the dedicated came to us, we did not attract passing trade. Various difficulties arose and so the shop was sold and we paid back the borrowed money. For a time, we rented the first floor over a shop in Marylebone High Street, where, because it was more central, trade was not confined to our dedicated supporters.

Following this we rented a shop on a long lease at 16 Chiltern Street, W.1., where, at the time of writing, every visitor seems charmed and trade is brisker than ever. This indicates that we are not simply a lot of solitary cranks, but that many people wish to purchase products that have caused no cruelty to animals.

Some of our branches have started boutiques of their own and I think it is the dream of most of the others to follow suit.

After we had been operating in a fairly informal manner for about two or three years, I received a letter from a firm of solicitors – then unknown to me – asking for twelve copies of a booklet we published, which listed all the products which do not cause cruelty. For some reason, this official-looking letter, on headed notepaper, perturbed me. I felt that the legally-significant figure of twelve must mean a jury!

I rushed to see a solicitor friend in Tunbridge Wells. He agreed that it did look potentially disturbing, but said he would telephone the firm of solicitors and find out what it was all about. On doing so, he discovered that the other solicitor, Mr. Noel Gabriel, merely wanted the leaflets for people who might be interested in our movement. Mr. Gabriel wrote to me saying he was sorry that I had had to get my own solicitor onto him and that his request had apparently been so formal and formidable. But he himself had long been interested in our work. What had puzzled him was how our operation was financed: who paid for everything?

That, I told him in my reply, was the one-million-dollar question. When we had started we had been able to pay for the postage and some printing out of our own pockets, but we had grown very rapidly. My husband, I explained, paid for my secretarial help, otherwise I would have been unable to cope.

Mr. Gabriel replied that he thought we were doing something which no other organisation in the animal welfare movement was doing, which was perfectly true. Although there were many other societies denouncing cruelties, Beauty Without Cruelty had come into being by offering the cruelty-free alternatives.

Noel Gabriel's gift to us was to convert us into a registered charity and thus enable us to have members whose fees would pay for running costs. This he expedited, drawing up all the necessary documents. Dr. Monica Latto, who became a Trustee, celebrated the occasion with a Beauty Without Cruelty garden party at her home in Caversham, Berkshire.

We were rather bewildered at first to find that Mr. Gabriel had also made us a limited company. But he explained: 'As I see it, in order to get your ideals over, at some period you will have to enter trade. As charities cannot trade, we are also a limited company under which our boutique and the products that are cruelty-free which we manufacture can be sold.'

The emblem of the Charity is an angel with wings out-stretched in protection over the animals; we call it the Angel of Compassion.

The emblem for the limited company is my own coronet, intertwined with some herbs and flowers which we use in our products.

It was never intended that Beauty Without Cruelty should become an organisation at the outset. I felt there were far too many animal welfare movements already in existence. But we were more or less forced into the position because no other organisation at that time was attempting to produce alternatives to fur, cosmetics, soaps and some of the cruelly-obtained leathers. All we had ever thought was that we would be the backroom girls, giving the alternative direction and impulse to the other move-ments. But it simply did not work out this way. We had to become an official organisation to get the message finally and firmly across to the people in this country and internationally.

Although Hugh and I did not actively seek out messages from mediums, during the various sittings we attended, we kept get-ting a very persistent one, pointing out the tragedy and suffering of animals and imploring me to do something for them. Always, the promise seemed to be: 'If you do, allies to your side we will bring.'

This promise, from unseen spiritual helpers, has certainly been fulfilled. For not only is there a wonderful Council who work so selflessly for Beauty Without Cruelty, there are branch leaders, lecturers, and hordes of other volunteers, and my son David, who gave up a much better job to work for a literal pittance for Beauty Without Cruelty. There are also the countless other dedicated ones who give their entire lives in working against vivisection.

In the early days of Beauty Without Cruelty and, perhaps, in a way, understandably, a good many journalists, newspapers and television media-people, really tried to take the proverbial mickey out of us.

I remember having to appear on a television programme in Cardiff and, when I arrived, there was a table laid out with a most peculiar array of objects upon it, including a tennis racquet. Realising that my interviewer really intended to goad me, I said: 'I don't think I will do this programme.' And I turned to leave. As the programme was scheduled to go out live after

13 David Whiting – Lady Dowding's son by her first marriage – makes friends in Rhodesia with a cheetah, whose fur is on its rightful owner! *Photograph © David Whiting Beauty Without Cruelty*

the nine o'clock news, the interviewer became rather perturbed at this turn of events.

'All right,' I said. 'I will do it on condition that you will first ask me three questions.'

I delineated them: 1. Why do you not wear an animal fur? 2. Why would you not use that particular lipstick? 3. Why would you not wear that perfume?

If he asked me these, I said, 'then you can do your funny stuff afterwards.'

He agreed. When the programme went on the air, I managed to take quite a long time explaining why I didn't wear animal fur, this perfume or that lipstick. The interviewer was getting impatient and wanted to start his Smart Alec stuff, but we had less than a minute to go. He then asked, I suppose in desperation:

'Why, Lady Dowding, would we not find a tennis racquet in your house?'

I did not realise at the time that the strings of some tennis racquets were made from animal-gut, no doubt involving some form of cruelty – and that he was trying to trap me. However, perfectly truthfully, I answered:

'You wouldn't find a tennis racquet in my house because I do not play tennis!'

End of programme. This interviewer was so furious that I was not even offered the usual drink before I left to catch the night train back to London.

The train seemed to be very crowded and the station attendant spotted me trying to get on. He called me and took me to my seat.

'That was very clever of you to have known who I was,' I said.

'Let's say I'm psychic,' he replied. Although I rather think it more likely that he had been watching the TV interview.

As my work drew me more and more into the public eye, I seemed to generate the most curious reactions among people in the news media. I can recall one reporter – among many scores – coming to see me for an interview about Beauty Without Cruelty. When I came into the room, she would not believe that I was Lady Dowding.

'But ... you are ... attractive!' she spluttered.

'What did you expect?' I asked.

'Someone in sandals, crazy hair, earphones and a weird kind of dress,' she said.

I am afraid that during the nineteen-fifties – era of the so-called Beat Generation – that was the mental image that someone who was a vegetarian seemed to evoke ...

*   *   *

One of the women who very quickly joined Beauty Without Cruelty was the renowned medium Mrs. Gladys Osborne Leonard (1882-1968). She was probably the most famous medium of the early part of this century. She was a beautiful singer, very blonde and, when appearing in a show in Drury Lane, she would often hold seances with some of the cast to pass the time.

She was originally rather fond of chicken, until one night when she had a dreadful dream. In it, she was with all the chickens who had had their heads cut off in slaughter. Next morning, one of the men who had attended her seances came rushing around to see her and said: 'Gladys, I don't think I will ever be able to take you out to dinner again. I have had a ghastly dream!'

He described it – and it was the same dream that Gladys herself had experienced.

Sometime later, Gladys had another vivid dream while in trance. She was with cattle which had recently been slaughtered. Their feeling of betrayal was, she said, evident. They were used to the rough kindness of farm-hands, they had worked and given of their milk to man, but they could not understand what they had done that he should betray and kill them.

Next, Gladys found herself in a kind of terracotta mist in which she saw people wandering about. The thing that struck her most was their reddish-brown, pottery-like skins, and she wondered to which race they belonged. Close by was a woman with her head cradled in her arms, sobbing. Gladys felt strangely drawn to her, put her hand on her shoulder and said: 'My dear, what is the matter, can I help you?' The woman turned and looked at her and, with a terrible shock, Gladys realised that she was looking at herself – with terracotta skin. The shock of this brought Gladys out of her trance.

She asked her spiritual helpers what was the matter and they told her: 'All who partake of the flesh and blood of animals must go through this stage.'

Overnight, Gladys Osborne Leonard turned vegetarian – not an easy decision, because at the time there were not the health food shops in every town, as there are today.

'Is this done to all mediums?' Mrs. Leonard asked her spiritual helpers. 'Why have the powers-that-be gone out of their way to give me these experiences?' She was told: 'Because you have a work to do which you would not be able to fulfil successfully unless we could refine you, and part of this refining would be to have you off the flesh of animals, for this is against the law of love, to eat Fish, Flesh or Fowl.'

Gladys was to become the medium of Sir Oliver Lodge (1851-1940), the well-known scientist and a founder-member of the Society for Psychical Research. She worked under test conditions with the Society and helped to bring greater spiritual enlightenment to many people throughout the world.

Gladys' marriage to her producer-husband was an ideal one and, although she was about eighty when I met her in 1962, she could still high-kick over her head and had the fair and beautiful complexion of a natural blonde of twenty.

To conclude this section on our work in trying to relieve the suffering of innocent animals, I can do no better than to quote a poem by Elspeth Douglas Reid, one of our founder-members:

MEAT

(On seeing some sheep driven into this town one summer day)

> Coming down the busy street
> On little, tired, stumbling feet,
> Here, O Christians, comes your meat.
>
> Dusty, dirty – one is lame,
> He is driven just the same,
> Driven to his Gethsemane,
> That you may have lamb chops for tea.
>
> Mouths are open, panting, wide;
> You may see the tongues inside,
> Tongues you shall tomorrow eat.
> Rejoice, O Christians, here is meat!

14 Lord Dowding at home: a photograph taken about three weeks before the retired Air Chief Marshal's death in 1970.

14

A Trial for Hugh,
a New Charity Is Born
and a Great Man Dies

AFTER HUGH AND I had been married for a few years, to our horror – because we had such a full and happy life together and we each had a son of our own previous marriages – I realised I was pregnant. What worried Hugh chiefly was the fact that I had almost died at David's birth. I think what worried me most was that the wonderful life we led together might be marred.

Hesitantly, I asked Hugh: 'Shall we try to do something about it?'

But he was quite adamant.

'No, my darling,' he said. 'I must get you through this somehow, but we cannot do anything about it – to me it would be wrong.'

I accepted Hugh's judgement. And it was fortunate that we made such a decision, because two weeks later I had a miscarriage. I think that, akin to other critical incidents in our lives, this period represented a test – this time one which Hugh had to face and to come through.

A few months afterwards, Hugh had to lecture to the Vegetarian Society. I was unable to go with him, as was my usual custom. I saw him off, but a moment later, he popped back into the house and said: 'By the way, darling, I think I had better add: "If your girl is a vegetarian, don't take risks!" ' Hugh was quite seriously of the opinion that Elizabeth of the New Testament, who gave birth to John the Baptist at the age of eighty, had been a vegetarian! It is postulated by some scholars that both the Baptist and Jesus themselves were vegetarians, having belonged to the Essene Sect. And it is certainly true, as I have already remarked, that vegetarians generally tend to look better and younger than flesh-eaters.

Although Hugh and I shared the same beliefs on most subjects, one which he could not quite fully accept was astrology. A man named Frankland, of Eastbourne, was one of the leading men in this field at the time. I had already, much earlier, become persuaded of the genuineness of Frankland as an astrologer. Especially since, a week or so before I had married Hugh, Frankland had told me that I would probably have the perfect marriage with great happiness ahead for both of us. But, he had added, it would not all be a bed of roses. When I asked him what might go wrong, he replied: 'Health.' His prediction had certainly turned out to be correct for myself, having been at death's door on two occasions and, ultimately, the same applied to Hugh.

When first I had been to see Frankland, I had taken along a close friend who had been widowed and left with a young son just before the War, and after only eighteen months of marriage. Being under the sign of Leo, she had since had quite a number of love affairs, but mostly unsatisfactory ones. She and her young son lived with her mother which was also very unsatisfactory for a woman who had had her own home. She was very anxious to re-marry and was engaged to a man some twenty or even thirty years older than herself. A friend who had been doing card and crystal readings for me suggested I take her to see Frankland and ask him to examine her aspects in the Seventh House, which astrologically speaking, is the area in which partnerships are signified.

When I took my friend, Frankland said he could not see more than a friendship link between her and her *fiancé* and did not see any likelihood of marriage. When he had finished, I put my own horoscope in front of him. After about ten minutes, Frankland looked at me very closely and asked: 'Are you two girls playing a trick on me?' He had obviously noticed that we both had the Leo 'look' about us – I being Leo Rising and my friend a Sun Leo. We assured him we had not switched horoscopes or anything.

'Well,' Frankland said, 'you are coming under Sun conjunction Venus and will have a very happy marriage to a man who I think is a great deal older than you are.'

At the time, I had kept my friendship with Hugh as secret

as possible and so my friend looked at me in amazement. I blushed scarlet and left as hastily as possible, before any more could be said.

Frankland had written an astrology book on the meaning of life and, like the contemporary Dutch psychic Gerard Croiset, had occasionally helped the police find missing persons. Because I held him in such respect, I asked Hugh if we might have Frankland to Oakgates once or twice a year, as I had consulted him in the past.

Hugh raised no objection and said, in fact, that he would like to meet the astrologer. And so Frankland came to see us and I booked various people for sittings with him.

At the time, Hugh still received many letters from people in distress and one of them was from someone who was deeply disturbed about her husband's peculiar behaviour. Hugh racked his brains, but could not think how to help her or how to answer her problem – which was unusual for him. He came to me.

'Would Frankland have time to give this woman a reading?' he asked.

'But Hugh,' I protested, 'you do not believe in astrology!'

He shrugged his shoulders.

'I cannot think what to tell the woman and, you never know, he might be able to help her.'

So I made a booking. Hugh accompanied the woman and, in his own peculiar shorthand, took down the results. Having made his calculations, Frankland looked at the woman and asked: 'When was your husband involved with black magic?'

It was the first time Hugh had heard mention of the subject and, to his amazement, instead of replying that her husband had not been involved with any such thing, she answered: 'Oh, about six or seven years ago.'

Frankland then went on to explain that it was as a result of this that her husband had been having strange attacks. He suggested what counter-measures should be taken to free him from such influence.

When they had left, Hugh said: 'I cannot understand it. How could that man, by adding up apparently the latitude and longitude and positions the planets were in when the woman's husband was born, manage to put his finger on the fact that the trouble had started six years ago with black magic?'

It was after this and other curious incidents that Hugh became convinced that genuine astrology was not simply some distorted old superstitious system which had refused to die out.

*   *   *

Drawing public attention to loopholes in the law was only one way of trying to get something done about cruel experiments on animals. Another and more positive step was to try to encourage experimenters themselves to devise fresh, alternative techniques – or to develop existing ones.

It was with these latter concepts in mind that the Joint Consultative Council of the various anti-vivisection societies met in January, 1960. This was an *ad hoc* body formed so that representatives of the NAVS and the British Union for the Abolition of Vivisection – the two largest organisations of their kind in Britain – could discuss and implement joint action.

The first idea put forward was the offering of a Research Prize to stimulate work in this direction. But, after discussion, this kernel, which had been inspired by a suggestion of my husband, was developed into the possibility of setting up a permanent Trust Fund which would sponsor research directly. The BUAV wholeheartedly supported the NAVS in this and throughout the ensuing year detailed plans were drawn up to launch a suitable Fund. The Scottish Society for the Prevention of Vivisection, based in Edinburgh, was also invited to join the venture, which it readily accepted. Eventually, it was agreed that these three key anti-vivisection groups would jointly set up the Fund.

An important proviso of the Trust, insisted upon by all three parent societies, was that no researcher holding a current licence under the 1876 Cruelty to Animals Act, which entitled them to experiment on live animals, would receive any financial support from the Fund. This, it was hoped, would encourage genuine and humane licence-holders to relinquish their authority to vivisect.

The Fund – known as the Lawson Tait Memorial Fund, after the famous 19th-century surgeon – was approved as a charity. It began to function on November 16, 1961.

The Trust Deed was worded to meet the requirements of the

three sponsoring societies and each contributed a substantial sum to launch the project. The Societies each appointed a Trustee who would, in turn, appoint their own successors. Although this was unfortunately not incorporated in the actual wording of the Trust Deed, it was the understanding of the NAVS that each of the founder organisations would always be represented on the Board of Trustees. This, it was felt, would ensure the continuity of the original societies' involvement with the special work of the Trust.

The Trust bought the lease of 51 Harley Street – thanks to a substantial loan of £36,000, at an extremely low interest rate, from the NAVS. The Lawson Tait Memorial Trust was thus established in the heart of the medical world and, with the financial and practical help of the NAVS, it attracted a lot of attention. More and more researchers were drawn to the idea of developing alternative and replacement techniques to that of vivisection.

The NAVS also took a sub-lease from the Trust and set up its own headquarters in the same building. For several years, the work progressed ideally, with the three sponsoring societies co-operating and the late Wilfred Risdon, who was Secretary both to the Trust and the NAVS, providing a strong and stable link between both organisations. The NAVS staff, being in the same building, were enabled to help in the work of the Trust.

There were, however – although we were not to realise it at the time – problems brewing on the horizon. Problems which were to lead to an eventual severance of the Trust from the NAVS and which will be described in due course.

*   *   *

Although he remained extremely active into his seventies and early eighties, my husband had a fall at the United Services Club in 1965, and developed arthritis which, as sufferers of this complaint will know, can be extremely painful. But having been a keen and expert ski-er and skater and, until he met me and began to support animal welfare work, a polo, fishin' and shootin' type, his active, outdoors life had served to keep him in otherwise good physical condition.

However, earlier in 1961, Hugh had also suffered a fall while ski-ing and broke his hip. What with the onset of arthritis, the old oak staircase at Oakgates was obviously painful for him to negotiate. I called in an architect to see if it were possible to have a lift installed, but the only suitable place where it might have been located would have meant ruining our guest bedroom and was therefore impractical. I also inquired whether it were possible to build on a bedroom and bathroom at ground-floor level, but I was told it would be difficult to secure planning permission to extend upon 500-year-old tiles and oak.

The only practical solution was to look around for another house, where we could have a bedroom and bathroom on the ground floor and in which Hugh would not need to use stairs. I went to look at many houses in the Tunbridge Wells area, but none seemed anywhere near as charming as Oakgates. At length I began to think that, so long as we could live on one floor, even if I didn't particularly like the house, I could probably make it cosy and pretty inside. Then, an estate agent took pity on me.

'Lady Evans of 1, Calverley Park, has bought another house,' he said. 'Would you like to see if she is wanting to sell?'

Lady Evans had waited until she had moved before putting up her home in Calverley Park for auction. When she discovered that it was Lord and Lady Dowding who were interested in buying, she invited us to tea the following weekend. Her husband, she said, wanted to meet Lord Dowding.

I didn't remember much about the house after that first visit, except to note that there were no steps for Hugh and that it seemed otherwise suitable in every way. It was then agreed that I could have the house if negotiations were completed within three weeks. To this day I cannot think how we managed to get all the paperwork and legal documents through in time, but we did.

Workmen converted the downstairs cloakroom into a bathroom for Hugh and, what had once been the butler's pantry was transformed into a bathroom for me. As our bedroom, we chose a lovely big ground-floor room which had probably been intended as a library. The dining room became Hugh's study and the sun-parlour, a dining room. There was a big lounge with a small dining table in it, which could be used when there were just the two of us.

Upstairs we had our guest rooms and my sister Totty had her own little apartment. The local council kindly gave permission for Beauty Without Cruelty – the Charity section – to operate from here, so we set up our office at Calverley Park.

It is a lovely house and we were very happy in it, as we had been at Oakgates. Hugh used to go out into the surrounding private park daily for walks and it is perfect for taking out my dogs and allowing my cats to roam about. There are twenty-four Regency houses in the Park and I do not think anyone who lives here ever wants to leave. It has its own, unique atmosphere, is within only minutes from the station and main shopping areas, and yet, inside, you could easily imagine yourself in the depths of the country. Perhaps the very thick walls of an earlier century help the place to retain its peace and quiet.

Hugh and I placed a stone bird-bath in the garden, as we had done at Oakgates before leaving. It is inscribed:

> In the hope that future occupants will care as we did for the birds and all life.
> All things weak and lowly are dependent on man solely.
> Care for them, we beseech thee.
> Placed in this their home by Lord and Lady Dowding.

During his last three years, Hugh became very crippled with arthritis. But he never complained and insisted that he would have a nurse so that I could carry on my animal welfare work. That way, he was cared for whenever I had to attend functions, give lectures and speeches or sit on committees.

Despite the fact that we had an immense bed, one of our cats who was particularly fond of Hugh, always insisted on lying pressed up against him, either behind his knees or in his back. On several occasions, I had told Hugh: 'You know, you will fall out of bed one of these days.'

One night there was a terrible crash and the cat had indeed pushed my husband over the edge of the bed. Because of the arthritis in his knees, he was unable to kneel and help himself up. And as he was a large man, I could not lift him. The only thing to do was for me to arrange our pillows and eiderdown on the floor, where we spent the rest of the night, our animals all curled up around us.

As soon as I thought it a respectable hour, I telephoned a doctor who lived in Calverley Park and he kindly came around. He found Hugh no worse for the fall and managed to get him back into bed.

It was at this time that I had to begin giving my own lectures on animal welfare – a task which Hugh had always carried out for me in the past. It was something I had always dreaded.

Hugh offered to write my speeches for me, but I found through experience that the only way I could speak at all was simply to stand up and talk. The one speech I did try to learn was hopeless; I sounded just like a parrot.

I still don't like lecturing, but I have become used to it. Generally, I hold a watch to which is attached a miniature of Hugh. I then invoke my husband and the patron saint of animals with a silent prayer, which usually goes something like: 'Now, come on Hugh, come on St Francis! You got me into this – now get me out!' And off I go.

During Hugh's illness, if I had to go out lecturing, he would always ask: 'What time will you be home?' And I would always give him a time about two hours later than I really expected to be home. Then, when I came in at perhaps 7.30, 9, or even 11 p.m., his face would light up.

'You are a clever girl,' he would say. 'How ever did you manage to get away so early?'

On one occasion, however, my driver missed his way while taking me home. Hugh's nurse, meanwhile, began to get a little anxious, even though my husband did not really expect me early. However, it seems that, somehow, he managed to sense that something was wrong – no doubt through the strong psychic and emotional link we shared – and when I did arrive home later than expected, he was in a terrible state of anxiety. The next day I could see that he was still very upset.

The following night Hugh went into a coma and, three days later, his soul slipped away from his body on Sunday, February 15, 1970. He was eighty-seven.

Despite his illness and the pain he must have suffered, Hugh was always such fun and encouraged me in everything I did. Although I am convinced that Hugh and I will meet again, the dreadful sense of loss of his physical presence could not at the time be alleviated, even by my firm belief in survival after death.

I remember little of those sad, sad days following his death except that, in some strangely sweet and fleeting way, with so many people sending flowers, it reminded me of our marriage. With the help of Hugh's secretary, Joyce Funnell, I attempted to send out acknowledgement cards to something like 8,000 letters of condolence – literally from all over the world.

Hugh's funeral and cremation on February 18 was, at his own wish, private. In fact, with great and typical thoughtfulness, he had made arrangements that three of his airmen would be at the private service and ensure that no-one who might have caused me distress would be allowed to attend. This was a precaution in case a particular person – who, although treated kindly by the Dowding family, had tried everything to cause unhappiness – attempted to create further upset.

I should like to end this chapter with the address, kindly delivered by Father Geoffrey Nixon, a friend and neighbour of the family, at the private service in Tunbridge Wells:

'On Sunday, February 15, Hugh Caswall Tremenheere Dowding slipped peacefully out of this life to one to which, we believe, he was not a complete stranger. The manner of his going was in keeping with a man for whom fuss and pettiness were equally abhorrent. He would wish the manner of his reception into that other world be likewise marked by that matter-of-factness which during his long and noble life enabled him to seize the heart of many problems which attended his career in Her Majesty's youngest service. But the Lord who alone sees to the depths of the human heart, who alone comprehends the full generosity of this, the most modest and self-effacing of men, may well see fit to accord him a glorious entry into His Kingdom. This is indeed the wish and the prayer of those who were permitted a glimpse of the greatness of this man's soul.

'Rightly was he hailed as the victor of the Battle of Britain and the principal architect of that victory. But this title, this achievement and this service were possible because he was a humble man; one who recognised his abilities, true, but having recognised them, saw them not as a weapon of personal aggrandisement, but an instrument of service to his country; and so used them without fear or favour single-mindedly. Such is the objectivity of the humble man who sees himself part of the whole with a holy part to play; and such men are commonly crowned with a greatness that in the selflessness of their service they did not think to seek.

'But no crown is won without suffering and it fell to him to bear the cross of seeming ingratitude and perhaps, too, misunderstanding from many of those whose standards were not his own. This he bore with fortitude, as too the later cross of painful disability which crippled his declining years without however halting or diminishing the energies of his active mind. It was his lot to discover another arduous path to the stars, not on Spitfire wings, but on the pinions of patient endurance. On this path he was ever graciously and lovingly assisted by his Lady, whose sympathy with all things living matched his own. Independent in mind and character he remained to the end, but the balm of her peaceful presence he acknowledged from the beginning.

'To her we extend the commendation he would have owned as her due; but much more our commiseration in her loss, offering her the consoling hope, that as her affinity with the spirit world knows not the barrier of physical distance, so even in the pain of bereavement she may find herself in communion with him. For this indeed is his finest hour, an hour not measured by the hands of any earthly clock, but by the rhythmic beat of those waters of everlasting and fulfilling life promised to those who serve in truth the God who will wipe away every tear from their eyes, who dwells where is no more death or mourning, or cries of distress, no more sorrow; for these old things have passed away. Who says; Behold, I make all things new.'

15

Memorial for an Unsung Hero ...
and Trouble for the Trust

ABOUT THREE WEEKS after Hugh's death I had such a vivid
'dream' of him, in which he looked so young and well and
handsome. We were driving around, not in a car but in a kind of
chariot, seeing a lot of friends and we were so happy. I looked at
the time. It was 5 a.m. and, so realistic was the experience, that
I actually thought: as soon as it is eight o'clock I must try to get
through to the Air Ministry and tell them how well Hugh is and
that the Memorial Service must be cancelled. It took quite a lot
to convince myself that it had been a dream ... or a psychic
experience. Yet it was this very spiritually uplifting experience which helped to get me through the Memorial Service,
at noon on Thursday March 12 at Westminster Abbey. It
was a beautiful affair and the Abbey was simply packed with
people.

Hugh's ashes were placed in the Battle of Britain Chapel,
under the memorial window, only a few feet from Lord
Trenchard, founder of the RAF. Opposite is the grave of Oliver
Cromwell and all around the graves and chapels of the Kings of
England.

Washed as I was with so many conflicting feelings and
emotions – the great sadness at my loss, and a feeling of awe at
the utter beauty of the occasion – I did not at the time recall
who the many VIPs were who attended. But I later learned that
among the crowd of an estimated 1,700 who came to pay their
last respects were representatives of the Queen, Prince Philip,
the Queen Mother and the Duke and Duchess of Gloucester.
Also represented were the leaders of the three major political
parties.

Lady Spencer-Churchill was present, along with many men whose names became famous during the Battle of Britain. There were five marshals of the RAF, 15 retired air chief marshals, 13 retired air marshals and 13 retired air vice-marshals. They were joined by members of the then new Strike Command.

I also learned that Hugh had made arrangements for two RAF police officers to be at the Abbey, to ensure that the person already mentioned earlier who had tried to cause great unhappiness between us, would not be able to make any attempt to approach myself or Hugh's family. Hugh had left provision in his Will that a sum of money would be left to this person on condition that no contact was ever attempted with Penelope, the widow of his brother Arthur, or myself. When an application had been made by this person for a ticket to the Memorial Service, I had agreed. But it was only later that I discovered that special precautionary measures had been taken to protect myself and Penelope.

Fleet Street's national newspapers had all paid their tributes to Hugh at the time of his death, with headlines like: DOWDING, THE HERO WE SNUBBED, HERO WHO SAVED BRITAIN – AND WAS AXED, and DOWDING … UNSUNG WAR HERO. Each, in their own way, had pointed up the behind-the-scenes battle Hugh had fought in Whitehall and other famous RAF figures added their comments. It was bemoaned that Hugh had never been made Marshal of the Royal Air Force as was his due, and Wing Commander Robert Wright was quoted as saying: 'In the way he saved Britain he stands with Nelson and Drake.' The newspapers had also noted that, the previous September, Lord Dowding had been given a standing ovation by 350 pilots he had once commanded – at the premiere of the film, *Battle of Britain,* in which my husband was played by Lord Olivier.

At the Memorial Service, the address was given by the-then Defence Minister Denis Healey, who described Hugh as 'a great airman and a very remarkable man … one of those great men whom this country miraculously produces in time of peril.'

He spoke of Lord Dowding's years of service in the RAF

before he became chief of Fighter Command and how he had encouraged the development of radar and the production of the Hurricane and Spitfire, ensuring that his pilots were equipped by the highest standards. He paid tribute to Hugh's vision, foresight, genius, singleness of purpose, deep humility and steadfast courage.

'He occupies a very special place in the hearts of the British people because he was one of the architects of our deliverance in the Battle of Britain, which was of supreme importance in this country's history,' Mr Healey said.

'Our success in that Battle was therefore a complete vindication of all Lord Dowding stood for.'

*   *   *

I do not feel overtly sad at having been widowed twice. The last private words to me of my first husband, Max – for he must have had a premonition – had been: 'Nine years is not nearly long enough to be married to you.' And Hugh remained my romantic and wonderful lover always in the nineteen years of our marriage. So I am indeed fortunate, unlike many who have much longer, though less happy marriages – and certainly more so that those who suffer the upsets and bitterness of divorce, which must be worse than widowhood.

Hugh sometimes used to say to me: 'My darling, I do hope you have a peaceful death in bed – and not a furrier's knife in your back.'

That is not so improbable as it sounds.

*   *   *

It is often said that troubles never come singly – and this certainly held true at the time of Hugh's death. Only three days after he died, my little black cat, Minnie, kept miaowing at the door leading down to the boiler house in the cellar. Finally, I went down to discover that the oil unit, which provides the hot water and central heating, was standing in about two feet of water.

Then, not much longer afterwards, the organisation which Hugh had inspired – a successor of which now bears his name – ran into trouble. Because of legal considerations, the full details of this unfortunate business cannot be entered into here. However, Colin Smith, general secretary of the National Anti-Vivisection Society, has kindly provided the ensuing account of the affair. He takes up the story of the Lawson Tait Memorial Trust at the point when new Trustees came to be appointed.

'With the passage of time new Trustees were appointed and, while Lady Dowding chose as her appointee someone from the Council of the NAVS, the other two Trustees made their choices outside the governing bodies of the other sponsoring societies.

'An ex-Army officer was appointed as a Fund Raiser for the Trust. By profession he was a veterinary surgeon with no experience of the anti-vivisection movement and, as it appeared later, no commitment to the ideal of abolition of animal experimentation.

'Before long disturbing reports were reaching NAVS Headquarters as to his comments on the anti-vivisection campaign.

'The NAVS Council, dismayed at this turn of events, sought an explanation from the Trustees and received in reply a most unsatisfactory answer. The NAVS was told by the chairman of the Trust that it "did not appoint a puppet" when the Fund Raising ex-Army man was engaged. The NAVS was thus obliged to continue to press the Trustees to ensure that their employees kept strictly to the official policy and not to give expression to their own private views. No satisfactory answer was ever received. Even more disturbing was the fact that one of the Trustees was attending NAVS Branch meetings and openly indicating disagreement with NAVS work, particularly our desire to see the establishment by the Government of a medical research institute for the specific purpose of developing and extending the use of alternative methods of research to the use of animals.

'With a number of resignations and new appointments made, the eventual constitution of the Board of Trustees left Lady Dowding and Bernard Conyers the only Trustees

directly connected with the governing bodies of the original
sponsoring societies.

'The NAVS Council became increasingly perturbed at the
attitude of the remaining three Trustees and alarmed when it
was learned that two of them had made representations to
the Charity Commission regarding the operation of certain
clauses of the Declaration of Trust relating to the award of
grants.

'On learning of this development, which in our view was
quite contrary to the principles enshrined in the Trust Deed
and certainly completely opposed to the wishes of the
original founding societies, the NAVS itself submitted to the
Charity Commission a statement, urging that the Trust Deed
should not be altered.

'The statement pointed out that the Trust was founded by
three anti-vivisection societies, each of which made substantial financial contributions totalling £5,000 and since the
Trust's inception, the NAVS had by annual donation contributed more than £16,000 to the Trust funds. In addition,
numerous and substantial contributions had been made by
NAVS Branch Societies and individual members, on the
recommendation of the NAVS. Finally, the NAVS had loaned
£36,000 to the Trust at a low interest rate and various
secretarial and accountancy services had been provided by
the NAVS free of charge, for the Trust.

'The statement pointed out that the modification of the
clauses suggested by the Lawson Tait Trust would enable
grants to be made to those holding a licence to perform
experiments under the Cruelty to Animals Act of 1876. This,
it was made clear, went against the stipulations governing
the disbursement of Trust funds as understood by the three
founding societies and that any alteration of the Trust in this
direction would be in direct opposition to the original aims
and intentions of these societies.

'The NAVS did not accept that the work of the Trust was in
any way hampered by adherence to the stipulations of the
Trust Deed. There were innumerable research projects
deserving of awards and prizes which were of value to
medicine – without the use of live animal experiments. The
Trust's previous catalogue of grants and prizes already

demonstrated this fact. Furthermore, the latest report of the Medical Research Council provided evidence of grants for research not involving live animal experiments which was, by its very nature, encouraging the adoption of techniques in line with the objects of the Trust.

'It was also pointed out that the Trust had already made grants for research into the study of homoeopathy and to the Humane Research Institute of the University of Ankara, run by Professor Dr S. T. Aygun, scientific director of the International Association Against Painful Experiments on Animals.

'Alteration of the Trust Deed, therefore, was entirely contrary to the purpose for which the Trust was formed. And the Trustees, it was made clear, had failed to show that it was impracticable to carry out the terms of the Trust in accordance with the original provisions. The statement concluded: "It is submitted therefore that the Commission have no power under section 13 of the Charities Act 1960 to make a scheme and that the said section does not apply to this Trust."

'The clash of opinions and attitudes on this and other issues between the Trustees on the one hand and the Trust and the NAVS Council on the other, led to a period of considerable difficulty and unpleasantness which was potentially damaging to the work in which we were all engaged.

'An impasse had been reached and Lady Dowding and Bernard Conyers, after consultation with the NAVS Council, decided that there was no option open to them but to tender their resignations from the Trust. The NAVS concluded that it could have no confidence in the remaining Trustees and therefore withdrew both its financial and practical support from the Trust.

'The Trust proceeded to sell the lease of the Harley Street property and repaid in full the loan to the NAVS, and removed its offices to Cheshire. The NAVS, having also considered the possibility of moving to more suitable premises, then decided to retain its sub-lease and to remain at 51 Harley Street from where it still continues to operate successfully today.

'The whole unfortunate episode caused great sadness to Lady Dowding and to others, like myself and the late Administrative Secretary, Mrs June Joynson, directly concerned.

'The NAVS Council, having withdrawn support from the Trust, was thus left with no direct means of sponsoring research projects which would demonstrate the viability and potential of "alternative" research techniques to the use of animals. After a period of consolidation and assessment of the situation it was decided to establish a department within the NAVS for the promotion of alternative techniques and the name chosen for this venture was *The Air Chief Marshal the Lord Dowding Fund for Humane Research.* The "Lord Dowding Fund" was established in 1973 and quickly emerged as probably the most significant body in the United Kingdom for the promotion of alternative techniques. In the five-year period 1973-78, it not only collected and disbursed £150,000 in research grants, but attracted the enthusiastic support of eminent scientists anxious to see a reduction in the number of animals used for experimental purposes.

'No grant may be made by the Lord Dowding Fund to a person holding a licence under the Cruelty to Animals Act 1876 and control of the awards made is vested in the NAVS Council of Management. It is an entirely anti-vivisection venture.

'We learned a painful lesson. It is one we will not need to learn again.'

16

The Saving of a Sanctuary

MY CONTEMPORARIES AND I in animal welfare stand on the shoulders of those who have worked for animals earlier in this century. And, I sincerely hope, future workers will be able to stand on the shoulders of people like Colin Smith, myself and many others who have also laboured towards the relief of animals' suffering. One of the great workers in this field in the early part of this century was Louise Lind Af Hageby.

She was born in Sweden and her compassion was originally aroused by the ragged, shoeless and impoverished little girls who sold matches on the streets. Later, she learned about the vivisection of animals. She came from an aristocratic family and, at the age of eighteen, she spoke out against this cruelty at a public meeting to which her social position gave her access. She was opposed by vivisectors themselves, who criticised her ignorance of the subject.

She then travelled to England with a friend and, in order to learn more first-hand, they took a medical course and in a book, *The Shambles of Science,* she recorded the experiments she had had to witness.

A major vivisector sued her and, although she brilliantly defended herself in court, she lost the case. However, the publicity generated gained her many supporters and sufficient donations not only to pay for the costs, but to found an organisation dedicated to relieving the suffering of animals.

One of her great supporters was Nina, Duchess of Hamilton, one of the first people to expose the cruelty of the fur trade. During the Second World War, she threw open her home, Ferne, in Dorset, to all animals belonging to people in the Services who had to go to war. The creatures would be fed and looked after and, if their owners did not return, would always be cared for.

This was the inauguration of the Ferne Animal Sanctuary, in which the Duchess and her great friend Louise played leading roles.

Upon the death of the Duchess, Louise inherited and took over the running of the Sanctuary. I came to know Louise through my own interest and work in animal welfare and she took me to the Sanctuary on two occasions and outlined to me exactly what needed doing to improve it. I politely pointed out that, at that time, I was nothing to do with the Sanctuary and that she should make these improvements herself. Later, she told Hugh that she intended to leave the Sanctuary and her organisation to me in her Will. My husband became very depressed at this prospect; since we lived in Tunbridge Wells, and the Sanctuary was in Dorset, he did not see how we could possibly continue our own full, busy and happy life and at the same time take on the responsibility of running the Sanctuary. Louise, however, never did make a Will.

When, after her death, I was asked to become a Trustee of the Ferne Animal Sanctuary, I felt that I could not refuse, in view of her original wishes. Like so many organisations, it did not have a straightforward or smooth course.

It developed into a situation in which we lost the Duchess' estate, yet ultimately were able to see that her wishes were still carried out.

It was in 1965 that events took place which would result in the Ferne Animal Sanctuary becoming a trust and a charity, registered under the Act of Parliament of 1960. One would have thought that the careful planning and discussions which took place in preparation could only have resulted in a smooth running basis for all time. But this was not to be.

Ferne had been run by a Committee under the care of the Animal Defence League and Anti-Vivisection Society and I served on that Committee. It was essential that the Sanctuary should be protected as a Trust and our first meeting was on November 5, 1965. To me, this was the beginning of a new era and I accepted the invitation to become a Trustee.

Because Louise did not leave a Will, a long, drawn-out legal problem arose. And, had the results been in accordance with the Duchess' wishes, the Sanctuary would still have been at Ferne today.

Others, however, felt that they had a right to stake a claim in Louise's estate. And the Animal Defence Society staked its own claim.

The ultimate court ruling was that the Animal Defence and Anti-Vivisection Society were the owners and so the Ferne Trustees carried on the work of the Sanctuary by permission of the Society. But during the actual court hearing and even after the result, the position of the Trustees as tenants remained in doubt.

At our Trustees' meeting in August 1968 we were reminded that it was the intention of the Council of the Animal Defence and Anti-Vivisection Society to transfer the Ferne Estate to the Trustees by Deed or Gift. But it came as a great shock to myself and my co-Trustees when the Society then offered to sell us a part of the Estate. It was offered at £55,000, but this was a valuation with vacant possession. The Trust had already spent £22,000 in improvements and repairs and so the Trustees made an offer to the Society of £25,000.

The Society rejected this figure and, in 1971, revised their original figure, to £40,000. We simply did not have this money.

The rejection of the original offer of £55,000 brought a reply from the Society giving us notice to quit. The Trust appealed for funds and was finally able to accept the second figure of £40,000 and the withdrawal of notice to quit.

But, to our great surprise, a further reply arrived stating that the Estate was no longer for sale, although the Society had no aims or plans to use Ferne itself.

This uncertainty forced us to engage an agent to look for a suitable alternative place in which to locate a permanent Sanctuary. Inflation of land prices made this task very difficult. Meanwhile, plans were also put into motion by the Society to sell the estate by auction, with vacant possession and no measures of consideration for the animals in our care.

The Society continued, meanwhile, to increase its offers to the Trustees, the figure climbing to £70,000 and finally to £160,000. We were eventually able, through appeals and fund-raising efforts to meet the first of these figures, but the final figure was out of the question.

As a result, the Society rejected all previous offers by us and issued a Writ against us threatening eviction, in which all the

Trustees would be summoned to court. And so our dreams of retaining a permanent Sanctuary, as the Duchess of Hamilton would have wished, on her own estate, sadly faded.

There was, however, one ray of sunshine to follow. In the New Year of 1975 we learned of a small estate of some thirty acres near Chard in Somerset. We bought it and, after many months of hard work, managed to establish the new Ferne Animal Sanctuary – a home of which we feel our foundress, the Duchess of Hamilton, would have been justly proud.

17

An Interlude – the Ultra Secret

ALTHOUGH THE behind-the scenes battle that my husband fought in Whitehall eventually became obvious to observers and commentators on the Battle of Britain, there were other, lesser-known reasons for the stance he took on aerial strategy and defence policy. The newspaper tributes to Hugh at the time of his death recounted his hard fight to dissuade the Government from sacrificing his fighter planes in the battle for France. They described how he won that fight – and was vindicated in this stance when The Few won the Battle of Britain against fantastic odds.

It was also noted how Lord Dowding was criticised for his preference for small, rather than massive formations of fighters – yet it was later conceded by some experts that scrambling an entire wing of aircraft would take longer than single squadrons.

But what was not generally known and what did not emerge until as recently as 1974, was some of the behind-the-scenes information which guided Hugh in his strategy and decisions. Information which only came to light with the publication of *The Ultra Secret,* by Group Captain F. Winterbotham, Chief of Air Intelligence, MI6.

Here, then, is a personalised glimpse of those highly secret operations – an ex-Wren's view, to be precise. This account grew from a telephone conversation from the former Wren, a complete stranger to me then, following publication of Group Captain Winterbotham's book:

'I am the "stranger" who telephoned Lady Dowding when *The Ultra Secret* was published in 1974, to draw her attention to the tributes to Lord Dowding and his involvement in this Intelligence triumph. She responded generously and immediately by inviting me to lunch. And now, as an ex-Wren who worked in "Ultra", I would like to add my own tribute to Lord Dowding.

'Patriotism and integrity are sadly lacking among many of our leaders in society today, and so a salutary lesson can be learned by studying the life of Lord Dowding, who had the responsibility of guiding the small but magnificent RAF to win the epic Battle of Britain in 1940.

'Before the War, he warned the authorities of the growing power of Germany, and asked for more defences and modern planes for his airmen. At the same time, another patriot – Group Captain F. Winterbotham, Chief of Air Intelligence MI6, was collecting information in Germany as to the strength and intentions of the German Luftwaffe. His warnings went unheeded, except by Winston Churchill.

'And so in 1940, Lord Dowding and Winterbotham were to be in close contact over the incredible "Ultra Secret". This was the breaking of the German Enigma codes which enabled us to read secret messages sent out by all the German Armed Forces. This organisation centred at Bletchley Park, Bucks., had assembled a formidable army of talent, which included cryptanalysts, mathematicians, chess players, post office engineers and about two thousand young Wrens who had the soul-destroying job of working on the monster decoding machines. The outcome of a most complicated procedure meant that messages were decoded in a remarkably short time. The rigid security and distribution of this priceless knowledge of the Nazi plans was organised by Winterbotham, who set up a direct line to Lord Dowding at Stanmore, Middlesex. Goering's plans and intentions were known in advance, which enabled Lord Dowding to use his slender resources to the best advantage. Warning of the great Eagle Day battles when Goering hoped to smash the RAF was the signal which finally decided the turning point in the rout of the Luftwaffe.

'Bitter criticism of Lord Dowding's strategy for not adopting the "Big Wing" plan suggested by some of his junior officers, was a disgraceful episode. I look back with gratitude to his great sense of reverence for life in not sacrificing his airmen without good reason. The integrity and genius of Lord Dowding remains intact in British history. Quite naturally, he never revealed the secret source of information which would have silenced his critics.

'The debate continues as to the effect "Ultra" had on the outcome of the war. Maybe the full truth will never be known by the public. General Eisenhower said, "It has saved thousands of British and American lives and, in no small way, contributed to the speed with which the enemy was routed and eventually forced to surrender."

'In my humble opinion, this country would not have survived the German onslaught without this vital intelligence organisation which, at its height, actually employed 10,000 people.

'It was a miracle that the Germans never suspected Winston Churchill's "Most Secret Service" which he described as "my chickens who laid so well without clucking."

'The story of "Ultra" is incomplete and will continue to be so until the Ministry of Defence releases the relevant documents. Perhaps the full truth will never be known. But Group Captain Winterbotham's book *The Ultra Secret* is the most complete account at present.'

18

Profits, Vanity – and the Terrible Cost in Suffering

HAVING EXPLAINED HOW I came to be involved with, or helped to establish the various organisations for which I work in animal welfare, I should now like to give some of the details and background behind the work that we do.

Few people, it is obvious, stop to wonder exactly *how* animals die to provide the fur garments they see in the furrier's shop window. What follows is a glimpse of the stark and ghastly reality.

Millions of animals are trapped and slaughtered for the fur trade every year. The clothing that these creatures provide does not help some primitive tribe to survive, or act as its only barrier to a cold climate. Instead, it represents commercial value and feeds man's vanity – poor substitutes for millions of creatures' lives.

Animals such as the beaver, bear, wolf, wildcat, otter, lynx, coyote, badger and countless others, fall foul of the cruel, steel-toothed jaws of an inhumane trap. The leghold, steel or gin trip is the most common type for wild furbearers. The unsuspecting creature steps on the trigger plate, causing the powerful springs to snap the jagged-toothed jaws on its leg.

A trapped animal may wait days for the relief of death ... from exposure, exhaustion, starvation, being eaten by a predator or, ultimately, being killed by the trapper. If it is fortunate, it might be able to wring off its own leg, or even bite through its already mutilated limb to gain freedom. But even these macabre possibilities have been reduced by the 'ingenuity' of man: modifications of the leghold trap, such as the jump and

15 A raccoon – one of many thousands of animals whose fur is coveted by the trade – met an excruciating death in this sprung steel trap. *Photograph © Friends of Animals Inc., New York.*

spring-pole traps, catch the victim higher up the leg, or hoist the poor animal by its leg into the air.

In a recent publication produced by the Animal Welfare Institute, the following analogy is given:

'If you want a rough idea of the leghold trap, just imagine that the door of your car has been slammed across the fingers of your bare hand. Imagine that the door is jammed shut and that you are then left with your hand so caught until you either starve to death, or freeze to death, or tear your hand apart.'

There are, it is true, humane traps which kill relatively quickly. But considering the enormous scale of the industry, few are used. No traps, however, discriminate and the number of animals caught which have no 'value' to the fur trade is staggering. Statistics indicate that for every 'target' fur-bearer held and killed, three non-target creatures are caught for the trapper's club. The trapper calls these 'trash': Dogs, cats, birds, turtles and endangered species, such as eagles.

Apart from the animals already mentioned, there are many more which stand out as specific areas of exploitation. Tigers, cheetahs, leopards, polar bears – all are endangered species. Yet every year they appear on the fur market. There is documented evidence of the revolting and unspeakable way in which larger members of the big cat family are killed. After capture, long needles – in some instances, red or white-hot iron rods – are inserted into the anus and up into the heart. This is so that the skin, which will be worn by some member of so-called civilised society, will not show any signs of damage. Snakes, crocodiles and lizards are often skinned alive to facilitate the process – again so that some fashion-conscious person may sport a 'genuine' crocodile-skin wallet or handbag, a pair of snakeskin shoes or a lizard-skin hat-band.

Cases of unnecessary, painful exploitation for the fur trade would nauseate all but the seasoned trapper and the utterly heartless.

One other creature highly prized by the fur trade is the seal. Many varieties are hunted, the main sealing nations being Canada, Norway and Africa. In recent years international charities have gained ground in their fight to expose the barbarism of the annual seal carnage.

A representative of Beauty Without Cruelty recently visited

the coast of Labrador to observe the slaughter of harp seals. Both pups and adult seal were slaughtered, the kill being shared between Norwegian and Canadian fishermen. The pack-ice is a dangerous region for both the hunters and observers: it drifts south at the rate of about 20 miles a day and the seal herds drift with it to warmer waters.

The harp seal pup is the first to be killed. But for the two groups of hunters the method of killing them is distinctly different. The Canadians use a regulation 30-inch club. This resembles a baseball bat and the pup is pounded on the head until it is unconscious. The animal is then turned over on its back and slit from navel to chinbone. A knife is inserted into the body and the auxiliary arteries of the heart are cut. Skinning is then normally completed in about one minute.

When watching such a kill, one cannot help feeling horrified at the cold-blooded act of converting a ten-to-fourteen-day-old baby seal, with its loveable puppy-like face and huge dark eyes, into a bleeding pelt. Even when unconscious, the pup's reflexes often make it wriggle and convulse upon the ice. To see it skinned while still moving is a thoroughly sickening sight.

The Norwegians use a hakapik, a wooden shaft with an iron hammer-head and spike. Here, the method is to render the pup unconscious by stunning it with the hammer – and then to drive the spike immediately into the brain. While the killing is in process, the mother, having retreated to the safety of a water-hole, waits. She listens to the cries of her young but stays there until the hunters have moved on for, unlike her uncomprehending pup, she fears man. Eventually she returns to the pathetic, naked, bleeding carcass and nuzzles up to it.

Later in the killing season – it runs from March 12 to April 24 – the adults are shot. Any suffering endured by the pups when being hunted down must be comparatively less than that of the adults killed in this way.

Marksmen from the bows of ships fire at the seals before they can escape into the water. But weather conditions are usually bad and often the men are shooting at moving targets. There are numerous reports of three, five, or even seven shots being fired into a seal before it finally dies. Their suffering must be great, for they feel pain as we all do.

And for what? For commercial gain and to pander to the vanity of both men and women.

Good quality simulated seal furs are readily available and yet, in a recent season, 160,000 harp seal pups and adults were slaughtered by commercial hunters.

The harp seal is only one species: many others, such as the grey and the hood seal are also exploited.

Those who defend the slaughter of seals tend to claim that systematic culling is necessary because of the effect that seals have on the fishing industry. But there is a powerful counter argument.

Dr Harry Lillie, who is an authority on whales and seals, has this to say:

'Seals are part of the essential biological cycle of the creatures of the sea. I am convinced from study of the balance of all sea life that the mammals play a part in maintenance of plankton on which the higher forms depend. My investigations up to now from the North Sea to the Antarctic indicate that the body excreta of sea mammals, birds and fish acts as a catalyst in the production of the essential plankton. Where seals are concerned they are, in this way, providing their own fish. And the destructive interference with seals in any way will be followed by destructive damage to fisheries by depletion of fish food.'

Today, farmed animals constitute a large proportion of the pelts used by the fur trade. Among those animals are mink, sable, chinchilla, and silver and blue fox. During 1970-71, Norway alone accounted for 165,000 blue fox skins. In that same period Poland farmed a further 150,000 skins and smaller numbers are claimed for the USSR, Finland, Canada, Denmark and Sweden. The farmed mink production for 1970-71 is estimated at 24 million pelts.

Farmed animals are kept in confined conditions and their lives are controlled to provide the best quality fur. These animals suffer from mental anxiety because the environment is totally alien to their species.

Silver foxes are mated in February or March. The cubs are born 51 days later. They are reared in individual wire-floored pens approximately 8ft by 4ft by 4ft and are killed in their prime, that is, in their first winter.

Next time you see a woman in a fox fur, think of the events which led up to the pampering of her vanity.

Thankfully, more and more women are turning away from furs, thus refusing to subsidise so grotesque a cult.

However, there remain those men and women who continue to turn a blind eye to the wholesale slaughter of countless animals – an offence against nature in itself.

Is it simply that they don't care? Or are they remnants of a human sub-species which will ultimately be replaced as man evolves – or is forced by nature to evolve – into a more enlightened, humane example of development, which respects all forms of life throughout the universe?

19

Re-Enter the Powers of Darkness

MY SECOND MAJOR – but this time indirect – encounter with the Powers of Darkness occurred some five years ago. The targets on this occasion were my friends and colleagues in animal welfare work, Prince Alexander Galitzine, his late wife Anne and their family.

Prince Galitzine, who is of noble Russian stock, was first brought to Britain as a babe-in-arms, by his parents in 1917. One day in 1975 he came to me, asking for advice and help. I could see he was deadly serious.

Although, in a religious sense, I am non-denominational – thanks to the widely differing beliefs I have experienced in my life, from the Judaism of the Epsteins, the Protestant and Catholic backgrounds of my parents and my later personal studies in Theosophy, healing and other spiritual areas – I had no hesitation in suggesting the course of action I thought he should take.

But because the terrifying events were actually experienced by Prince Galitzine himself, I am leaving him to describe it in detail in this next section of my book. I have no doubt that the reader who is inexperienced in these areas will thus come to realise the very real and deadly dangerous nature of the dark forces at work in the world today.

EVIL –
A Positive Force in the World

by

Prince Alexander Galitzine

IT IS NOT too fanciful to say that the world today is under attack by a ruthless enemy who is difficult to identify and, curiously enough, even more difficult for most people to believe in.

Belief in the spiritual nature of man implies belief in his continued existence in another form and it is in these more rarified spheres of existence that events take place which can have either a good or bad effect on human beings. Recent much-publicised events have shown that certain things do happen which have no rational or scientific explanation, and it is highly dangerous to laugh them off or always to seek an explanation in psychiatric theories of mental disturbance.

There has been an enormous increase of interest in recent years in the occult. There are a number of reasons for this. Dissatisfaction with the shape of modern society, in spite of its material comfort, is widespread. The great advance in this material comfort has removed from man the necessity to struggle against the more obvious difficulties (although these have been replaced by other and more subtle pressures which are harder to withstand.)

The experience of two cataclysmic World Wars have shaken traditional religious faith to its foundations and orthodox religion has not really been able to shore it up again. Added to this, the tremendous interest in scientific knowledge has caused us to question all our most deep-seated beliefs as to the nature of man and his place in the universe – and even the nature of matter itself.

Faced with the failure of established, orthodox religions to come to grips with their spiritual problems, people have turned to occultism, witchcraft and a number of esoteric cults and beliefs. These are not all bad in themselves and through a study of them man has begun to realise the enormous powers locked within him. But when he tries to release these powers he may suddenly become aware that the genie is out of the bottle and is towering over him – a terrible and demanding ally. In other words, experimentation with spiritual power has opened the door to a world as yet undreamt of by most people (although the Roman Catholic Church has always known of its existence) and to powers which are going to be hard to contain.

Things are happening today which we ignore at our peril: ritual Black Magic in remote parts of the country accompanied by desecration of churches, demonic possession, totally unexplained suicides, occult attacks on innocent people for evil purposes. These things we hear of from the newspapers or second-hand, but it might be of interest to have an account of such an attack from one who has actually experienced it.

I think that one should consider the matter on a factual basis and from the point of view of solid evidence and one should not stray too far into the realms of theory or sophisticated theological discussion. Having said that, however, I think also that one can only explain these happenings and formulate a defence against those that cause them on the basis of a fundamental (non-sectarian, if you like) belief in God and a corresponding realisation of the existence of the Devil.

The experience of myself and my family took place over a period of about three months, during which we were attacked quite violently. (We are, in fact, still the subject of attention – although rapidly diminishing.)

Occult, or Black Magic attacks are made on individuals sometimes for selfish reasons: for gain, to achieve an ambition, or for revenge. They are also made if the individual is engaged in some kind of work which benefits society or relieves human or animal suffering. Attacks are sometimes made on institutions or organisations for the same reason.

At this particular time I was involved in such work. I do not want to be too specific because I do not want certain people or places to be identified, but suffice it to say that I worked for an institution that was dedicated, in its broadest sense, to the relief of human suffering.

I had not been there long before I became aware that the place had an 'atmosphere' which some might call psychic. It was also obvious that there was considerable conflict among the staff and others who lived there, for no apparent reason. The unrest, to put it no higher, appeared to have two sources and seemed – although I was only aware of this later – to form a two-pronged attack, one on the institution as a whole and one on me personally. Each attack was complementary to the other and I believe that I was vulnerable simply because I had been engaged to do certain work which, if successful, would benefit the organisation. I therefore had to be got rid of.

My particular 'enemy', as I came later to identify him, was an individual who worked for me and of whom I very soon came to the conclusion that he was mentally unbalanced. He sometimes spoke of a 'healer' whom he used to visit and whom he was very anxious that I should meet. However, some warning bell rang in my mind and I always avoided doing so. (It should be said in passing that the dark forces of which we are speaking often use mentally disturbed people to do their work because they have less resistance. At the same time they are difficult for their occult masters to handle and frequently go off on a line of their own.)

My family have since told me that about this time I underwent what they have no hesitation in describing as a personality change. We are normally an unusually close family and yet I became aloof and withdrawn from the others and appeared totally unconcerned with their doings. I developed a violent temper and yet occasionally gave the impression of being in a trance, as if hypnotised. Physically, I felt drained of strength and found it increasingly difficult to make the effort to work.

The situation with my assistant steadily deteriorated and, although nothing had yet been said, it became obvious that he would have to go. At this point my family came under attack. My wife began to lose strength in the same way that I did, but much more severely, and to feel extremely ill. On one occasion she became so alarmed that she decided to call the doctor, only to find that she had not strength enough to reach the telephone – let alone leave the house to go to him herself. My daughter, in London, was walking along a gallery in the building where she works when she was seized and an attempt was made to throw her over the railing to the floor below. This was in broad daylight and there was no one else in sight. Fortunately she summoned enough strength to resist and was merely thrown to the ground.

On another occasion, one Sunday evening, my wife (normally the most well-balanced and least neurotic of people) was almost overcome with the desire to commit suicide and was with great difficulty restrained by my son and daughter. To their distress, I was simply a rather disinterested spectator of the whole incident.

In relating briefly these events, and to forestall any question of auto-suggestion, it must be emphasized that none of us had the least inkling of what was behind these happenings. Our acquaintance with the occult had up to now been theoretical and intellectual and attacks such as these were something that happened (if they really did happen) to other people in such places as Haiti or West Africa.

My family grasped the situation before I did. My daughter came down to see me and having met and talked to this man, went straight out and bought four crucifixes which she then took to a priest to be blessed. But for her immediate psychic awareness of what was going on, I shudder to think what the end might have been.

The family finally convinced me of the connection between the attacks and my assistant. The fact that I was so reluctant to believe it shows, I think, the strength of the influence that was being brought to bear upon me. However, I realised that he had to go. The final interview was prolonged and hysterical. At the end, he said, looking at me very intently, 'If I go you will regret it.'

He went, and I breathed a sigh of relief. My wife and I went out that night and celebrated. Our celebration, however, was a little premature. In the small hours of the next morning I awoke with a sense of something amiss and found my wife wandering distractedly round the room. She appeared to be packing our belongings in a desultory sort of way. When I spoke to her she answered confusedly and I urged her to come back to bed. She thereupon fell unconscious on the bed and ceased to breathe. I could not rouse her nor could I detect any signs of life in her inert body. To all intents and purposes she was dead.

What happened then, what brought her back to life, can only be described as the operation of a powerful beneficent force – called upon by me and working through me – which was the power of God in combat against the Evil which was taking place. I held her in my arms, I called upon God and I invoked the name of Jesus Christ. I also repeatedly made the sign of the Cross on her forehead. After a few minutes a tremor showed that life was returning and tears started from her eyes. (I have since learned that tears are the first sign of relief in these attacks.) She then stretched out her arms towards me, opened her eyes and the attack was over.

Some hours later, when we were able to think calmly, we assessed the situation and realised the extreme danger we were in. We also felt very defenceless because the miracle of deliverance which had taken place that morning was too recent to have sunk into our minds and we could not feel sure that prayer would always 'work.' Prayer, after all, or communion with God (to give it its real name) is not, in the Western world, taken very seriously. One should pray sometimes, yes, but it is not really a part of daily practical living in a materialist society. In desperate trouble one prays, of course, and hopes that it will 'work', but without any very great faith that it will. 'Praise God and keep your powder dry', as Cromwell's soldiers used to say, but nowadays the first part of that exhortation is usually left out.

So we felt unprotected and panicky and wondered to whom we could turn for help. We did not think of the Church, any Church, so much has organised religion lost its hold on one's imagination. We turned, instead, to what we considered would be a body of experts in matters of occultism and Black Magic – to Spiritualism, in fact. The individual whose help and advice we sought was Muriel, Lady Dowding, a remarkable woman; well-known in these circles, of great intelligence and wide human sympathies and a tireless worker in the cause of animal welfare. She understood at once and her advice was immediate, if a little unexpected.

'The Roman Catholic Church,' she said. 'They are the only people who can really cope with this sort of thing. Go to Father Nixon and mention my name.'

Father Geoffrey Nixon lived some distance away in Sussex and I immediately telephoned him and made an appointment for the next morning. We set out by car and about half way there, my wife, who was sitting in the back, was suddenly seized with the most violent pain in the solar plexus. She explained later that it was as if a large, sharp knife had been driven through her body. The pain was so intense that she could hardly breathe or speak, but she did manage to say, 'I'm not going to give in – I'm going to beat them' and (as she told us later) a wave of anger and determination flooded her mind. I stopped the car and we all three of us gathered round her and put all our forces of will and spiritual strength – and we prayed. After a few minutes of what seemed to be an immense struggle between two powerful forces, the pain ebbed and then quite suddenly left her and we were able to continue our journey.

Father Nixon at once accepted, as do all others of his religion, the reality of what had happened to us and it was a very great relief to talk to him and to have his advice. He explained that he would certainly offer prayers for us and that others would do the same but that he was not a practising expert, as it were, in these matters. He did, however, recommend us to one who is an acknowledged authority on all forms of occultism and Black Magic and who spends a great deal of his working life helping and healing those who have been injured by evil forces. This man, Dom Robert Petitpierre, is an Anglican monk of the Order of St Benedict and he is one of a community in an Abbey in Hertfordshire.

It was then about midday, but we were prepared to drive to Hertfordshire there and then if we could see him. It is very difficult to convey the state of mind of all of us during those few days; to communicate the nightmarish sense of running from something from which there was no escape – the incongruity of driving through beautiful countryside in bright sunshine with a sense of doom hanging over us and the nervous tension of fearing another attack at any moment. We were prepared to drive all day and all night, if necessary, to go anywhere and see anyone if we could get help.

However, Dom Robert was not available until the next day and so we went home and hoped for the best. Looking back on this period from a distance of a few months, I now realise how effective were the prayers of Father Nixon because never, from the time of our meeting with him, were any of us subjected to quite such violent physical attack again, although other and subtler attacks were to continue.

Our visit to the Abbey is worth describing in some detail.

Nashdom Abbey is a large house built in about 1920 as a country seat for a Russian Prince Dolgorouky, who spent a good deal of his time in England. Although it houses an Anglican community the atmosphere to me, a layman, was much more Roman Catholic than Anglican. We were introduced to the Abbot and to Dom Robert and we then attended a short, simple but rather beautiful service, after which we were shown into a small room in which was a prie-dieu and a large crucifix. Dom Robert listened intently to our story and then said that he had no doubt that we were the target of a Black Magic attack. This was one surprising but heartening aspect of the whole affair and one which we were to meet with again and again – the immediate acceptance and understanding of our predicament and the certainty that if one sought help in the right way, protection would be provided.

Dom Robert also told us that our troubles were very far from being unique and that many institutions, as well as individuals, are today being subjected to the same attentions by dark forces. So serious has the situation become that the Church has formed a special 'flying squad' to deal with such attacks.

We were then given a short service which included the Laying On of Hands and anointing with the Oil of Salvation. After further discussion with Dom Robert, during which he impressed upon us the essential need for regular prayer, we left to return home. We also bought a crucifix from the Abbey and this was solemnly blessed by Dom Robert. (This blessing was extremely important, as will be seen later.) In addition, we were given a quantity of Holy Water – that is, water that has been blessed – with instructions as to how to use it.

We returned home and thereafter the attacks on my wife, who was the main target, diminished in frequency and in strength until they ceased altogether.

This, I think, could be considered a classic case of occult attack and it is important to realise the exact nature of the forces mounting the attack, the measures taken in defence, and the reasons why these measures are successful.

The important thing is, first, to know that you are being attacked and for this we are indebted to my daughter's keen psychic perception and instant action as soon as she grasped the situation. Second, one has got to decide what measures one is going to take to save oneself. Because – let there be no mistake – the logical end, indeed the object, of these attacks, is destruction and death.

Now, opinions on the form of defence may differ. Those experienced in occult matters sometimes advocate learning the techniques of psychic self-defence. This can be hazardous since it requires a knowledge and a spiritual strength that few possess. It is like fighting an individual war without transport or means of communication, without any organisation to sustain you in the field, to replenish your stores and ammunition when they run low or to come to your aid if you are badly wounded.

I am in no doubt as to the right course. I speak as one who, although believing in God, has not since childhood followed any religious observance or owed particular allegiance to any Church. Nevertheless I have become convinced that an onslaught by the forces of Evil, very real and controlled by the Devil, can only be countered by the forces of Good, which are no less real. And when we say 'the forces of Good', we mean, quite simply, God. How then does one get the forces of Good – or God – to help?

It is not as simple as getting on the telephone to the local police. Communication with God – in a specific sense – is difficult. Although prayer is sometimes dramatically answered, one can think of many instances where it is not. However, in cases such as we are considering there is no doubt that if such communication can be made, no cry for help will go unanswered. Help will come and with such strength and constancy that eventual victory is assured. How, then, does one summon help?

Communication can only be achieved by those who have the knowledge, the power, the technique and the authority – above all the authority – to do so. However disillusioned one may have become with the modern Church – any modern Church, of any demonination – whatever one may think of its materialism, its lack of courage or its sheer inability to cope with present-day spiritual problems – the Christian Church, as an institution, has a direct and continuing historical link with the Founder of Christianity. Through Him it derives its authority and in conflict with Evil it can call upon Him and know perfectly well that He will bring His immense power to bear in order to defeat it. The lines of communication have been kept open, the path is a straight one and has not been allowed to become overgrown or impassable.

This is not to say that every priest, of whatever demonination, is necessarily a good instrument in this kind of work. Many are obviously not, but I am convinced that, generally speaking, it is only within the confines of the established religious orders that help and protection can surely be found against the kind of evil we have been discussing. (Comparisons are invidious but I am bound to state that my own leaning – and I am not a Roman Catholic – is towards the Roman Catholic Church, whose priests seem to have a power, a certainty and a self-confidence, as well as a knowledge, that other denominations lack.)

How is this help and protection given? We are not talking about faith, we are talking about practical steps which are taken to counter a specific danger. We are not talking about 'exorcism' either, which, if not handled by a properly qualified person, seems to me to be a highly dangerous proceeding which could well play into the hands of the dark forces opposing us. Here again I can only recount the experience of myself and my family.*

On our first visit to Father Nixon he undertook to pray for us and to see that Masses were said for us in a number of other communities. He also gave us a quantity of Holy Water with advice as to how to use it. After this visit there were, over the next weeks, only two more attacks of a purely *physical* nature, although those of a mental or psychological nature continued for a time.

Dom Robert at Nashdom Abbey continued and strengthened this process and he also paid a visit to my place of business in order to conduct a short service of exorcism. He also presented us (as mentioned earlier) with a crucifix which he solemnly blessed and sprinkled with Holy Water. He pointed out the necessity of regular prayer and some kind of regular religious observance, particularly the service of Communion.

Now follows the most remarkable part of the whole story.

---

* See *To Anger the Devil,* by Marc Alexander. The Story of The Rev. Dr Donald Omand, exorcist extraordinary. Neville Spearman. 1978

Over the next few months the danger receded. But during those months there were many occasions when my wife was under attack. It was not at all unusual, in the first few weeks, to wake in the small hours to find her wandering about in a distressed state, confused in mind and utterly depressed in spirit, convinced that life was over and that there was no hope in anything. On one or two occasions she apparently contemplated getting out of the window – whether suicide was in her mind I do not know and nor did she.

On all these occasions something awoke me immediately (and I am sure this was no accident) and I always tried to make her hold the crucifix in her hand. She invariably refused and struggled not to do so. I then forced it into her hands and the effect was immediate. Her expression changed, she gave a deep sigh and she was relaxed and happy. The evil force had gone.

It is difficult to explain adequately such a miraculous happening, which I have witnessed many times. The crucifix and the Holy Water are not significant in themselves as objects. In other words, they are not White Magic opposing the Black Magic against them. But – and I can find no other words in which to express this – God goes with them and God is where they are. They have been solemnly blessed by a priest and the power of God resides in these material objects and affords protection and help to those who need it. This, I believe, in some way explains the significance of Holy Communion. Further explanation is not possible. This thing happens. The Devil attacks and one calls upon the name of Jesus and takes up the crucifix and the Devil is routed.

To sum up, I think it is important to realise that evil is a positive force in the world, that the Devil is real and that the entities at his command do attack and destroy human beings when they have the opportunity or *when they are called upon to do so*. But God is real also and, to quote the words of Father Nixon, 'most assuredly the powers of darkness, terrible as they are, cannot prevail over the forces of light when arrayed against them.'

20

Through Other Eyes

FOR A PERSON who dislikes travel, I suppose I have done rather more than my share in the past few years. But most of it, I hastily add, has been done to help support the cause that is dearest to me – that of animal welfare, in any of its many forms. Over the last two years or so, on behalf of Beauty Without Cruelty and the International Association Against Painful Experiments on Animals, which was founded by the National Anti-Vivisection Society, I have visited America, New Zealand, India, Germany, the USSR, Poland and Norway.

Naturally, I did not go alone and, since travelling to so many places in short order, making speeches, arranging shows and lectures and being interviewed by the media is exceptionally time-consuming, I am not a very good diarist of my travels, either. The following accounts, therefore, have been prepared by those who accompanied me: Jon Evans, President of the International Association Against Painful Experiments on Animals and secretary to both the NAVS and the International Association Against Painful Experiments on Animals; Joseph Piccioni, Managing Director of the trading company, Beauty Without Cruelty Limited, and Daphne Charters, official Fashion Show Organiser for Beauty Without Cruelty, and currently manager of the company's London boutique.

Hence the title of this chapter.

BEAUTY WITHOUT CRUELTY – 'NOT FAIR TO AMERICAN FUR'

by

Joseph Piccioni

IN THE WINTER of 1978, Beauty Without Cruelty learned that the fur industry was planning an exhibition in New York, under the somewhat contradictory title of 'American International Fur Fair.' The show was, so we heard, to be one of the largest exhibitions of furs ever held in the world. It was also an important attempt in the fur industry's campaign to rehabilitate itself with the public who are becoming increasingly aware of the atrocities committed on many millions of animals every year, purely in the name of financial profit.

It was decided that Beauty Without Cruelty would also make its presence felt in New York when the exhibition of furs was to be held during the week of March 18, 1979.

The planning for the Beauty Without Cruelty counter-exhibition was immense, involving the commercial operations of our movement, the New York Branch and our Public Relations consultants. The funds available to us were very small in comparison to what the fur industry was spending, but we resolved to maximise the effect of every dollar spent. We also had the advantage of the spirit of people whose motivation was not financial profit, but compassion for helpless animals.

The effect of our New York campaign would have been very limited had not Lady Dowding agreed to accompany our party to open our activities.

She was enthusiastic about our plans at the very beginning and when, in the autumn of 1978 she became seriously ill, her main concern was not for her personal well-being, but for the possibility that she might not be able to be in New York for the forthcoming exhibition of March 1979.

During the period of her illness in October, November and December of 1978, I felt considerable concern for her state of health. During the initial and more serious part of her confinement, I was in America, but kept in daily contact with her. She continually assured me that she was recovering, but it was all too obvious from her voice that this was not the case.

Gradually, she started a slow recovery and all the time her concern was to be able to be in New York to head the campaign opposing the American International Fur Fair. Many people advised her to forget the idea, but she would hear none of it.

Finally, the day for our departure for New York came – on the evening of March 12, 1979. Both Lady Dowding and I had been working very hard in the days leading to our travels, trying to clear as much work as possible, and when we met in Tunbridge Wells to be driven to Heathrow Airport, she was in great spirits, despite considerable stress.

We arrived at Kennedy Airport at what would have been 2 a.m. in Britain but was 7.30 p.m. local time. Despite the lateness of the hour, she showed no sign of tiredness and was delighted to be met by Dr. Ethel Thurston, our New York Branch leader, and Jill Haley, one of our public relations consultants who had flown out the day before. Happily, we made our way to the Roosevelt Hotel in midtown Manhattan and prepared for the following day's activities.

The pace of work in New York was immediate, with Press and radio interviews and preparations for the Press Conference which was scheduled for March 15. There were also many major preparations for the big Fashion Show, which was to be held on the evening of March 19.

Despite great efforts on our part, things started going badly for us during the first half of our visit and we were not getting the response for which we had hoped. On my part, I confess to having been very worried during that period, but Lady Dowding seemed unaffected and sure that if we did our best, all would be well.

The tide turned for us on the evening of the Show. By this time we had been joined in New York by Lynn Zimmerman, who is in charge of our distribution centre for cosmetics in Milwaukee, Winsconsin, and Marcia Pearson, a dedicated vegan and model, who had flown out from Seattle, Washington, to organise our own Fashion Show. Both these ladies worked extremely hard towards making March 19 a day not to be forgotten.

The Show was scheduled to start at 7.30 p.m. Until that

evening, the Hotel appeared to have been full of furriers who were in New York for the Fur Fair. There had already been many unpleasant incidents. By 6.30 p.m. the situation had reversed and the Hotel seemed to be full of people who cared about animals and the furriers were keeping a very low profile.

The Broadway actress Gretchen Wyler was preparing to commere the Fashion Show, which was to be opened by Lady Dowding. Another notable speaker was Cleveland Amory, President of the Fund for Animals and one of the American Vice-Presidents of Beauty Without Cruelty.

Cleveland Amory had just returned from a voyage on the *Sea Shepherd,* aboard which he had been to Canada to oppose the seal hunt. Within six miles of the baby seals there had been so much ice that the *Sea Shepherd* could not get through, so Mr. Amory and his party of observers walked across the ice-bound sea and were able to mark with indelible dye some 1,000 baby seals so that their coats would be useless for fur. They were arrested, but eventually got out on bail and back to the States by helicopter.

The unexpected arrival of a camera team from New York's Channel 7 Eye-Witness News delayed the opening of the Fashion Show for half-an-hour. There were numerous other Press representatives on hand and the queue of people entering the Show was enormous. Despite extra chairs being brought in from other parts of the Hotel, there were still about 100 people left standing. We later learned that many of these people had come from places as far away as Vancouver, on the West Coast of British Columbia, to be present that evening. One group of young men to whom I spoke had motored from Ohio and were sleeping rough in church premises. Their efforts had been to express their support for the Beauty Without Cruelty campaign.

The Show was one of the greatest successes in the history of the movement to date. The interviews with the media had been quite numerous before the Show – after it, they became an avalanche. As a more modest follow-up, another Fashion Show was held in Riverdale, New York, on the evening of March 21, which also proved a great success.

After the exposure of our activities by the media, people everywhere congratulated us on what we were doing – everyone, from chambermaids in the Hotel to waiters in restaurants.

16a & b An African civet in its natural state and (inset) the cramped and cruel conditions in which musk is extracted from the creature for perfume. *Photograph © David Whiting, Beauty Without Cruelty.*

17a & b   A baby karakul (Persian) lamb is skinned for its fur. Inset: the karakul in its natural – and highly vulnerable – state. *Photograph © David Whiting, Beauty Without Cruelty.*

In addition to our campaign, a splendid series of demonstrations and picketing had been organised to coincide by Friends of Animals and members of the American Society for the Prevention of Cruelty to Animals.

On March 21, we said goodbye to our friends and collaborators who returned to various parts of the United States, while Lady Dowding and I returned to England. We were all very tired but considered our efforts had placed a very uncomfortable thorn in the side of the fur industry.

One thing which gave us a great deal of satisfaction was a conversation of two furriers' wives, overheard in a ladies' room of the Hotel. They were loudly complaining about the news coverage being devoted to the 'poor animals' campaign – rather than to their American International Fur Fair!

*   *   *

Within five days of our return to England, Lady Dowding and I were off again – boarding a plane at Heathrow for New Zealand, a twenty-nine hour flight. The entire trip involved a very long journey, but we were expecting a more leisurely tour of Australasia without the worries, stresses and conflicts of the American visit. But this was very far from being the case, as it turned out. Certainly the worries and stresses were not there, but the actual workload was enormous.

On the day of our arrival in Auckland, New Zealand, Lady Dowding was interviewed on radio and on South Pacific television. The following weekend was crammed with enormous Press interviews and she also read the lesson at a large Auckland church.

As in America, the pace quickened and, by the end of our tour of New Zealand, she had been interviewed by every newspaper of any standing and by every radio and television station in the country. In addition, she attended many functions for members of the public and made appeals on behalf of animals to the Prime Minister, Mr Muldoon and the Mayor of Auckland, Sir Dove Myer-Robinson.

We found our New Zealand Branch very highly efficient and with many thousands of members. Due to import restrictions, however, we had been unable to supply these members with cruelty-free cosmetics, so part of our job was to initiate arrangements for contract manufacturers, which we hope will come to fruition in the latter part of 1979.

Our five-day tour of Australia was no less hectic. Again Lady Dowding was in great demand and once more appeared on every national television channel, radio station and in every major newspaper. She addressed innumerable meetings and the enthusiasm she instilled in her audiences was overwhelming.

There was never any chance of her being able to take her prescribed afternoon rest and most nights she was unable to sleep for more than five hours because of the great amount of work she was doing. I could see that she was very tired, but refused to give in, fulfilling all her engagements by the sheer strength of her will.

At the end of our tour, it was apparent that she had made Beauty Without Cruelty a household name in New Zealand and Australia. No doubt, because of her efforts, countless animals have been spared much suffering. I truly feel that she did a magnificent job for our movement and I do not think that anyone else could have done the same.

TO RUSSIA WITH LOVING CARE

by

Jon Evans

BECAUSE OF MY long friendship with Lady Dowding and working with her as I do in a common cause to end abuse and suffering inflicted upon animals by man, I have been invited to contribute to this book. I do so with infinite pleasure.

As representatives of the National Anti-Vivisection Society and the International Association Against Painful Experiments on Animals, we have visited many countries together in an endeavour to persuade world governments and scientists to relinquish the cruel and immoral practice of experimenting on

living animals and give a meaningful lead in the development
and use of humane alternatives. What we saw and experienced
during our travels would sadden the stoutest heart; often the
journeys were tiring and irksome, sometimes dangerous, but
always there were lighter moments, without which we would
have submerged in a quagmire of despair.

Throughout the following pages I have endeavoured to reveal
a little known facet of Lady Dowding's life; the personal hazards
resulting from long and tedious journeys abroad are seldom recorded and I doubt whether more than a handful of close friends
know, how by sheer determination and often a complete dis-
regard for personal safety, these missions were accomplished.

Alas, Lady Dowding has a very human flaw; she is endear-
ingly inadequate in coping with the exigencies of travel.
Airports, she believes, are fiendishly constructed to lose a
passenger in a labyrinth of glass corridors from which they
never return. Whether it is a distrust of modern bureaucracy's
handling of time-tables, I do not know, but it is one of her
cardinal rules to be at the airport at least two hours before
baggage check; if you should be late, life can be very unpleasant,
but only for a little while. Perhaps I may claim, with due
modesty, some credit for being a mentor, guide, physician and
friend responsible for her safety while travelling through two
continents in the service of her friends – the animals.

It was in Moscow during 1972 that there occurred one of the
most dramatic events in the history of the anti-vivisection
movement; a meeting between Russian scientists and officers of
the International Association Against Painful Experiments on
Animals. Preparations for the visit to the Soviet Union had
taken months and had only been made possible because of the
splendid co-operation between the British Embassy in Moscow,
who undertook negotiations on behalf of the IAAPEA and the
Soviet Academy of Medical Sciences.

The British party consisted of Lady Dowding, IAAPEA
Secretary-General, Colin Smith, and myself. Fortified with the
knowledge that at least the Soviets had agreed to meet us, we
left Harley Street on a cold February afternoon. Little did we
realise that this was the beginning of one of the strangest
adventures ever undertaken in a quest for the humane treatment of laboratory animals.

We were met at Moscow airport by an official from the British Embassy who immediately took charge of the clearance formalities. These were nearly completed when the customs officer noticed a copy of the NAVS sponsored film *Did You Ever See Such a Thing in Your Life*. Lady Dowding had insisted that we take this to show scientists in Iron Curtain countries how in the U.K. we were campaigning for a more humane law to safeguard research animals, as well as pressing for the wider use of alternatives. The customs officer disappeared with the reel. An hour later he returned, saying we would be allowed to keep it as he had found nothing 'undesirable'.

The Metropole, one of Moscow's older hotels, built during the regime of the ill-fated Tsar Nicholas II, faces the grey stone facade of the famous Bolshoi Theatre and is only a few minutes walk from Red Square. After a perfectly ghastly meal which consisted of soup, stale bread and beetroot we decided to retire; tomorrow was our meeting with the scientists. Colin and I escorted Lady Dowding to her room, a vast chamber soberly furnished with only the bare necessities. The noise of passing traffic was dulled by several inches of snow which covered the City. For security reasons we entreated Lady Dowding not to leave her room until morning when we would identify ourselves by a special knock. As Colin and I retraced our steps along the corridor we distinctly heard the sound of a chair being drawn up against the door.

The following day, accompanied by our guide, a loquacious Russian lady who appeared like the 'genie of the lamp' whenever we were about to leave the hotel, the three of us set off for our assignation with Dr. Dushkin, Director of the Soviet Academy of Medical Sciences. After about twenty minutes' drive through the streets of Moscow, the car halted opposite an impressive building with wide steps leading to a great portico of smooth granite; it was a heritage of the Romanovs and had survived the ravages of the revolution which had changed the destiny of Russia.

Dr. Vasili Dushkin rose from his seat at the long table which occupied most of the room, and greeted Lady Dowding with a gentle smile; a moment's hesitation and we all shook hands. The ice had been broken. An attractive girl, a biologist and personal assistant to Dr. Dushkin, interpreted. Her English was so fluent that language differences proved no problem. We were introduced to four men who had remained in the background – all scientists who worked with our host in his laboratories outside Moscow.

With traditional hospitality, vodka, coffee and sweet biscuits appeared. We talked of the problem of animal experimentation and the need to develop alternative techniques. The sincerity with which Lady Dowding put the case for an international campaign against the present inhumane treatment of research animals made a deep impression on the Russian scientists. Dr. Dushkin agreed that the treatment of experimental animals in the USSR, as elsewhere, left much to be desired, but he said a committee had been formed to develop rules for the humane treatment of laboratory creatures. The conversation then turned to alternative methods of research, and Dr. Dushkin claimed that 'ninety per cent of all vaccines in the USSR were produced by tissue culture techniques'.

Colin was engaged in the subject of breeding establishments when I whispered to Muriel, 'Shall I ask him if we can visit his laboratories?' She gave me an excited nod. To our utter amazement he instantly agreed, saying he thought it would prove very useful, and if we could be ready by 10.00 the next morning he would send a car to take us to a breeding establishment 40 miles outside Moscow.

We returned to our hotel in a daze. The seemingly impossible had happened: a group of anti-vivisectionists had been discussing with Russian scientists practical means of improving the plight of research animals, and they were actually going into Russian laboratories. I thought of the veil of secrecy which shrouded similar establishments in the United Kingdom.

The next day during breakfast, I was intrigued by the rapid disappearance of bread rolls of which there had been ample supply, when I noticed that Muriel, with the dexterity of a conjurer, was transferring the last slice to the inner regions of her muff, which I knew also served the purpose of a handbag. I murmured to Colin, 'I think Lady D gets hungry during the day,' nodding towards the now empty plate. The enigma of the missing bread was soon to be solved when Muriel asked us to take her out into the street so that she could feed the sparrows.

We staggered along a slippery side street, clutching each

other for support, snow blowing into our faces hard enough to cause tears. After a few minutes in blizzard-like conditions, we saw a low hedge in which sparrows had taken sanctuary against the arctic winds. The muff now revealed its secret and the bread was thrown lovingly to the birds. I was thankful the streets of Moscow were free of elephants!

Hardly had we returned to the warmth of the Metropole when a car arrived to take us to Dr. Dushkin's laboratories. It was an unforgettable journey. After leaving the city, the road ribboned through pine forests; everywhere there was snow.

The complex of buildings where Dr. Dushkin and his team conducted their research consisted of several two-storey cement blocks; the peeling paintwork and strange atmosphere of desolation was in complete contrast to the splendid edifice in Moscow where we had been entertained on our arrival. However, we were made most welcome and encouraged to partake of vodka and small cakes, sweetmeats and lemon tea. Colin Smith had brought with him the NAVS film *Did You Ever See Such a Thing in Your Life,* and after it was shown there were a number of appreciative comments from the technicians who crowded into the small hall to see an English science movie.

Lady Dowding had been anxious for us to see some of the laboratories where animals were bred for experimentation, and when to our utter surprise Dr. Dushkin agreed to our request, I asked for the impossible: 'May I use my camera?' Glancing at Lady Dowding I saw the flicker of a smile.

'Certainly,' said the interpreter, 'Why not?'

My camera was busy. Not only was our visit to the Soviet Union the first ever of its kind by an anti-vivisection organisation, but never before had a British anti-vivisectionist taken pictures in a Russian research laboratory – with permission.

As we boarded the plane for Warsaw, the next stop in our journey behind the Iron Curtain, I felt that we had left burning one small candle in a vast sea of darkness. Without Lady Dowding this might never have been lighted.

After endless engagements in Poland and Finland where important links were forged between animal welfare movements and scientists working in the field of humane alternatives, we returned to London. At Heathrow Lady Dowding was hustled to a crowded press conference to talk about her work in Russia

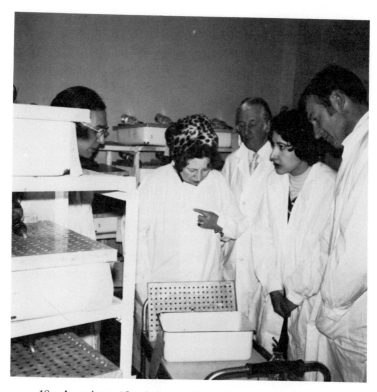

18 A unique 'first' for anti-cruelty campaigning.
Lady Dowding is seen here with IAAPEA Jon Evans
(centre) inside an actual Russian animal laboratory.
Photograph © Colin Smith

for laboratory animals. A few hours later she was interviewed on the BBC radio programme *World at One,* where she related her views and experiences on the delegation's highly successful visit to three European countries. Colin and I were amazed at her fortitude and vitality – but after all she is a very amazing lady.

*   *   *

The historic Rajaji Hall in Madras, once the home of Clive of India, was packed with delegates attending the first National Conference on Animal Welfare. The State Governor, His Excellency, Shri K. K. Shah, had just begun his welcome address. Suddenly a uniformed messenger jostled through the crowded assembly to the platform, saluted, and thrust an envelope into the hand of the governor. Mr Shah read the message, then announced that Pakistan had declared war on India. He asked for unity in India's hour of need. The Indian national anthem was sung. At least for that day, all thoughts of the Conference were abandoned.

Lady Dowding and I had been in Madras barely 48 hours, having flown from London to address India's first national conference on all aspects of animal welfare. It had been organised by our old friend Rukmini Devi Arundale, one of India's outstanding humanitarians who had possibly done more than any other individual to enrich her country's artistic and cultural heritage. Rukmini, dedicated to the cause of suffering animals, was once a member of parliament in Mr. Nehru's government. She introduced in the Rajya Sabha in 1954 a Bill for the Prevention of Cruelty to Animals, which she later withdrew under pressure from the Prime Minister. When the government approved the establishment of the Animal Welfare Board, Rukmini was elected Chairman. She has visited London many times and holds office of a Vice-President of the IAAPEA.

No conference could have opened under more foreboding influences, but in spite of the political catastrophe and its most serious implications, the sponsors decided upon its continuance, with an abridged programme. Packed into two and half days, this well organised conference proved to be a magnificent success. Lady Dowding spoke of the suffering of the animals in the cosmetic industry, and I remember well the impact her speech made on the vast audience who were visibly stirred by her plea for the manufacture of animal-free products. As a result, Beauty Without Cruelty branches were established in India during the next few years.

The opening ceremony at the Rajaji Hall was one never to be forgotten; the traditional garlands of flowers and sandalwood which bedecked the necks of principal guests, and the temple elephant which, it is purported, gave a blessing when placing its trunk upon our heads. Learning that it lived near a remote temple some distance outside Madras, Lady Dowding asked if several large bunches of bananas could be stowed in the boot of our car as she wished to visit its forest home to feed it before our return to London.

During our stay in Madras, we were guests of His Excellency the Governor, at Raj Bhavan, the most beautiful Residency, a few miles from the city. The three days however were spent in talking with the representatives of the many animal welfare societies who had converged on Madras for this huge educational get-together. The speeches seemed endless, and everyone wanted to talk to us about legislation controlling animal experiments in the United Kingdom, and how could we help Indian scientists develop alternatives? At the end of the first very tiring day, we were invited to a civic dinner given by the Mayor of Madras. An excellent vegetarian meal of Indian dishes was served on large palm leaves, much to Lady Dowding's delight.

The worsening political situation necessitated a premature return to the UK. The Governor insisted that we leave that night and arranged for a car to take us to a small airfield from which we would fly to Bombay. Sadly we took leave of our many friends and with hastily packed bags started on the first stage of the journey home. The road to the airstrip, hemmed on one side by thick forests, was brilliantly lit by a full moon. Suddenly Lady Dowding said, 'How far are we from the temple with the baby elephant?'

The driver replied with some alarm: 'Four miles, Lady memsahib.'

She turned to me, 'Jon, the bananas are in the boot. Have we time to feed the elephant? I promised ... '

'No, Muriel,' I replied, 'The country's at war, Bombay is likely to be bombed, we don't know how we shall get home, and anyhow the bloody animal, apart from being over-fed, will probably be asleep.'

She did not say another word. I had won my point, and thank God.

The Bombay airport was seething with people clamouring to leave the city. There was complete chaos everywhere. 'No, there are no planes going to London; in fact everything that *can* fly has left,' the one official that I managed to approach was quite definite.

I turned to Lady Dowding. 'I will try to contact someone at the British Consulate. I want you to sit on the cases. Don't move until I return,' I said.

By extraordinary good fortune I found an official who had received a telephone call from the Residency in Madras; he knew of our plight and had reserved for us the last two seats on a London-bound Air India plane, which we later learned was hidden behind a hangar on the far side of the airstrip, so it would not be mobbed by the crowds intent on getting away from Bombay. I returned to find Lady Dowding peacefully perched on our piled-up suitcases, blissfully unconscious of the crisis around her, writing postcards to her grandchildren.

At last we were air-borne, but our troubles were by no means over. Four hours later, two fighter planes appeared, uncomfortably close to the London-bound aircraft. Our course was diverted and the pilot was ordered to land at Baghdad. Air India had been 'blacked' by countries sympathetic to Pakistan. We remained on the runway for hours in a high temperature with no air-conditioning while the plane was searched for arms by the Iraqui authorities. Much later, very tired and weary, we landed at Heathrow. Lady Dowding had conveniently just finished reading her last paper-back.

*   *   *

In November 1977, Lady Dowding made a second visit to India and again I was her travelling companion. We had both been invited to speak at India's third and largest animal welfare conference to be staged in New Delhi. If Muriel felt any trepidation after her past experiences on our earlier visit, she showed nothing but obvious enthusiasm.

During the flight we spoke of the possibility of seeing the Indian Prime Minister, and appealing to him for a ban on the export of monkeys and songbirds. I felt doubtful whether the man who shouldered the problems of 600 million people would have time to discuss animal abuses with two British anti-vivisectionists. However, I kept my thoughts to myself.

We were greeted at New Delhi airport by our old friend Rukmini Devi Arundale, who drove us to the hotel where we were to stay for the duration of the conference. During a meal we raised the question of an interview with Mr. Morarji Desai, and Rukmini, a close colleague of the Prime Minister, promised to do whatever possible to arrange a meeting, and later that evening she rang to say that Mr. Desai had agreed to see us the following afternoon at Parliament House.

As the car drew up at the official entrance of the great stone building designed by Edwin Lutyens for the British Raj and now the seat of parliament for the Republic of India, two soldiers wearing gold and red head-dresses jumped to attention, and almost immediately an official appeared in the doorway to guide us to the Prime Minister's office.

Mr. Desai rose from behind his desk to greet us. The 80-year-old statesman, who only recently had suffered a plane accident in the jungle and walked miles in darkness to find assistance for his injured companions, showed nothing of this traumatic experience. We shook hands. The talks began. Lady Dowding spoke with great feeling on the vexed question of exportation of Indian monkeys and drew the Prime Minister's attention to the U.S. ban on the killing of whales for sperm oil, pointing out that a non-animal alternative had been found to replace the needs of industry. We pressed for prohibition on monkeys which found their way to U.S. research laboratories, pointing out the horrendous suffering inflicted upon these creatures by scientists who regarded them as mere 'laboratory tools'. I asked the Prime Minister for his views on vivisection and he immediately affirmed his total opposition to any experiments on any living being. We were with Mr. Desai for an hour and a quarter before he was called into the debating chamber; I know he was much affected by Lady Dowding's passionate and reasoned appeal for a law which would safeguard animals in India against the cruelties forced upon them by researchers. The cry for compassion was particularly apposite in a country where 'Ahimsa' (sacredness of all life) is a fundamental creed.

We returned to our hotel exhausted, but happy with the knowledge that at least we had seen the Prime Minister and made a strong plea for his support for our campaign to reduce animal suffering. Feeling very tired I excused myself from further conversation, wished Muriel goodnight, and retired to my room. I had scarcely fallen asleep when there was a thundrous knocking on the door, repeated every few seconds with urgency. With thoughts of some awful catastrophe skimming through my mind, I opened the door to find Muriel in a state of feverish excitement. She had just received a telephone call from Diana Ratnagar, leader of Beauty Without Cruelty in India, to say that Mr. Desai had spoken to her and asked her to tell Lady Dowding that the ban she had asked for on the export of monkeys would go through, and he was to make an announcement to this effect when he addressed the Animal Welfare Conference the next day. Our delight knew no bounds; this courageous decision would mean that every year at least 20,000 monkeys would be spared the horrors of experimentation.

There was an air of expectancy in the Conference Hall as the Prime Minister began to speak. If his message could be reduced to a single sentence it was to ask mankind to adopt a more civilised and humane behaviour towards every form of life. Mr. Desai then made his historic announcement, that there would be the enactment of a law prohibiting the exportation of monkeys and certain other creatures from India. As he stepped from the rostrum and returned to his seat, Mr. Desai smiled at Lady Dowding, and the sustained applause from the hundreds of delegates continued for several minutes.

While in New Delhi we accepted numerous engagements to speak on the work of the NAVS and the International Association Against Painful Experiments on Animals. There were occasions when I grew anxious lest Muriel should overtax her strength – during one afternoon she gave six recorded interviews for radio – but in spite of the heat and the many calls made upon her she showed no sign of strain.

There was one incident which made an indelible impression, as it clearly typifies Lady Dowding's concern for 'all creatures great and small'. We had been interviewed on a special television programme which meant being confined in an unbearably hot studio for at least two hours, because of the necessary preparations for the transmission. With a little time to spare before our next engagement, and a dire need for fresh air, I suggested we take a taxi to the outskirts of the City and visit the place where Gandhi's body was cremated, now a beautiful garden with green lawns, carefully and lovingly tended by the devotees of the saint-like man revered by the world for his reverence for life. We asked the taxi driver to wait, removed our shoes, and with other visitors walked towards the grass quadrangle. The lawns were being cut with an ancient heavy iron mower drawn by a solitary bullock. The old gardener who guided the contraption seemed unaware of the animal's fervent desire to eat the spray of fresh cuttings thrown up from the blades. Muriel watched for a few moments and then, completely unperturbed by onlookers, crossed the path of the approaching bullock, motioned the man to stop, and insisted that the box of rich green cuttings be fed to the tired and hungry beast. Her brief lecture on animal welfare to the perplexed and somewhat alarmed gardener was translated by a willing passer-by who fully appreciated the Englishwoman's concern for an old and tired beast. I am quite sure that Gandhi himself would also have approved.

NEPTUNE STILL RULES THE WAVES

by

Daphne Charters

WHEN PRIMITIVE MAN developed faculties beyond those needed for his simple existence, he began to observe the natural phenomena around him and to wonder what caused certain events to take place. He needed both sun and rain for the crops which were essential for his survival, but often he was obliged to contend with floods and drought. As his flocks and herds had to multiply to keep pace with his growing tribe, he pondered on the wonders of birth and death and he came to the conclusion that each river, forest and valley had an invisible Guardian, like himself in nature, but transcending him in power. The sun, moon and wind were also personified and he sought to gain favour from these superior beings by raising temples and effigies in their honour; making sacrifices to them; beseeching them for favours and worshiping them.

It was out of man's need that the gods were born; his need for something or someone greater than himself to invoke for aid or comfort when events went against him and with whom to rejoice when life was good.

When reading about one of the ancient cults, we may shudder at the description of the flashing knife and the sacrificial beast falling to the ground, its lifeblood a propitiatory offering to the gods. We may self-righteously congratulate ourselves that now mankind is 'civilised' such useless and horrific rites are no longer performed.

But sacrifices still take place. Not in ones and twos on special occasions, but in their millions. The research laboratory has replaced the Temple, the vivisector the priest, and no longer is blood considered a sufficient gift. Terror is now added and the mutilation and long, drawn out suffering of millions of defenceless creatures are offered yearly to the god of our modern age, Science.

To many, the old gods no longer exist, even the One, the Prime Cause of the great religions and philosophies of the East and West is scorned, to be replaced by an ideology, often a false one, or even a poor little slogan.

It is true that the form of the gods and their dwelling places, built of wood, stone, metal and jewels, were man-made. But the Highly Intelligent forces flowing through them when invoked, were Cosmic or real. If we believe in them or, preferably, know how they function, it is possible to contact them today.

Lady Dowding works tirelessly for many branches of animal welfare. The organisation, Beauty Without Cruelty, of which she is joint-founder and Chairman, spreads through its literature the truth concerning the agony of animals caught in traps for their fur, and the suffering or death inflicted on defenceless creatures to produce the ingredients for many cosmetics. These are the sacrifices of this Age, not to the Goddess of Beauty, but to her ugly sister, Vanity.

This organisation sends lecturers all over the country and shows the alternatives to trapping by giving Fashion Shows of simulated fur coats. It also manufactures cosmetics made from vegetable oils and flower essences, kinder to both skin and conscience than those in which animal cruelty has been involved.

Voluntarily, I work for this Charity, and in my capacity of Fashion Show organiser, I accompanied Lady Dowding and another member, Miss Ruth Plant, to Norway, a land steeped in folklore and legend, of Trolls and Nordic gods. It is the birthplace of Peer Gynt, the ageless story of Everyman's journey through life, his frailty and folly and ultimate redemption.

A great deal of work is involved before and during any of these Fashion Shows, augmented this time by the paperwork and special packing demanded by Board of Trade regulations. We were travelling by road and boat with two loaded cars, one of which I was driving. It was important that we should all have a good night's rest on the ship carrying us from Aarhus in Denmark, to Oslo, especially as we were bearing our message of compassion to a fur-producing country.

On the way to our cabins we noticed a life-sized effigy of a bearded Viking, his aged eyes closed, deep in thought or sleeping. We were told that he was the national hero, Holge Danske, after whom our ship was named. Legend relates that he still sleeps beneath Elesmere Castle and that he awakens to protect his country when it is in danger.

'A pity he did not bestir himself during World War II,' the sceptic may sneer. Yet, in his own way, he did fulfil his mythical purpose during the War years. For the code-name of the Leader of the Danish underground was 'Holge Danske.'

We slept well, the sea being no more turbulent than a pond and, in spite of the early hour and teeming rain, we were met by our kind hosts. Amid a jostle of umbrellas, they greeted us with: 'Oh, you poor ladies, did you manage to get any sleep?' Surprised, we replied that we had had a most restful night.

They then told us that gale-force winds had raged all night. We had obviously slept much better than they.

Our anti-cruelty message delivered, our promotional work done, several days later we drove back up the gangplank of the *Holge Danske* and were not reassured to see that all car-wheels were being lashed to the deck.

The Captain had been on leave on our outward journey, but this time we met him and at dinner he laughingly advised us to take our sea-sick tablets and told us that he would be spending the night on the bridge. Later, he took us there and we nervously eyed the barometer, which had slumped to the depths as though brooding over the coming storm.

But the barometer was misleading; the Captain wrong. He spent the night, not on the bridge, but in his cabin. We slept.

We heard later that savage storms had lashed the coastlines on both sides of the North Sea and a yacht was lost off the Channel Isles. Other ships were obliged to prove their sea-worthiness, but not the *Holge Danske*.

Coincidence? Possibly. Or could be it that the gods prefer sacrifices to be in terms of time and energy from those who are seeking to *save* animals, rather than the bloody corpses of defenceless creatures? And that if they are invoked, they can and do still come to our aid?

21

Mysteries for the Aquarian Age

I BELIEVE THAT under the influence of this Aquarian Age, many mysteries will be elucidated and many skeletons of the past will emerge reconstructed from their cupboards. Several such enigmas have, to varying degrees, haunted and fascinated me during my life. I have already written of some of them, such as the UFO experiences related by Desmond Leslie, George Adamski and many thousands of other people all over our planet. In this chapter, I would like briefly to examine a few more which have involved me directly or indirectly.

When I first visited Stratford-on-Avon at the age of fifteen, I was bitterly disappointed. Always having been rather sensitive to 'atmospheres' of places, I had a strong, distinct feeling that the much-lauded and publicised birthplace of Shakespeare was nothing but a sham. I could not, then, have said why – it was simply something inborn, instinctive in my psyche which told me that Stratford was not precisely all it was trumped up to be.

I was not to think of this again for many years, when I came across the great Baconian controversy which, I have come to believe, has a great deal to support it. Although I should quickly make it clear that I do not subscribe to the simplistic view that Francis Bacon wrote all the Shakespearean plays.

The theory, as I have come to understand it and which appears to be most reasonable, is as follows:

Francis Bacon was the son of Elizabeth the First and Robert Dudley, Earl of Leicester, who were secretly married after the death – or murder – of the Earl's wife, Amy Robsart. Amy died in mysterious circumstances in a fall from a balcony at night and there are reasonable grounds for believing that a balustrade upon which she leaned gave way, because someone had tampered with it deliberately. At any rate, the marriage of

Elizabeth and Leicester could not have been revealed at the time because it would immediately have thrown light upon the reason for Amy's death.

Elizabeth's best woman-friend was Lady Bacon and it is thought that on the birth of the child, he was smuggled to Lady Bacon and brought up as the second son of herself and Sir Nicholas Bacon. (They already had one son of their own, Anthony.)

The actual registration of Francis Bacon's birth is rather curious in that he is entered as *Mr.* Francis Bacon – a strange appellation for a newly-born child – almost as if to ensure that any inquirer would not find any title connected with his name. The place of his birth was given as York House, in the Strand, where his proxy 'father', Sir Nicholas, was tenanted as Lord Keeper of the Great Seal.

It is strange, also, that in his will Sir Nicholas left nothing to Francis, indicating I think that Francis might be supplied from another source. Elizabeth had miniatures of Francis painted and, about the time of his birth, caused the Correct Education for a Young Gentleman to be written.

Among the letters of Lady Bacon is one to her son, Anthony, asking him to obtain a list of medicaments, because Francis was not well. She adds, ' ... for I could not love him more if he were my own.'

It is known that Francis was sent to the court of France at the express command of the Queen. There he met with a group of young men, savants of the famous Pleiade group, under Jean Daurat and later, the poet Pierre de Ronsard. This group was trying to restore the language of France to the beautiful form in which it exists today. Francis fell in love with Marguerite de Valois, but for reasons both personal and political, Elizabeth refused to entertain the idea of his marriage to the French Princess, and he was ordered back to England.

It is here that I diverge from the Baconian theory that Francis wrote *all* the Shakespearean plays. I believe, rather, that Francis and a group of intellectuals, including Robert Greene, whose *Pandosto* (1588) suggested the plot of *A Winter's Tale,* attempted to do for the English language what was being done for France and a number of their writings were produced under the name of Shakespeare. Since it was treasonable to write about the deaths of kings or queens in that time and because the theatre was considered an extremely low calling, it is thought that the name of Shakespeare – an actor Bacon and his friends knew – was used. This had an esoterically phonetic significance for Francis also, for as was the fashion of literati of the day, he had for his Muse the goddess Athene, the Greek deity of wisdom, who *shakes* the *spear* of knowledge in the face of ignorance.

There is no space here to go into all the complex arguments and explanations involving secret ciphers and encoded messages believed to have been incorporated into the writings of Shakespeare and other works to indicate that Bacon and his fellow collaborators were the true authors. But such evidence is quite extensive and would seem much more than circumstantial. A fairly elaborate summary of these considerations may be found in *The Secret Teachings of All Ages,* by Manly P. Hall, who believes that Bacon was a high initiate of the mystic fraternity known as the Rosicrucians, or Brothers of the Rosy Cross. The entire story of the royal intrigues which enveloped Francis Bacon as a result of his true parents' clandestine marriage, is contained in Comyns Beaumont's book, *The Private Life of the Virgin Queen,* published in 1947.

Perhaps over the next century or so the truth behind this mystery will come to light, for I do not believe that the generation now being born will be pressured into suppressing information, simply to support the financially-motivated preservation of Stratford-on-Avon as a commercial attraction. In any case, the Shakespearean cycle of plays and sonnets will always stand on their own upon the strength of their content and beauty – regardless of their true authorship.

*   *   *

Another, more contemporary mystery which has intrigued me for some time surrounds the publication* of a book called *Witch-Doctor's Apprentice,* written by a naturalised American woman of French/Canadian origins named Nicole Maxwell. She

*Victor Gollancz Ltd. 1962

was a botanist, explorer, ex-journalist and a Fellow of the Royal Geographical Society, and was commissioned by an American pharmaceutical company to journey up the Amazon, to try to discover rare, little-known herbal remedies and medicines. Among these was an alleged contraceptive plant believed to be used by some of the more remote Indian tribes of South America.

Her book told of the many herbs and roots she found on her adventures and described her difficulties in tracking down the contraceptive until, almost about to return in despair, she decided to visit one last tribe, the Maina Indians, who live off an Amazon tributary in Peru.

En route, she stopped off to visit another family and, while there, heard of a neighbouring Jivaro Indian woman whom she thought might be able to help her in her search. While her hosts were enjoying a fiesta of heavy drinking, Miss Maxwell went off to meet the Jivaro woman and established a rapport with her, the woman speaking broken Spanish and using sign-language. The woman asked why Miss Maxwell, who was very attractive, had no husband. The author could not put across the 'civilised' concept of divorce, so simply said that her husband had another woman. This aroused great sympathy in the Jivaro woman and gave her confidence in the white *gringa* visitor. She too had had 'bad man' as a husband, she confided. And her uncle, who was the local witch doctor had said that because she was married to a 'bad man' she should have no children – and gave her a 'no baby' plant. And although she lived for a further two years with her 'bad man', before he eventually deserted her, she did not conceive.

Miss Maxwell also, she said, should take the 'no baby' herb – until she found herself another, decent man. For, said Tesa, the Jivaro, when she herself had found a second suitable husband, her uncle had then given her another 'baby herb' which once more permitted her to have children. In the next room of her jungle, riverside shack, her baby son lay sleeping – as living proof of the effectiveness of this native medicine.

Without being asked, Tesa offered to get some of the plants for Miss Maxwell and waved her hand, indicating that they grew 'out there.' She would give her the 'no baby' plant and if, after she found herself a good man, she returned in three years, she would then also give her the 'baby herb.'

After a long and trying search, Miss Maxwell had at last found what she wanted. Along with the other remedies she had collected in her herb press, she returned to New York. As she said, these plants had completed the full circle, from the witch doctors with painted faces and feathered crowns to the witch doctors with scrubbed hands and white coats, who attempted to assess their value in large, shiny laboratories.

But what eventually became of the contraceptive plant remains a mystery. It is now some eighteen years since Miss Maxwell's book was published – and nowhere has there been any forthcoming information about the tests on the plants. The book seems quickly to have vanished from the market and from neither the publishers nor Nicole Maxwell's agent is one able to get any satisfactory information.

Were the white-coated 'witch-doctors' of the laboratories unable to find out the effective ingredient of these supposed natural, organic contraceptives? Or were they tested and found to be ineffective? (Certainly, Miss Maxwell gathered evidence that they worked for the native tribes she encountered.)

One is tempted to wonder, on the other hand, whether it was feared that such simple methods – with no apparent side-effects – might interfere with the marketing of the Pill. For it was about the time of Miss Maxwell's book that chemically-produced contraceptives began to be widely distributed ...

Perhaps, in an age when more and more people – especially the young – are turning back towards herbal and naturally-obtained remedies and medicines, we might yet see the re-discovery of Tesa's intriguing no-baby plant.

*   *   *

Since the Treasures of Tutankhamun exhibition toured the world seven years ago, including its period in London when more than half-a-million visitors thronged to see its wonders at the British Museum, practically everyone knows of how the Egyptologist Howard Carter and his patron, Lord Carnarvon, together opened the boy-king's tomb in 1922.

In 1971 I was invited to go to Vancouver, British Columbia, to speak to the Vancouver Psychic Society. Since we also had a branch of Beauty Without Cruelty in the west coast Canadian city, I accepted. (The Psychic Society had already invited me the previous year, but because I did not want to leave Hugh, I had politely declined.)

While there I received a message from a Mr Charles Carter, asking if I could go to visit him at his home. Mr Carter was elderly and suffering from cancer and could not leave his house to come and see me, so I accepted his invitation.

As we talked in his pleasant living room, it became quickly obvious that Mr Carter, like myself, had spent much time studying Theosophy, the occult and spiritual matters in general.

While I am aware that controversy still continues about the details surrounding the actual discovery of the tomb, the protocal followed (or ignored) and the stories of a curse upon anyone who disturbed the funerary relics and mummy of King Tutankhamun,* I found Mr Carter's remarks on the subject very intriguing. In fact, it was I who raised the subject of Tutankhamun, for, noticing that Mr Carter had a television set in his home, I remarked that I had recently seen an interesting documentary on Tutankhamun in Britain and wondered if the programme had appeared on Canadian television.

It was then that Mr Carter revealed that he was a cousin of Howard Carter. He also gave me a written account of what, he said, his cousin had told him about the discovery of the tomb – one of the greatest and most sensational archaeological finds in all history.

Here is what he had written:

Howard Carter viewed the desolate rubble heap that was the Valley of the Kings, now marked with excavations and debris, where the last resting places of the pharaohs who had hoped to rest in peace had taken every care to place their remains.

Carter was in a deep depression, for this was to be the last

---

* See Philipp Vandenberg: *The Curse of the Pharaohs,* (Hodder & Stoughton Ltd., 1975), for an account sympathetic to the curse-theory; Thomas Hoving, in *Tutankhamun: The Untold Story* (Hamish Hamilton Ltd., 1978), and others, remain sceptical.

season of research wherein he hoped to find a famous tomb. Six years had been spent in searching. He knew the Valley of the Kings perhaps better than any other Egyptologist who had laboured there and had been successful in many valuable discoveries, including that of Queen Hatshepsut's tomb. Lord Carnarvon, his patron, had been most generous in terms of both time and money ... but there was a limit to everything.

On the morning in question, Carter stood by the Tomb of Rameses VI and gazed upon four stone huts which ancient Egyptian masons had built to shield themselves from the pitiless midday sun.

'I had a most unusual urge to get my men to clear away these four huts,' Howard later told me. 'It was really a superstitious urge that seized me ... it carried the message that down under those huts would be a fabulous tomb ... perhaps that of the famous Tutankhamun. So I gave my men orders to pull down the huts and clear away the rubbish so as to make a good start the following morning.

'When I arrived the next morning I was surprised to find my workmen standing in a silent group awaiting my arrival. "What has happened?" I asked the head man. "We carried out your orders regarding the huts," he said, "and found a step cut into the rock in the centre of where the huts stood."

'In five hours we did more excavating than we had done in five years. And at the end of the sixteenth step we came to the first chamber of what proved to be a most famous tomb – the greatest tomb in all that desolate valley – the Tomb of Tutankhamun.'

What is most astonishing is the way Howard Carter totally ignored both warnings over the entrance arches of two chambers which, in ancient Egyptian hieroglyphics, plainly stated: 'Death will come on swift wings to those entering this chamber.'

If he made any comment upon the death of Lord Carnarvon – less than two months after the opening of the tomb – there is no record of it. If there were any proof that the genii sealed in the tomb of Tutankhamun by the High Priests of his time, who knew more of black than white magic, it was only revealed in Lord Carnarvon's hotel in Cairo, when the entire electric lighting system suddenly failed. For if there is anything that lends itself to an easy psychic build-up it is electricity, which can be increased terrifically in voltage that races down from globes to dynamos with loud explosions.

When Lord Carnarvon's nurse went to his bedside – he had been confined for some fifteen days with a fever and high temperature – after the electric current had been restored, he was quite dead. And upon his left cheek was the imprint of a Swastika in exactly the same place as a similar mark upon Tutankhamun's cheek when his mummy was examined months later.

During his six years' search Howard Carter (who made no secret of his dislike for tourists) seldom crossed the Nile to Luxor or Karnak, but spent most of his time with Sheikh Abu Shrump, who was noted for his power over the dreaded genii which sent the Bedouins hurrying from the Sphinx, Pyramids and the Valley of the Kings before twilight. They had a wholesome fear of the genii and could never be induced to go anywhere near these places after dark. Perhaps their knowledge of the lingering powers of the ancient priests was first-hand, for they had indulged in tomb-robbing for centuries.

Sheikh Abu Shrump of Kurna, a small village six miles from the Valley, had made Howard Carter welcome in his white villa. Indeed, as the list of victims who passed into the tomb of Tutankhamun grew larger, the Sheikh made it known that he had protected his friend Carter from the wrath of the genii during their years of friendship.

Whether Howard Carter placed any faith in the Sheikh's avowal will never be known. But it is very significant that Lord Herbert, son-in-law of Lord Carnarvon, before leaping from his hotel window left a note upon his dressing table that stated: 'The damned thing has followed me even here, and I can stand no more of it!'*

* *Publisher's note:* No reference can be found to the death alluded to here by Mr Carter, although he may be confusing the death of 'Lord Herbert' (which was Carnarvon's family name) with that of Lord Westbury. According to Vandenberg, op cit., Lord Westbury aged eighty-seven, plunged to his death from the seventh storey of his London house after learning that his son, Richard Bethell, Carter's

*   *   *

On one of the occasions when I had to travel abroad – this time to Rhodesia and Africa – on animal welfare work, I did not want to leave my sister Totty alone at Calverley Park. There were also my animals to be cared for, so a good friend, James, agreed to stay during my absence.

When I returned James told me that he thought the room in which he had been sleeping – the guest room – was haunted. I knew that he was rather psychic and that this gift had apparently been intensified by severe head injuries during the Second World War. (James had come over to England with the American forces in 1944.)

I did not take too much notice of his remarks that there was a presence of a young man in the guest room, although I did recall that another psychically sensitive friend of mine who had used the room for some weeks had told me there was a 'young man' in the room. When one has psychic faculties, one is inclined to be rather blasé about such things, yet it did remain in the back of my mind that the room *could* be haunted, since the house was of the Regency period.

One day when a friend, Gerald Gough, came to lunch I happened to mention my previous guest's remarks about the guest room. He asked to see it. Here are the impressions he felt at the time:

'As I entered the room, I knew at once what the trouble was. It could not have been picked up telepathically from Lady Dowding, as she did not know anything of the background, beyond being told that the room was haunted.

'I knew at once that it was a young British officer, who had been killed on the Indian frontier. One might say that he died a long while ago, but who is to measure the nature of "time" on the inner planes?

'This young man seemed rather a loner, without strong

secretary, had died in 1929, of a circulatory collapse. According to Vandenberg's thesis, by 1929 twenty-two people who had been directly or indirectly involved with the Tutankhamun tomb had died prematurely, thirteen of whom had participated in the opening of the chambers.

emotional attachments to other persons. Perhaps that is why others in his present whereabouts have failed to get him to start a new life.

'His only strong emotional attachment seems to have been to the place where he was born and which he so loved. It is remarkable that this was strong enough to hold him back and to cause slight manifestations.

'The freeing of him from past attachments was not difficult when one felt great sympathy for him and was able to arouse trust on his side, so that one seemed able to get it across to him that this world no longer concerned him acutely, but that if he looked around, he would find those who would help him in adjusting to his new conditions.'

Some months later, along with another friend, James Durran, I took my dog Trudy for a walk in Calverley Park and met one of the Trustees of the Park. At the time there had been arguments as to whether the church built along with the twenty-four houses in the Park, by the famous 19th-century architect Decimus Burton, should be pulled down or restored. The church was considered unsafe in its present state and had been closed for twenty years.

The Trustee we encountered on our stroll said: 'If the decision is to pull down the Decimus Burton church, there is something you should have from it. It is in a very dark corner and is a plaque to a young man killed in the Indian wars, who lived at No. 1, Calverley Park.'

This completely confirmed what Gerald Gough had told me some months previously. As he himself points out: 'Naturally, as Lady Dowding says, I could not have known anything of him. Nor could I have known that there was a long-closed church in which there was a plaque to his memory.'

*   *   *

There is often much debate in esoteric circles as to whether animals, as well as man, possess a soul or some spiritual form in which they survive in an after-life. Although it is difficult, if not inadvisable, to be dogmatic about such matters, I believe that the next little vignette may speak for itself. It was passed on to me by Mrs Feo Montgomery who, as Jane Baxter, was a well-known actress in the Thirties. Her husband, Clive Dunfee, a racing-driver, was the 'James Hunt' of his day. My first husband, Max, was at school with Clive's brother and although I did not know Mrs Montgomery personally, we have a mutual friend in James Durran, of whom I have written in the previous anecdote. Here is Mrs Montgomery's account:

My husband, Clive Dunfee, was killed at Brooklands in September, 1932. In November of that year, when I was driving my mother back to Wimbledon from Leatherhead the car hit a sparrow. We stopped and I walked back to pick it up and see if it was dead. I found it alive but seemingly hurt and unable to fly. My mother and I were both very fond of birds and animals and were deeply concerned for it. First, we put it on a little bush in the sun and then, thinking it might fall down we put it on the ground under the bush. Then we thought a cat might catch it, so I picked it up again and we decided that it would be better if it were killed rather than left to some horrible fate.

'We had pulled up at a place where country bus drivers changed over and there were a couple of drivers there. I kissed the little bird and told it to go straight to Clive and give him my love. I then approached one of the men who looked a kindly soul, and asked him if he would finish the poor little thing off for me.

'We drove home and never mentioned this event to anyone, and had quite forgotten about it when, in January, I had a letter from Lady Conan Doyle, whom I did not know, asking me if I would come for tea with her one day as a friend of hers had a message for me.

'I went to tea with her and she told me that a clairvoyant friend of hers had a message for me from my husband. We were both very well known at the time and often had our photographs in the papers.

'This lady lived in Maida Vale and did not practise her clairvoyance for money. She suddenly received messages and felt she had to pass them on. In fact, this gift was a positive nuisance to her. I went to see her.

'She first told me that she had seen Clive dressed in his

racing overalls and he had what appeared to be a lease or a contract in his hand and he told her that I should sign it. At that time my mother and my brother were trying to decide whether to sign a seven-year lease on a house in Kensington, which we subsequently took with happy success.

'Then she asked me: "Did you have a little pet bird? He had a little bird on his hand and it kept fluttering round him and alighting on his hand again."

'I asked what the bird was like and she said, "Oh, a little greyish-brown bird." '

*　　*　　*

As well as solving mysteries, I believe the Aquarian Age will usher in greater knowledge and wisdom and a true benefit from the hidden sides of nature. In a sense, this is now being demonstrated in the way that more and more people are turning to alternative, natural remedies from old and half-forgotten systems and through intelligent investigation and experiment are finding them to be beneficial. Meanwhile, orthodox scientists and members of the medical profession are beginning to re-examine their own rigid standards and values and, at the same time, they too are occasionally seeking the reaons why systems of ancient knowledge are so attractive and, in many cases, why they work.

While I fully realise that there are many areas of controversy as the unorthodox and the orthodox follow their still irreconcilable paths, I feel that ultimately only good can come of this intelligent seeking. The naturopath, the healer, the homeopath each asserts that his system works and brings health and well-being. The scientist looks on with curiosity – then begins to investigate to try to discover *why* such alternative methods appear to work.

In the face of much controversy, especially in the United States, I know personally of one friend who put her faith in an alternative form of medicine and, so far as she is concerned, that faith was justified. Although this particular method may not be suited to everyone, I am giving her own account, in the hope that it may give heart to other sufferers. Here then is her own story by my friend, Marjorie Osborn:

'Cancer is the disease that someone else gets. In your case, I am that someone else. In 1976, I became a statistic, one of the numbered women in the UK who contract cancer of the breast between the ages of forty and fifty.

'The previous year I had entered the hospital for the removal of a harmless lump from my left breast and in 1976 I was back again with another lump on the same site. Instinctively, I knew it was cancer, although none of the doctors who examined me had indicated in any way that it was anything but another harmless lump. After removal, the tissue was analysed and it fell to a very young doctor to tell me that traces of carcinoma had been found and a mastectomy was recommended. I refused the operation and there followed days of countless interviews with doctors and consultants, but the advice was always the same: mastectomy was the best and surest way of treating the disease.

'Although the news had shocked me and despite the fact that my self-control was stretched to its full limit in the dreadful weeks that followed, there fortunately remained my belief that a mutilating operation was not the answer.

'Very slowly my physical condition was deteriorating and when I found a hospital that suggested radiotherapy instead of an operation, I accepted that treatment. It was not the ideal course to take but quick action was needed to try to arrest the disease.

'Summer 1977 I was in hospital again. A third operation was made on my left breast and a lump was removed from the right breast. Mentally, I was as low as I could be when my loved friend, Muriel, told me she had heard of a new treatment for cancer. The treatment consisted of an easy-fo-follow diet supplemented by B17, a substance taken from apricot kernels. I have followed the regime since then for two years and today I feel better in health than at any time prior to my illness! Looking back, I realise my progress has been a steady, daily matter; the effect of the treatment would appear to be cumulative.

'Now, I attend the hospital every four months for a check-up. Everyone says I look wonderfully well. And last week (early

September, 1979) I received the finest compliment of all. I visited a small hall where I was to give a talk on Beauty Without Cruelty. No one there knew me or my history. When the evening ended, the leader of the group shook my hand, thanked me for an interesting evening, and concluded with the comment, "Your appearance has fascinated us. You positively glow with health. Do come back another time and tell us the secret."

'The secret is LAETRILE – that is the name of the treatment that has brought me back to joyous living.'

22

Astrology – the Light on the Person and the Path

by

Betty Midderigh

ABOUT TWO YEARS after the launching of the Beauty Without Cruelty Movement a friend, knowing my interest in animal welfare, said: 'You should write to Lady Dowding. The Beauty Without Cruelty Movement sounds just right for you.' I did – and it was!

As it was anathema for me to offer myself to any movement just as a part of the scenery, I tentatively suggested to her ladyship that I was an earnest student of astrology and that I also lectured on the subject. Could I perhaps lecture for Beauty Without Cruelty and could I advise her astrologically, both in regard to her personal horoscope and the horoscope of the Beauty Without Cruelty Movement? Understandably cautious – for all humanitarian movements tend to attract a lunatic fringe – Lady Dowding, although gracious and polite, said that due to her mother's interest in the subject, all the family had been very adequately 'horoscoped', but would I care to attend a Council Meeting and make myself known personally to her? That was the beginning. I shall never forget that first meeting and the wonderful atmosphere that prevailed; also the strong impression, which remained with me, that somewhere in the dim and distant past this same band of gracious, dedicated women had met before.

In time I was asked to join the Council and eventually to become a Trustee, and I did have the privilege of casting the horoscopes of Lord and Lady Dowding and that of the Movement itself; also to advise on the best days for Beauty Without Cruelty events. With regard to the latter, however, it is seldom my policy to say: 'Don't on any account choose

such-and-such a day for the fashion show, etc.' On the contrary,
I prefer to say of an unfavourable day: 'Choose another if you
can, but if it must be that day, be prepared to work harder and
try to remain calm in the face of irritations and setbacks.' In
other words, eventually we have to learn to rule our stars and
cease from allowing them to rule us!

Astrology is as old as the dawn of wisdom. It springs from the
same roots as the great myths, legends and religions of the
world and, in common with them, has become debased and
materialised over the centuries.

The Twelve Gates of the Nile (Egyptian); the Twelve
Labours of Hercules (Greek); the Twelve Nidanas (precepts) of
the Buddha; the Twelve Signs of the Zodiac – all represent the
twelve labours of the Soul until, like the Prodigal Son, it is
satiated with experience and ready to return to 'the Father' (its
Divine Source), after which the 'fatted calf' (Taurus, represent-
ing the body) is 'slain', since there is no need thereafter for
further incarnation.

The doctrine of reincarnation is implicit in esoteric astrology,
just as it was a tenet (many will be surprised to learn) of the
Christian Faith, until the sixth century. Thus, when we have a
natal horoscope in front of us, based not only on the day but the
precise hour of birth, we are studying the balance sheet of a
soul – a very sacred document indeed. Lady Dowding has given
permission for her own map to be included in this chapter.

From this chart one observes that the Sun is in Aries, 1' 3".
This means not only that the native is endowed with fire,
energy and initiative of Aries, she is close enough to Pisces to be
imbued with the compassion for animals so much associated
with this latter sign. The Sun is in conjunction with the planet
Saturn, denoting power and responsibility; also the probability
of an older husband. The Sun is also in conjunction with the
Part of Fortune which the ancients believed represented the
stored knowledge of the soul from its past incarnations. Sun,
Saturn and Part of Fortune are placed in the ninth division or
House of the higher mind, just out of the transmuting and
refining influence of the eighth House, but still influenced by it
to some extent. All are in Trine (beneficial) aspect to the planet
Jupiter, indicating Lady Dowding's rise to fame and the success
of the movements to which she has chosen to dedicate herself.

The Sun is in wide Square or stressful aspect both to Neptune and Pluto in the eleventh House of friends. Taking the Neptune Square first, this inclines to bring some deception from those in whom she may have placed a too-implicit trust. The Pluto Square inclines to bring an abrupt end to friendships which are not based on a solid-rock foundation of proven trust and affection. She certainly numbers the wealthy and powerful (signified by Pluto) in this House and a Sextile, or benefic aspect between Pluto and her Leo Ascendant shows that much benefit will be obtained from people in high places.

The Ascendant (the sign which appears over the Eastern horizon at the very moment of birth) is our special unique point in this incarnation. Lady Dowding has 17′ 45″ Leo rising. Leo is the sign of the leader and administrator. Born in the middle ten degrees or Sagittarius decanate of the sign, she is so resilient that she can be literally at death's door, yet live on to confound doctors and prophets alike. This decanate of the sign expands the Leo nature and emphasises the humanitarian and 'caring' aspects of the sign.

The Moon is in Scorpio in the fourth House. Thus, both by sign and House the personality is shown as having considerable interest in psychic matters. Moon in opposition to Mars, with the latter planet in good aspect to Uranus, makes the native both a fighter and a formidable opponent. It is unlikely in this incarnation that she will extend the loving Leo nature to include the trapper, the vivisector or the clubber of seals.

Uranus occupying the fifth section of the horoscope in good aspect both to Venus and Mars confers unusual children, talents and close friends. During the whole of her life, Lady Dowding is never likely to lack the male admirer!

Mercury, denoting the mind, is 4′ Pisces and in seventh House of personal relationships including marriage. The 4′ Virgo to 4′ Pisces line is noted for the gifts of compassion and healing, and she is destined to have relationships with people of this type. The mind is shown as humane and very psychic, both of these facets being supported by a beneficial aspect between Mercury and Neptune.

It is noteworthy that in the tenth House of profession and vocation Lady Dowding places her Venus. There could hardly be a more 'Venus' profession than the Beauty Without Cruelty

Movement, and the success this has attained is due partly to her own effort of will, and partly because of the highly beneficial aspect between her Venus and the planet Uranus in the fifth House of creativity.

Finally, eight out of the ten planetary bodies are above the horizon, denoting one who has the power to rise above circumstances. Secondly, the two Lights – Sun and Moon – plus Mercury, Saturn and the Part of Fortune are in the 'western' half of the map, denoting that the native is 'paying back' to life in this incarnation in the form of some kind of dedicated service.

In the *Book of Revelation,* Chapter 12, verse 1, there is written what I regard as the astrologer's 'Lord's Prayer.' It reads: 'And there appeared a great wonder in Heaven, a Woman clothed with the Sun, and the Moon under her feet, and on her head a crown of twelve stars.' The Woman is the Soul: the Moon (personality) is under her feet, i.e., no longer required, and she wears the crown of twelve stars because she has triumphed over all the signs of the Zodiac and they no longer have the power to bind her.

When it comes to Muriel Dowding's turn finally to 'wear the crown' I feel two of the stars will shine with especial brilliance: Aries for courage and initiative, Leo the lion-hearted for the loving strength to succour that part of creation now abandoned and tortured almost to extinction which the Divine Being originally placed under Man's sovereignty.

ASTROLOGICAL LINKS – MURIEL AND HUGH

Magnetic and Emotional

Mars in the one chart EXACT conjunction Venus in the other. This is a very powerful stimulus; indeed, it is the most powerful which can occur and shows the greatest possible physical, harmonious link. The resulting interchange of magnetic energy each to the other is mutually beneficial and revitalising

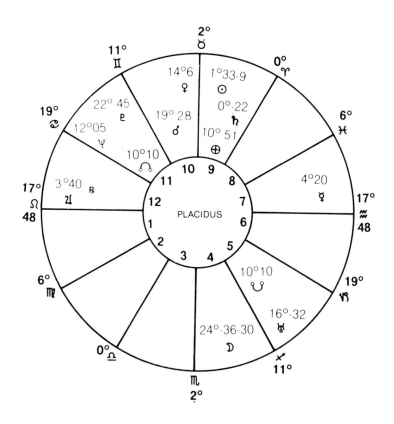

Sun in Aries
Moon in Scorpio
Leo Rising

19 Horoscope of Muriel the Lady Dowding.

to the magnetic centres. It is noticeable that the interchange is exactly the same degrees of the sign Taurus in both cases, which is the sign of true lovers.

Intellectual

Mercury in the one chart in EXACT sextile harmonious aspect to the Sun in the other, showing that the strong psychic intuition of the one (Mercury in Pisces) will blend in great harmony with the powerful intellect of the other. (Mercury in the other chart is also within a few degrees of the first-named's Midheaven, another indication of harmony on the intellectual plane – similarity of views and intellectual aims and aspirations, etc.)

Business, Financial and Social

The rising Jupiter and ascendent of the one chart is the sign on the second House (Leo) of the other, so association of these two very powerful focii would *attract* material concord. Any sort of partnership or amalgamation of interests would therefore stimulate astrological centres previously dormant which would attract what on this plane we call material good fortune.

Past Links

These links between the Higher Octave planets and the Moon interchanges make it evident that neither is a stranger to the other. There must have been very close association in the past to have formed such strong links. In fact, work has evidently been started of which the meeting this time is just a logical and necessary continuation, and with such strong associations these links are not in the least temporary, but will surely continue for many lives to come.

23

What I Believe and Why

PROBABLY AS A result of many previous lives, I firmly believe that everything has something of God in it – every blade of grass, flower, plant, animal and human being. That over the centuries, or even millennia, we evolve through these different kingdoms in succession and, as my mother often said, life on earth is but a term at school; when we die, we go home for the holidays.

Because this 'school' is not always pleasant, many people reject the idea of reincarnation, because they do not want to return. But I believe that, in the early stages of evolutionary incarnation, they have no choice; their natural instincts and bonds are all of the earth and, deep down, they automatically have an affinity for it and wish to return. When, occcasionally, glimpses are caught of the great, god-like creature that a person will ultimately become – in flashes of inspiration, intuition, illumination or in the mystical experience – they will willingly return to the 'school' of earth to learn the lessons that will allow them to overcome their faults. Then they can progress and eventually achieve this wonderful, ineffable state of the perfected being, which is only vaguely hinted at by the greatest of the mystics and occult teachers.

I believe that Jesus and many other great teachers are examples of this attainment and that they returned to help the rest of mankind. But, ultimately, each must alone evolve to a similar state of spiritual elevation which in turn leads to sublime perfection and oneness with the godhead. I certainly do not believe that Jesus was the only Son of God. Humanity and all creation are the sons and daughters of God in the most profound sense.

I think that the story of the Prodigal Son in *The Bible* expresses this concept perfectly. Humanity itself is the Prodigal

Son, who goes forth and sinks to the lowest depths. The most angelic – or highly developed – of beings remain ever close to the Father; they do not descend to the levels of physical incarnation.

As a child, I always thought it was so unfair that the 'naughty' son returned home to all the rejoicing in his honour and nothing was ever said about the 'good' sons who had remained at home with the father. But this, I now believe, is simply to illustrate that when the Prodigal Son, which is man, has sunk to densest matter and has probably committed many crimes and transgressions, he eventually turns and goes back to the Father. Upon his return he has learned wisdom, love and compassion and is thus a god himself, ready to carry out the work of the Father. Because he has taken the most difficult path, his brothers who remained behind – the 'angelic' beings – must always respond to any appeal from man to the angelic, or fairy kingdom – call it what you will.

For this reason – and it may seem silly on the face of it, until proper meditation on the subject brings about realisation – whenever I lose anything, I call upon the fairies (angels) or upon St Anthony, the saint of lost articles. I cannot tell you how often I have found that this has worked. In fact, it has never failed.

*   *   *

What first attracted me to the Theosophical Society was a book by the clairvoyant Geoffrey Hodson, called *Fairies At Work And Play.* Having seen fairies myself as a child, it was the first independent confirmation I had of their existence.

Theosophy is derived from *theosophia,* a Greek composite word meaning 'divine wisdom' or 'wisdom of the gods.' In the Society's literature I also encountered the concept of reincarnation and I quickly realised that many of the seeming half-memories which I have had since I was a child were probably of past incarnations.

Now, although the soul may be fundamentally male or female, it cannot possibly gain all its necessary experience for total fulfilment by incarnating as one sex all the time. I therefore believe that the soul – the immortal essence which manifests in many physical incarnations – returns to experience both male and female roles.

This, of course, poses some problems. Having perhaps been a woman for many incarnations, the idea of suddenly finding oneself in a male body would seem to be a very difficult and daunting prospect, especially for the first, second and maybe even the third incarnations in a different sex. I believe that many of the fears, phobias and difficulties about which people consult psychiatrists and theologians may originate in some experience of a past life in a different sex-role which has made a deep and lasting impression.

Hugh appeared to have a deep awareness and sensitivity towards previous incarnations. It will be recalled that when I told him of the recurrent dream in which I believed I was being executed for breaking the vows of an Egyptian temple maiden, he remarked upon the fact that the experience hinted of memories of a violent death while still young. Hugh himself would seem to have undergone some similar form of unpleasant experience in a past life, as the following will demonstrate.

Whenever I went into his study when he was writing and put my hand on his shoulder or on his head, he would always respond lovingly and kiss my hand. But if I placed my hand on the back of his neck, he would say quite suddenly: 'Oh, don't do that!' And although we never discussed the matter, I felt that he might have been beheaded in a past life.

I know of a man whose wife had to accompany him to have his hair cut, because he was so terrified of the feeling of scissors on the back of his neck. Perhaps he, too, had undergone execution of some form of violent death involving cold steel, in a previous incarnation. The guillotine?

On the question of who one might have been in previous lives, I do not feel that I have been anyone important. There was a common joke among our circle of believers in reincarnation that, perhaps one day, six former 'Cleopatras' might turn up at one meeting! But from a serious point of view I think that perhaps one person might have one vividly-recalled and important incarnation, followed by a dull or rather less exciting existence, in order that they might readjust or recover.

I think I have been a Hetari – the women of noble birth in Greece who were married to men for political reasons and who sought concubines to relieve them of the attentions of their husbands; they often took lovers. This may explain the many men who have been attracted to me in this life. I feel certain that Hugh and I met in such a previous relationship and, possibly, another man with whom, I am amazed to find, I have developed a love relationship in this life.

My interest in the occult and in spiritual matters is probably because I have incarnated in ancient mystery temples and in early convents. This might explain why I felt so much at home during my schooldays in a convent. It might also account for the fact that I am still somewhat psychic – a legacy from my temple and religious training. My ability to dance, also, I strongly feel is a faculty which has remained from past lives in a temple environment. As I explained in an earlier chapter, my instinctive feeling for dancing seems to hark back to a time when dancing was sacred, a form of worship in which the soul expresses itself through the movements of the body. My fondness for dancing certainly did not stem from a desire to take up a career on the stage – such a life simply was not commensurate with the ecstasy and worship which I instinctively connected with dancing.

I also have a fairly strong feeling that I was once Hugh's page – my only recollection of a male incarnation – and died at the age of twelve. I cannot be sure of the period, but it was certainly in a time when spears were used and firearms had not been invented.

Nowadays, I feel much as Betty Midderigh has already indicated – that many of those with whom I work in animal welfare I knew in previous lives, possibly in temple incarnations. We probably wanted to do work of this kind even then, but the time was not ripe. Now that conditions are favourable, it is possible that we have been drawn together by some strange and wonderful evolutionary plan.

As far as the actual places in which one may have spent previous lives are concerned, I think it is often possible to gain an indication of this by a seemingly inbred interest of that country or time. I, for instance, have always been fascinated by the legends of Atlantis and Lemuria, by the Inca dynasties, the mysteries of Greece and, of course, Egypt, the Arthurian cycle and by the life and times of Henry VIII and the Tudor period.

There are other occasional and often seemingly superficial or even hidden indications of the reality of reincarnation. At one time, for example, I was always rather bewildered by the idea of a very ordinary man and a very plain woman claiming: 'It was love at first sight with us.' My attitude – unspoken, of course – would be: Well, I am sure you are both very nice people and, when you get to know each other will no doubt discover this, but what on earth could you see in each other at first sight? Now, I believe that love at first sight *is* possible and is a form of soul-recognition – the result of two people having known and loved each other in previous lives.

But of course one's succession of lives cannot always and invariably be a pleasant experience. Throughout our many lives we may have to learn numerous lessons, one of which might be reconciling oneself to accepting a former enemy as a friend. Because of this, it is not always possible to be born into a harmonious family environment or to have a harmonious and happy marriage. This may well form part of the training which the soul must undergo and which it cannot achieve in only one incarnation.

*   *   *

While I am not in any way in favour of Women's Lib *per se,* I think that one trend of the future is that woman, having been oppressed and subdued for so many centuries, may well become top-dog for a certain period. But eventually, I think the two sexes will equalise because they are naturally complementary and cannot exist or function ideally without each other. As I have already suggested, while each soul may be fundamentally male or female, they may have to incarnate in both sexes in order to obtain the necessary experience for this kind of eventual balance to be achieved.

*   *   *

I am convinced, as was my husband, that under certain circumstances communication between the so-called dead and the living is possible. But I also know through experience that it is nothing like as easy as many people may think.

During the Victorian era there were many great mediums, and I feel that this was an evolutionary stage in which the truth of survival and communication was being brought home to people in the West. Nowadays really great mediums are far fewer, but there are still some very genuine ones.

When Hugh died, his being a very famous man, I had the most utter rubbish sent to me by goodness knows how many so-called mediums, who thought he had come through to them. It might have been enough to put anyone off spiritualism for all time.

Why should this happen? I think that in the minds of these people – aside from the quite conscious charlatans – there was a subconscious desire to have some famous person use them as a channel. As the Theosophical Society – which knows far more about spiritualism than most spiritualists – has shown, a thought-form can build up in the psyche of such people because of their subconscious wish to be associated with someone famous. But what emerges as a result, is not of course a true communication.

On the other hand, Cynthia, Lady Sandys and Grace Cooke, neither of whom knew each other, sent me messages from Hugh which coincided quite remarkably and convincingly. And, just before beginning this autobiography, as I mentioned in my introduction, I had a most satisfactory sitting with the famous medium Ena Twigg.

I will deal with the communications of Cynthia, Lady Sandys, in due course. But first I will explain how Hugh and I came to meet Ena Twigg.

During the time that David was at co-educational school, under the care of John and Karis Guiness, they had been attempting to treat some of the children who were going through adolescent problems with the Dr. Bach remedies. On the whole, these proved very satisfactory, but there was one case of a girl who apparently burst into tears at the slightest thing – if her shoelace came undone, for example. Despairing, the Guinesses asked Hugh if he could help. We took the girl to Ena Twigg for healing – and she was much improved.

'Ena, what can we do for you?' Hugh and I asked, being so grateful. She asked to meet Dorothy Kerin and we invited both ladies to our home. But although Hugh and I never had sittings with Ena Twigg, we met her at various functions from time to time and always greatly admired the fact that, as probably the leading medium in this country, she gave up all her public demonstrations to retire and study how mediumship works.

Several months ago an overseas branch leader of Beauty Without Cruelty came to spend a few days with me and asked if I could get her a sitting with a medium. I eventually arranged for a meeting with Ena Twigg, after which she was positively radiant. We invited Ena to lunch a month or so later and she gave me a sitting.

The first person to come through was my sister, Totty, who had passed away in 1977. I knew it was her at once because Ena raised her arm in a way that was so characteristic of Totty when she greeted me as I would walk across the fields to my mother's home. 'Hello Poppet!' she said. She seemed very excited and told me that she had just met Ivor.

'You mean Ivan,' I said, thinking of Betty Midderigh's husband, who had recently died.

'No,' she said, 'Ivor of the beautiful music.'

I remembered only afterwards that my sister had been tremendously fond of the music of Ivor Novello and had, I believe, at one time sent him some of her writings to which he kindly replied. For many years Totty had kept a photograph of Ivor Novello in her bedroom. But Ena Twigg could have known nothing of this, since it had all happened years previously.

When it came to contacting Hugh, I had not the faintest doubt that it was he, talking to me through Ena, for no one else could have said the things he said; as I have already noted, he was very romantic and the perfect lover.

Although none of this was absolutely evidential, because the knowledge was already in my own mind and could have been discerned telepathically, it was nonetheless very convincing and typical. Hugh told me that he was engaged in his own work, but that whenever there was the slightest sign of distress in my life, he was immediately with me. 'I was with you when you packed up all my clothes,' he said, referring to the sad days following his death.

In fact, all Hugh's RAF uniforms and accessories had been immediately taken by museums, but his son, Derek, had disposed of his civilian clothes. I did keep one garment, however. It was rolled up in the bottom of my wardrobe and was a dressing gown. It had been a source of argument between us because it was the most terrible old grey affair and Hugh was loth to part with it. I once asked him how old it was and he replied: 'I don't know, I rather think I had it in my first term at Winchester.' During the nineteen years of our marriage I had given him something like ten other dressing gowns as presents, which he would dutifully wear. But if I happened on him unexpectedly, I would often find him in grey flannel trousers – with the awful old dressing gown on top.

Through Ena, Hugh told me he was very touched that I had kept the much-hated garment. Again, this is not what one would regard as cast-iron evidence, because I was already aware that I had kept the dressing gown.

What could be classed as irrefutable evidence of communication, however, was when my first husband Max told me that his aircraft had been flying towards Norway when it came down, while my own mind had been fixed upon Duisberg in Germany. This information was, as I have already explained, confirmed after my step-father met the Danish farmer on the train and learned of the memorial which had been set up.

I am, however, convinced to my own satisfaction that it was Hugh talking to me through Ena Twigg. It is difficult to convey such a feeling of certainty; all I can say is that it was so typically Hugh. One thing he did tell me was that immediately after his death, when he was out of his body, a young airman appeared and said: 'Happy landing, sir. I am Max.' Hugh's comment to me was: 'You never told me how good-looking your first husband was.'

* * *

At present there are so many self-styled gurus and self-appointed teachers, offering such systems as transcendental meditation, bio-feedback, astrology and various forms of yoga training. But it is my firm belief that there are no short cuts to enlightenment and I am always grateful for the teachings of the Theosophical Society, which has now been in existence for more than a century. Anyone who takes the trouble to look into the history of other systems, such as the Arcane School, the Anthroposophical Society of Rudolf Steiner and so many others, will find that they are more or less offshoots of Madame Blavatsky's Theosophical Society. In addition, of course, Madame Blavatsky frequently asserted in her writings that she was the custodian of initiated teachings dating back for centuries and passed from highly advanced master to chela (pupil) in an uninterrupted tradition. Aside from one or two rather shallow and not very well-founded attacks upon the character of H.P.B. in days when her opponents tended to demand rather trivial 'spirit-phenomena', this has never been convincingly disputed.

My main criticism of many of the Eastern religions and their Westernised developments is that they are so selfish; they are often only devoted to the improvement of oneself, of getting the aspirant off the hook, as it were, from the wheel of karma or reincarnation. Although the Christian churches have made such a complete and utter hash of the teachings of their founder, they could have done so much better, because this was, I think, the one religion which tried to teach not only self-improvement and spiritual progress, but a love and concern for others. Certainly, the Catholic countries are the most cruel to animals and many people refuse to go on holidays to these places for that very reason.

Indeed, as I write these final chapters, we have just once more passed through Christmas, the so-called Season of Goodwill, during which many Christians pay only lip-service to the principles and precepts of their founder. I have come to regard it as the Great Annual Slaughter, in which millions of animals are killed and butchered to assuage the vanity and greed of those who ought to know better. In any case, if one wished to be pedantic, it could be pointed out that there is absolutely no case for celebrating the birth of Christ at this particular time. Christmas as a festival was grafted by the early Church Fathers upon the ancient feast of Saturnalia, celebrated in honour of the god Saturn, bringer of old age and symbolic of the 'death' of the old year. It was the Winter Solstice – the time of the shortest hours of daylight – celebrated everywhere by early peoples who carefully watched and ritually observed the cycles of nature.

From it developed the curious custom – borrowed from the Romans – when masters and slaves or servants swapped roles and, in the Middle Ages, a servant was crowned the Lord of Misrule and held 'court' for the festivities. Similarly, the Mummers' Plays, still performed in rural districts, were a form of symbolic evocation to the Sun to return to the skies once more and bring forth the earth's fruits.

Since the actual birthdate of Christ is unknown, the celebration of Christmas – Christ-mass – was quite arbitrarily superimposed upon these age-old celebrations when Pope Julius I sanctioned the introduction of December 25 as the official date in the Roman calendar.

From a slightly more esoteric viewpoint, however, it seems to me more likely that the founder of Christianity, if one takes into account his association with the symbol of the fish, the early secret sign of recognition used by the Christians during their persecution, would have more likely been born in the Piscean period, corresponding approximately to February 20 to March 21.

It also seems obvious to me that a Christ-child who is depicted in the scriptures as being born in a stable, surrounded by animals, is not meant to be the figurehead of a Great Slaughter and a feast of gluttony and self-indulgence.

For some time I have nursed a growing conviction that Man is the greatest destroyer the earth has ever known and it may be that the earth will fight back and remove this parasitic menace which has infested it for so long, and with increased indifference. I certainly watch with mixed interest and alarm as more and more earthquakes, volcanic eruptions, floods and other disasters seem to increase in parts of the world which are not normally prone to them. It may be that – as so many prophets have forecast – only one relatively small release of nuclear energy will act as a trigger to a chain reaction which will devastate the entire planet, freeing it from the abuse of man in polluted earth, air and waters and the mass slaughter of animal life.

It would then, no doubt, take centuries before the earth could readjust back to its true purity and beauty. Perhaps then, in something between 1,000 and 2,000 years from now, the first representatives of the true Aquarian race will begin to be born. They will be naturally peaceloving – what, through my studies I have come to call for convenience, under the influence of a 'love ray' – and their parents will teach them a deep reverence and love for all forms of life. From their male parent, they will probably re-learn what today's esoteric schools call 'ancient wisdom', gaining a knowledge of healing, herbs and other beneficial latent powers. Hopefully then, a wonderful race will finally emerge which will no longer be destroyers of the earth, but instead its guardians and cruelty and war will cease to be known.

Whether or not this is a form of wishful thinking, I do not know, but it seems to be a natural development stemming from the various esoteric teachings of occult initiates.

*   *   *

To return, however, to the various spiritually-based organisations with whom I have come into contact, I found the White Eagle Lodge, of which mention has been made earlier, particularly attractive. For although its teachings are by no means as comprehensive as those of Theosophy, they are very much along the same lines and I feel that no one could gain anything but good by being a member of either of these organisations. For spiritualism of the superior type, I can do no better than recommend the College of Psychic Studies, 16 Queensberry Place, London SW7. The addresses of the other organisations which I have mentioned throughout this book are:

The Theosophical Society, 50 Gloucester Place, London W1.
The White Eagle Lodge, Newlands Rake, Liss, Hampshire;
or 9 St Mary Abbots Place, Kensington, W8.

There is an arcane saying that God sleeps in the mineral kingdom, dreams in the vegetable or flower kingdom, becomes conscious in the animal kingdom and self-conscious in the human kingdom. So that, as I said at the beginning of this chapter, every created thing has a little spark of God in it.

Thus we return in another body in another age to overcome the difficult school of earth and so that defects and weaknesses which prevent us from becoming the Beings of Light which can be used in God's many works.

24

On the Death of Trudy,
My Little Dog and Companion

TRUDY WAS A little dachshund pedigree. When her human family emigrated, she was left heartbroken, with neighbours who did not want her. Eventually, before the local RSPCA were about to put her down as too unhappy for anyone ever to take her, she was brought to me. I said: 'If my dog Timmy will accept her, I will take her.'

After three days, Timmy and I made Trudy feel part of a family again. And within only three weeks, we made her realise we loved and wanted her and she stopped crying for her original owners. I think she must have belonged to a young family, for bliss to Trudy was to sit beside a young man in a car, and when she heard children's voices she ran to them.

To all those who may be contemplating deserting an animal, I say this: Please, try to realise first how much they love and want you.

After many years, Trudy's kidneys failed and I had to make the decision whether to let her die in discomfort within two weeks, or try to help her to pass over. She was pretty ill and on her last day she was taken up to the top end of Calverley Park by car and then walked back with me. She had a lovely lunch of cats' fish, which she enjoyed, and everything else she wanted. Then she went to sleep in my bedroom and I got into bed.

The vet, whom she regarded as a dear friend, and his assistant arrived. Together, we gave Trudy lots of love and chocolates and, within only seconds of the injection, she was gone. I sat with her little body until the evening and she was so peaceful I felt sure she was happy and free from discomfort and that my late friend Princess Anne Galitzine, who loved dogs, was there, standing by to take her little soul.

Trudy was left in her box with her blanket for at least

forty-eight hours, so that her various subtle bodies could leave the physical – in the same way that we leave a human being to lie in peace while the subtle bodies free themselves.

To anyone facing the prospect of having to get rid of a much-loved pet, I would advise them to get a vet to visit their home; to be with the pet with words of love and comfort so that there is no fear or distress at the moment of passing.

I am a coward and, since I take in old animals, I have to face this experience often and I have loved and suffered for them all. If you cannot afford to have the vet to your home, do insist on staying with your pet to see that it is injected and suffers no anguish that you have deserted it, but are there to the last.

Stand up for your rights and be loyal, as your own pet would be loyal to you, and on no account allow the decompression chamber to be used. This is a particularly unpleasant way to dispose of an animal and in Australia attempts are being made to ban its use on the grounds of cruelty.

Although it is no longer in use in the state of Victoria, according to my informants, officials in Queensland and elsewhere seem to be indifferent to this horrendous method of animal execution. Unwanted pets are herded, often in their hundreds, into the large metal chamber and a vacuum pump sucks out the air. The animals scream and thrash about in agony, often taking up to ten minutes and more to die.

One veterinary surgeon, Dr. Edward Mintz, told an Australian newspaper that seeing animal exterminations in the chamber made him vomit. Animal welfare activist Mrs. Bette Rich is leading a public protest in Queensland, hoping that the government will ban the use of the decompression chamber.

The device was invented in 1941 by Dr. Sigmund Rascher, a second lieutenant in the Nazi SS. He used it to exterminate Jews at Dachau.

See for yourself that your own pet 'goes to sleep' without any fear or distress.

My Trudy never felt the injection. She just fell asleep and her heart stopped beating within seconds. She didn't even finish her last chocolate, but went over peacefully and happily.

If you cannot possibly bear this last act of love, you are a selfish creature, unworthy of anyone's love ... not even that of your pets.

Lady Dowding is Founder President of Beauty Without Cruelty, the charity, of 1 Calverley Park, Tunbridge Wells, Kent. Mrs. Kathleen Long, Lady Dowding and Mrs. Anthea Gough founded the cosmetic firm of Beauty Without Cruelty Limited. Lady Dowding no longer has any connection with the cosmetic firm, so all enquiries regarding the Beauty Without Cruelty cosmetics should be addressed to Beauty Without Cruelty Limited, 37 Avebury Avenue, Tonbridge, Kent. TN9 1TL